Fodor's Inside

Lisbon

Date: 8/15/19

CONTENTS

ABOUT THIS GUIDE

Inside Lisbon shows you the city like you've never seen it. Written entirely by locals, it includes features on the city's street art and galleries and plenty of insider tips. The result is a curated compilation infused with authentic Lisbon flavor, accompanied by easy-to-use maps and transit information.

Whether you're visiting Lisbon for the first time or a seasoned traveler looking to explore a new neighborhood, this is the guide for you. We've handpicked the top things to do and rated the sights, shopping, dining, and nightlife in the city's most dynamic neighborhoods. Truly exceptional experiences in all categories are marked with a ★ .

Restaurants, bars, and coffee shops are a huge part of Lisbon's appeal, of course, and you'll find plenty to savor in its diverse neighborhoods. We cover cuisines at all price points, with everything from enduring institutions and groundbreaking chefs to the perfect late-night street snack. We cover hotels in the Experience section at the front of this guide. Use the $ to $$$$

price charts below to estimate meal and room costs. We list adult prices for sights; ask about discounts when purchasing tickets.

Lisbon is constantly changing. All prices, opening times, and other details in this guide were accurate at press time. Always confirm information when it matters, especially when making a detour to a specific place. Visit Fodors. com for expanded restaurant and hotel reviews, additional recommendations, news, and features.

WHAT IT COSTS: Restaurants			
$	$$	$$$	$$$$
Under €15	€15–€20	€21–€25	Over €25

Prices are the average cost of a main course at dinner or, if dinner is not served, at lunch.

WHAT IT COSTS: Hotels			
$	$$	$$$	$$$$
Under €100	€100–€175	€176–€225	over €225

Prices are the lowest cost of a standard double room in high season.

DISCARD

AMEIXOEIRA

CHARNECA

LUMIAR

SANTA MARIA
DOS OLIVAIS

PARQUE
DAS
NAÇÕES

CARNIDE

AVENIDAS
NOVAS

MARVILA

SÃO DOMINGOS
DE BENFICA

BENFICA

CAMPOLIDE

BEATO

SÃO JOÃO

PENHA DE
FRANÇA

ARROIOS

MARQUÊS DE POMPAL E
AVENIDA DA LIBERDADE

SÃO
MAMEDE

ANJOS

INTENDENTE

SANTA
ENGRÁCIA

GRAÇA

CAMPO DE
OURIQUE

ALCÂNTARA

PRINCIPE
REAL

MARTIM
MONIZ

MOURARIA

ROSSIO

SÃO
VICENTE

ESTRELA

RESTELO

AJUDA

LAPA

BARRIO
ALTO

BAIXA

CHIADO

ALFAMA

CAIS DO
SODRÉ

SANTOS

BELÉM

WELCOME TO LISBON

After taking a serious hit in the global financial crisis, the Portuguese capital has recently undergone a stunning transformation and Lisbon has fast become a famously dynamic city of contradictions and constant evolution.

LISBON TODAY

A bustling port city on the northern bank of the wide Rio Tejo, or Tagus River, Lisbon is the largest city in a small country that has mostly retained its own way of doing things, even as internationalism and gentrification creep in. Right now, that hybrid is deeply compelling.

Only a half a million people live within the city limits, but hundreds of thousands more live in nearby suburbs in all directions (Cascais and Sintra being the most well known, and well heeled), bringing the population to 2 million for all practical purposes. The city is increasingly mixed, with lifelong Lisboetas living shoulder to shoulder with immigrants from the former colonies, plus a growing community of expats who have fallen in love with the laid-back, Portuguese way of life.

More and more visitors are discovering the joys of the capital city: leisurely coffees, outstanding but simple food, quietly beautiful architecture (both gloriously decaying and fully intact), and blue skies and sunshine more than 300 days a year. Still, a purely Portuguese current of melancholy (captured by the sentiment *saudade*, whose closest English translation is "longing") runs beneath it all, making this beautiful country all the more intriguing.

HISTORY

Ever since Neolithic and pre-Celtic times, Lisbon's location at the far southwest edge of Europe has given it special status as an escape exit, an entry point, a strategic military enclave, and a center of trade. Over the centuries, the Phoenicians, Romans, Celts, Greeks, and Islamic Moors settled, invaded, and fought over this slice of the Iberian Peninsula.

In 1147, Portuguese Catholics and crusaders forcibly reclaimed parts of present-day Portugal from the Moors, and 32 years later, the pope recognized it as an independent country. Lisbon became the capital in 1255. By the 16th century, Vasco da Gama sailed four ships to India and established new trade routes, making the Portuguese masters of global maritime trade and Lisbon the richest city in the world.

Things were good until an estimated 9.0 earthquake rocked the city, causing huge fires and a massive tsunami. An estimated 25% of the population was killed and Lisbon was in ruins. As the city got back on its feet, the 19th century was defined by class struggle and the decline of the monarchy. The Portuguese Republic was established after a coup d'etat, which was followed by years of political instability and financial chaos: there were 45 government changes over 16 years.

António de Oliveira Salazar, a right-wing dictator, established Estado Novo (New State), the corporatist authoritarian government that ruled Portugal from 1932 to 1974. Salazar maintained viselike control of the population through censorship, torture, and imprisonment. Democracy was restored on April 25, 1974, with the Carnation Revolution, a bloodless military coup coupled with a popular campaign of civil resistance.

Like many other countries, the great financial crisis of 2008 crippled Portugal. It received a bailout, trudged through the hard years of austerity, and has slowly reemerged as a hub of art and innovation.

THE PORTUGUESE DISCOVERIES

Portugal's sailors and mapmakers were among the best of the 16th century, and they had a knack for colonization, though they refer to places like Mozambique and Brazil as discoveries rather than what they actually were. Citizens of the one-time colonies see things a bit differently, but the Portuguese are proud of their seafaring heritage and their onetime management of resources from around the world. Lisbon is rife with monuments to those explorers, particularly in the nearby suburb of Belém, where many of their expedition ships set sail.

GENTRIFICATION

Lisbon is at something of an inflection point right now. After the depths of the financial crisis, the government was grateful to see an influx of tourist dollars, encouraged foreign start-ups to take root, and encouraged wealthy foreigners to buy property (hello, Madonna). Home prices and rents have been rising quickly, and many of the apartments in the city center are inhabited (or Airbnb-ed) by foreigners.

Regardless of the pros and cons of the current boom, it's an excellent reason to venture beyond the city center and into the suburbs, along the beach toward Cascais or across the river to the south, to experience how the Portuguese really live and to sample the most authentic—and least expensive—food and wine.

WHAT'S WHERE IN LISBON

Each of Lisbon's neighborhoods has its own allure. To help plan your visit, here's a rundown of the areas we cover in detail. The numbers refer to chapter numbers.

2. BAIXA AND ROSSIO

The central square in the downtown Rossio district is known for its towering statue of **King Pedro IV** and the distinctive waving pattern in its sidewalk tiles. It has been one of the city's main gathering places since the Middle Ages. Some of the shops and cafés around the square, like **Café Nicola,** date from the 18th century. Baixa means "low," and this area is downhill from everything else, right by the river. Most of the important tourist sites, such as the central, bright yellow **Praça do Comercio,** are there. Although there are some nice hotels, the majority of restaurants are overpriced tourist traps.

3. CHIADO AND BAIRRO ALTO

The SoHo of Lisbon, this is where many of the luxury (and less so) brands and Michelin-starred chefs have set up shop. The main reasons to visit are the shopping and the eating, but there are also some must-see attractions, such as the roofless **Convento do Carmo,** the most stirring museum in the city. Along with the massive clubs along the river, Bairro Alto's warren of steep streets is Lisbon's nightlife

hub. The sidewalk cafés are busy until late in the evening, and then the party moves to the many bars lining the streets—and into the streets themselves.

4. AVENIDA DA LIBERDADE, PRÍNCIPE REAL, AND RESTAURADORES

Probably Lisbon's most posh neighborhood, hilltop Príncipe Real is home to many high-end independent boutiques and well-regarded casual restaurants. The park in the center is one of the prettiest in the city and a popular gathering spot for locals and visitors. Down the hill, Restauradores is, as the name implies, home to a good variety of restaurants, ranging from overpriced tourist traps to very good seafood houses. The massive roundabout called **Marquês de Pombal** is the geographic heart of the modern city and the northern boundary of the tourist city. Above it is **Parque Eduardo VII,** which has gorgeous geometric hedges and a postcard-perfect view of the city below. Leading down the hill is the wide, tree-lined Avenida da Liberdade, often likened to the Champs-Élysées for its many international luxury boutiques.

5. ALFAMA

The historic heart of Lisbon, this district is still a place to get lost in a warren of tiny, hilly streets, buy all sorts of souvenirs, sample local food and wine, Instagram your heart out, and take in a fado performance.

6. GRAÇA, SÃO VICENTE, BEATO, AND MARVILA

Even farther up the hill from Alfama, Graça is a neighborhood that is still only mildly gentrified (though the restaurant scene is rapidly expanding) and is home to two of the city's most beautiful terraces with a view, **Miradouro da Senhora do Monte** and **Miradouro Sophia de Mello Breyner Andresen.** Nearby, São Vicente is largely residential but has one of Europe's best flea markets and some pretty examples of Portuguese architecture and decay. To the east, Beato and Marvila are the new creative hubs, where young professionals gravitated in search of affordable housing when they were priced out of the city center. The neighborhoods are still gritty but increasingly populated by art galleries, multiconcept art spaces, and craft breweries.

7. ALCÂNTARA, CAIS DO SODRÉ, AND SANTOS

The area surrounding the working docks is home to some excellent no-frills seafood restaurants. Santos is increasingly gentrifying and its vibe is pushing to the west. More and more businesses are opening around the **LX Factory,** a former factory turned into a hipster paradise of specialty shops, cool restaurants, yoga studios, coworking spaces, and rooftop bars. Cais do Sodré and Santos are rapidly gentrifying areas to the west of the city center and home to an increasingly international, trendy crowd. This means there's an abundance of cute and highly Instagrammable brunch spots and cocktail bars. **The Time Out Market** features food stalls from many of the city's best chefs.

8. ESTRELA, CAMPO DE OURIQUE, AND LAPA

This family-friendly hilltop neighborhood of Campo de Ourique has lots of cute shops and a number of good restaurants. Upscale Lapa and Estrela, surrounding the **Basílica da Estrela** and the beautiful **Jardim do Estrela,** are largely residential and well cared for. The azulejos (colorful tiles) are imminently Instagrammable.

9. INTENDENTE, MARTIM MONIZ, AND MOURARIA

Until recently, Intendente and Mouraria were no-go zones, full of prostitutes and drug dealers. Now these hilly neighborhoods of narrow, winding streets and small homes are being cleaned up by young, creative up-and-comers. Still largely off the tourist path, the area around Intendente's central square is packed with trendy bars, cafés, and restaurants. Working-class Martim Moniz is home to many of Lisbon's Asian immigrants.

Go here to experience how the culinary arts of China, Vietnam, and India have traveled and incorporated Portugal's super fresh ingredients.

10. BELÉM

Most of Lisbon's top museums and monuments are here, including the **Torre de Belém, Mosteiro dos Jerónimos, Museu Berardo,** and the groovy new **Museum of Art, Architecture and Technology.** It's also one of the best places in town to get a just-baked *pastel de nata* (eggy custard tart), at the famous **Pasteis de Belém.**

11. AVENIDAS NOVAS

The city's best museums (the must-see **Gulbenkian**) and a few little-known attractions, like the monumental **Fonte Luminosa,** can be found down these broad avenues collectively known as Avenidas Novas (New Avenues). The palatial mansions that used to line the streets have mostly been torn down and replaced by dull office buildings, but bike lanes and pedestrianized squares have revitalized the 20th-century district.

12. SOUTH OF THE RIVER

Just across the Rio Tejo are the spectacular beaches of Costa da Caparica, Sesimbra, and Arrábida and the cleanest ocean swimming closest to Lisbon. The scenic fishing villages and vineyards that dot the coast provide cheap and delicious local seafood, pastries, and regional wines.

13. ESTORIL, CASCAIS, AND GUINCHO

More than mere suburbs, the capital's backyard is rich with possibility. Go to Cascais and Estoril for a night of upscale entertainment or soak up the fresh air and glorious beaches in Guincho, where annual world-champion windsurfing competitions are often held. Pleasure seekers are nothing new here. Lisbon's 18th- and 19th-century nobility developed small resorts along the Estoril Coast and the amenities and ocean views are still prized.

TOP EXPERIENCES IN LISBON

Everyone in Lisbon has their own favorite things to do. We return to them again and again and recommend to friends and family. Our top 10 experiences will guide you to the best of the city.

NEIGHBORHOOD IMMERSION

You might as well ditch the map when you head into the historic center of Alfama. The narrow, winding cobblestone streets wend and weave in a fascinating maze. The joy of the neighborhood is getting lost, coming upon new holes-in-the-wall, and leaving full of memories that you can't quite describe.

WATERFRONT VIEWS

Lisbon has a funny relationship with its river. You can see the water from the central square and areas nearby, but other parts of the waterfront are blighted with warehouses and port facilities.

For the best views, get out of the center and stroll along the river's edge in Alcântara, where the Docas collection of waterfront restaurants offers sophisticated dining.

EATING AND DRINKING

Locals joke that eating is the national sport, and it's perfectly acceptable to assume that what's for dinner is a good conversation topic for lunch.

Although the traditional mom-and-pop *tascas* (simple restaurants), which serve hearty, heavy portions of typical home-cooked fare (whole fish cooked on the grill, platters of beef, and salted cod cooked 50 ways from Tuesday), are starting to get priced out of the city center, they still exist on the fringes.

And in upscale Chiado, Michelin-starred chefs like José Avillez (Belcanto) and Henrique Sá Pessoa (Alma) are turning out high-end fare that competes on the world stage.

HAPPENING NIGHTLIFE

There's a reason Lisbon is a draw for roving partiers. On warm weekend nights, entire neighborhoods become inclusive street parties, where you can take your beer or caipirinha to go and hop from bar to bar. Start in Bairro Alto, where an alfresco dinner easily turns into another round of drinks, or consider the bars of the city's famous Pink Street.

The famous dance clubs, like Lux Fragíl, get started around 2 am.

URBAN HISTORY

If the quiet grandeur of Lisbon's facades doesn't captivate you, the city is rich in historical and contemporary museums. Along with the seasonal exhibitions at the deservedly popular Gulbenkian Museum, a permanent collection of hundreds of years of propaganda posters is an illustrated crash course in Portuguese history.

Other significant museums include the Museu Nacional do Azulejo, the Museu Nacional de Arte Antiga, and an impressive variety of palaces that have been opened to the public as historical sites.

THE ART SCENE

Chiado's exceptional Design and Fashion Museum, or simply MUDE (which also means "change" in Portuguese), houses an outstanding collection of 20th-century design.

The stylish MAAT (Museum of Art, Architecture and Technology) is perhaps the most cutting-edge contemporary art museum in the country. Housed in a former electrical plant on the waterfront in Belém and in a newly built, heavily geometric (and heavily Instagrammed) structure designed by Amanda Levete Architects, the museum showcases the provocative work of contemporary Portuguese and international artists.

There is also a burgeoning gallery scene in the eastern precincts of the city, led by innovators like Underdogs Gallery and newcomers like Collectors—Vintage Department in Marvila.

PARKS AND GARDENS

Whenever possible, Lisboetas live their lives outside, be it having a pleasant alfresco meal or hanging out in the many parks, gardens, and *miradouros* (viewpoints). The kiosks that serve coffee, snacks, and gently priced adult beverages encourage a social scene. The Gulbenkian Gardens and Jardim de Estrela are the city's largest and most beautiful, but the more compact Jardim Botânico is a hidden retreat.

FESTIVALS AND EVENTS

Although Lisbon's climate is mild, the rhythms of life are governed by the seasons. People may muster some energy to go out in December, when a massive Christmas-tree-shaped structure lights up the Praça do Comércio, but they tend to stay home during the often-rainy winter months.

That changes in the spring, starting with the April 25 anniversary of the Carnation Revolution that marks the peaceful end of the country's nearly 50-year dictatorship. The biggest party of the year is on June 13, the day of Santo António, Lisbon's patron saint. Neighborhoods compete to see who has the best costumes and floats, and a procession of couples gather at the Sé Cathedral to tie the knot. Everyone else gets to eat grilled sardines and dance in the streets.

LISBON SHOPPING

The city has never really been a fashion hub, but a handful of young designers and makers are beginning to change that. At the malls and on the streets of Chiado you'll find Zara, H&M, and all the expected luxury and fast-fashion brands (often with different items than you'd find at home).

For local, independent designers, head to Príncipe Real—particularly the Embaixada, a collection of concept shops inside a former embassy—and the LX Factory.

PERFORMING ARTS

Lisbon is practically synonymous with fado, and there is no shortage of venues in which you can hear the soulful music on any night of the week. As for other types of music, the Calouste Gulbenkian Museum hosts an excellent concert series, and in summer, the Out Jazz festival brings musicians of all genres to play free shows in city parks on Sunday afternoons.

Drama is difficult unless you're able to understand Portuguese, but there is the occasional dance or non-word-driven theater performance around town.

TOURS WORTH TAKING

Aside from annoying pickpockets in many tourist areas, Lisbon is safe, compact, and easy to navigate. With a good map and a willingness to get lost, you'll most likely stumble across a few treasures that remind you of why you travel. Still, sometimes it's nice to have a local show you what's what. That said, avoid the random guides that might accost you at the major monuments and attractions. They're usually working in tandom with local shopkeepers and restaurants, drumming up business.

CULINARY BACKSTREETS

This company specializes in walking food tours around some of the world's best eating cities. The guides are culinary journalists, former chefs and sommeliers, and other gastronomic insiders. In Lisbon, the tours range from a broad overview of the best of the city's dishes, to a journey through ethnic restaurants run by chefs from the former colonies, to a moveable seafood feast along the docklands of Alcântara. The tours aren't cheap, but they provide enough food and wine for the entire day. Book at www.culinarybackstreets.com.

WE HATE TOURISM TOURS

The founders of the outfit really do hate the mass tourism that is changing the face of Lisbon. Their mission is to take visitors away from the city center and the inundated major tourist sites and into the heart of the authentic Lisbon, where locals still live and socialize, and to support restaurants and other businesses that don't run on tourist dollars. There are plenty of options that are guided, but they also offer DIY tours: guests plug in their itineraries and follow them at their leisure. Book at www.wehatetourismtours.com.

UNDERDOGS PUBLIC ART TOURS

Lisbon has some fantastic large-scale street art, including pieces by internationally known artists like Shepard Fairey and Vhils. This is largely due to the tireless effort of the cutting-edge Underdogs Art Gallery, whose members champion the work of urban artists. They offer periodic public tours (by minivan) of some of the most important works, with curators who explain the stories behind them. Private tours (by sidecar) are available on request. To learn more or book, email info@under-dogs.net.

SURF BUS

Surf Bus runs private and group trips to the best surf beaches surrounding Lisbon, including Guincho, Costa da Caparica, and Praia Grande. Full-day tours can take in farther-flung spots such as Ericeira or Peniche. Hotel pickup, lessons, and equipment are available. Visit www.surfbus.pt for more information.

GUINCHO AVENTOURS

This enduringly popular tour company runs adventure tours in and around Lisbon, including kayaking and quad biking. It has off-road motorcycle tours in Cascais, buggy tours to the most remote areas in Cascais, and more family-friendly excursions, like dolphin-spotting boat trips.

COOL PLACES
TO STAY

Although a few big hotel chains do exist here (mostly away from the city center), part of the delight of Lisbon is staying at a small, maybe historic, locally owned hotel that has a truly Portuguese sensibility. Here are a few of our favorites.

ALMALUSA
The name means "Portuguese soul," and this intimate hotel in a historic building in Baixa aims to fully embody that sentiment. ⊠ *Praça do Município 21, Baixa* ⊕ *www.almalusahotels.com*

CASA BALTHAZAR
Located in Chiado, at the epicenter of Lisbon's handsome downtown, the 17-room guesthouse is hidden from the tourist hordes on a quiet backstreet, and stepping inside feels like a wonderful wind-down after a busy day exploring the city. A pool and gorgeous views make a stay here even more of a treat. ⊠ *Rua do Duque 26, Chiado* ⊕ *www.casabalthazarlisbon.com*

LE CONSULAT
Ideally located on Praça de Camões, the central square of Chiado, the art-filled Le Consulat has a moody, intimate feel. ⊠ *Plaça Luís de Camões 22, Chiado* ⊕ *leconsulat.pt*

HOTEL DA ESTRELA
Off the beaten path in quiet, residential Estrela, the unique Hotel da Estrela's lawn and pond are particularly lovely, and ducks from the nearby Jardim da Estrela often find their way there. ⊠ *Rua Saraiva de Carvalho 35, Estrela* ⊕ *hoteldaestrela.com*

HOTEL VALVERDE
Stylish and discreet, Hotel Valverde is among the luxury boutiques on busy Avenida da Liberdade. With entry limited to guests, and a private garden in the back that serves lunch, after-work cocktails, and an excellent Sunday brunch, it feels like a private oasis. ⊠ *Av. da Liberdade 164* ⊕ *www.valverdehotel.com*

INTERNACIONAL DESIGN HOTEL
The restaurant here is popular with locals and a cut well above the typical hotel restaurant, and the hotel's playful Alice in Wonderland theme makes it a fun spot to bed down. ⊠ *Rua da Betesga 3, Baixa* ⊕ *www.idesignhotel.com*

THE LUMIARES

Absolutely everything in the stylish Lumiares is purely Portuguese. The views are great, and the rooftop terrace is a nice place to hang out. ✉ *Rua do Diario de Noticias 142, Bairro Alto* ⊕ *www.thelumiares.com*

1908 LISBOA HOTEL

A lovely art nouveau building-turned-hotel, 1908 Lisboa is a less-expensive option in an up-and-coming neighborhood that's away from the city center. ✉ *Largo do Intendente Pina Manique 6, Intendente* ⊕ *www.1908lisboahotel.com*

PALÁCIO BELMONTE

Nearly 4,000 blue-and-white tiles from the 18th century decorate the walls of this intimate, historic hotel. The building has a long history as a private home for a wealthy family that dates from 1449, and a terrific location near the castle. ✉ *Pátio de Dom Fradique 14, Alfama* ⊕ *palaciobelmonte.com*

POUSADA DE LISBOA

With a heated indoor pool, private sun-lounging deck, spa, and standout restaurants, the hotel has plush rooms with impressive views and is at the epicenter of all of Lisbon's downtown happenings, from sunset strolls along the waterfront to fine dining, late-night barhopping, and taking in the impressive architecture of the Pombaline downtown. ✉ *Praça do Comércio 31–34, Baixa* ⊕ *www.pousadas.pt*

SANTIAGO DE ALFAMA

This 19-room boutique hotel at the heart of Lisbon's Alfama neighborhood is a reformed 15th-century palace, long abandoned but now brought beautifully back to life as one of Lisbon's most stylish lodgings. ✉ *Rua de Santiago 10-14, Alfama* ⊕ *www.santiagodealfama.com*

SANTA CLARA 1728

This tiny, sophisticated bed-and-breakfast right by the Feira de Ladra flea market has a laid-back, beachy vibe. ✉ *Campo de Santa Clara 128, São Vicente* ⊕ *www.silentliving.pt*

VERRIDE PALÁCIO SANTA CATARINA

With grand public spaces and guest rooms, this intimate palace hotel has a spectacular rooftop that's perfect for afternoon cocktails. ✉ *Rua de Santa Catarina 1, Bairro Alto* ⊕ *www.verridesc.pt*

LISBON WITH KIDS

Interactive museums, nice playgrounds in well-kept parks, and even a swath of protected forest within the city limits make entertaining kids easy in Lisbon. Just note that the city's hilly nature makes it stroller unfriendly.

WILDLIFE ENCOUNTERS

The Oceanário, in Parque das Nações, is the largest oceanarium in Europe and home to penguins, sea gulls, sea otters, sharks, rays, chimaeras, seashorses, starfish, octopuses, jellyfish, and all sorts of fish and marine plants. The Jardim Zoologico is home to more than 2,000 animals of more than 300 species.

MUSEUMS

Near the Oceanário, the Pavilhão do Conhecimento science museum has plenty of interactive exhibitions, exploration routes, and a play space for kids. The Museu da Marioneta has an extensive collection of puppets from around the world. For kids who like boats and buses, the Museu do Marinha is dedicated to all things related to Portugal's history of navigation, and the Museu da Carris shows historic trolleys and trams. In Sintra, in addition to the palaces, the Museu do Ar is the aviation museum of the air force.

SHOPPING

A new toy is always fun. Find cute European-made ones at Cristina Siopa, Sigtoys, or Pires e Tadeu. For kids' clothes, check out Maria Gorda for flowery dresses and countryside skirts, Tuc Tuc for vivid prints and fun colors, and Naturapura for baby clothes made from natural materials.

PLAY TIME

Many of the city's parks have compact but innovative playgrounds. The ones in Estrela, Príncipe Real, and Campo de Ourique are especially good. Monsanto is a protected forest within the city limits that is a good place for hiking or playing in the woods. At the edge of Monsanto there's Hello Park, a supervised space where kids can climb on a simple ropes course, bounce on inflatables, or experiment in a painting studio. At the esplanade outside, parents can have a coffee or a drink as they watch.

BEST BETS

With so many places to go and things to do in Lisbon, how will you decide? Fodor's writers and editors have chosen our favorites to help you plan. Search the neighborhood chapters for more recommendations.

ACTIVITIES AND SIGHTS

ARCHITECTURE
Alfama

Convento do Carmo, Chiado

Mosteiro de São Vicente de Fora, São Vicente

Mosteiro dos Jerónimos, Belém

MAAT, Belém

Praça do Comércio, Baixa

Igreja e Museu São Roque, Chiado

Sé de Lisboa, Alfama

MUSEUMS AND GALLERIES
Casa Fernando Pessoa, Campo de Ourique

Galaria Baginski, Marvila

Galeria Filomena Soares, Beato

Galeria Francisco Fino, Marvila

MAAT, Belém

MUDE, Baixa

Museu Berardo, Belém

Museu da Carris, Alcântara

Museu da Marioneta, Santos

Museu de Marinha, Belém

Museu Nacional do Azulejo, Beato

Museu Nacional de Arte Antigua, Santos

Underdogs Gallery, Marvila

PARKS AND GREEN SPACES
Gulbenkian Gardens, São Sebastio

Jardim Botânico da Ajuda, Ajuda

Jardim Botânico, Príncipe Real

Jardim da Estrela, Campo de Ourique

Jardim da Parada, Campo de Ourique

Jardim do Príncipe Real, Príncipe Real

Parque Eduardo VII, Avenida da Liberdade

Tapada das Necessidades, Alcântara

VIEWS
Amoreiras Towers, Amoreiras

Café da Garagem, Graça

The Garden Rooftop, Santos

Miradouro da Senhora do Monte, Graça

Miradouro de Santa Catarina, Bairro Alto

Miradouro de Santa Luzia, Alfama

Miradouro de São Pedro de Alcântara, Bairro Alto

Miradouro Sophia de Mello Breyner Andresen, Graça

Park Bar, Bairro Alto

Portas do Sol, Alfama

Rio Maravilha, Alcântara

Sky Bar at the Tivoli Avenida Liberdade Hotel, Avenida da Liberdade

Topo Chiado, Chiado

Topo Martim Moniz, Martim Moniz

SHOPPING

CLOTHING BOUTIQUES

Embaixada, Príncipe Real

Fashion Clinic, Avenida da Liberdade

The Feeting Room, Chiado

Sapataria do Carmo, Chiado

Soul Mood, Chiado

TM Collection, Chiado

JEWELRY

Joalharia do Carmo, Chiado

Tous, Chiado

W. A. Sarmento, Baixa

LISBON MADE

A Vida Portuguesa, Intendente, and other locations

Chi Coraçao, Alfama

Cork & Co, Chiado

Cortição & Netos, Alfama

Fábrica Sant'Anna, Chiado

Pelcor, Príncipe Real

Maison Nuno Gama, Príncipe Real

Teresa Pavão, Alfama

VINTAGE STORES

A Outra Face da Lua, Baixa

Ás de Espadas, Chiado

Retro City Lisboa, Intendente

Retrox, Intendente

Sunday outdoor market at LX Factory, Alcântara

FOOD

BAKED GOODS

Gleba, Alcântara

Kasutera, São Bento

L'éclair, Avenidas Novas

Lomar, Campo de Ourique

Manteigaria, Chiado

Pasteis de Belém, Belém

Pastelaria Centro Ideal da Graça, Graça

Tartine, Chiado

SEAFOOD

Água Pela Barba, Bairro Alto

Cervejaria Liberdade, Avenida da Liberdade

Cervejaria do Ramiro, Intendente

Marisqueira O Palácio, Alcântara

Nune's Real Marisqueira, Belém

Peixaria da Esquina, Campo de Ourique

Pesqueiro 25, Cais de Sodré

Pinóquio, Avenida da Liberdade

Sea Me, Chiado

BRUNCH
Amélia Lisboa, Campo de Ourique

Comoba, Cais do Sodré

Ela Canela, Campo de Ourique

Cafe Boavida, Cais de Sodré

Dear Breakfast, Santos

DeliDelux Avenida, Avenida da Liberdade

Flora & Fauna, Santos

Heim Cafe, Santos

The Mill, São Bento

Café Nicola, Rossio

The Valverde Hotel, Avenida da Liberdade

BURGERS
Burger Factory, Alcântara

Cais da Pedra, Santa Apolónia

Hamburgueria do Bairro, Príncipe Real

Honorato, Chiado

Vegana, Cais do Sodré

HAUTE PORTUGUESE
Alma, Chiado

Belcanto, Chiado

Feitoria, Belém

Eleven, Avenida da Liberdade

JNcQUOI, Aveninda da Liberdade

Epur, Chiado

Loco, Estrela

100 Maneiras, Chiado

Prado, Baixa

ICE CREAM
Gelateiro d'Alfama, Alfama

Gelato Davvero, Santos

Nannarella, Príncipe Real

Santini, Chiado

ITALIAN AND PIZZA
Casanostra, Bairro Alto

Casanova, Santa Apolónia

Il Matriciano, São Bento

In Bocca al Lupo, Príncipe Real

Osteria, Santos

Zero Zero, Príncipe Real

OUTDOOR DINING
Cais da Pedra, Santa Apolónia

Casanova, Santa Apolónia

Clube de Jornalistas, Lapa

DeliDelux, Santa Apolónia

Lisbon Sud, Alcântara

Zero Zero, Príncipe Real

Terra, Príncipe Real

Jardim dos Sentidos, Avenida da Liberdade

Lost In, Príncipe Real

ROMANTIC DINING
A Travessa, Madragoa

As Salgadeiras, Bairro Alto

Clube de Jornalistas, Lapa

Faz Figura, São Vicente

Senhor Vinho, Lapa

Via Graça, Graça

TYPICAL PORTUGUESE

Cantinha Zé Avillez, Alfama

Maça Verde, Santa Apolónia

Taberna Moderna, Alfama

Taberna da Rua das Flores, Chiado

Toscana Casa de Pasto, Alcântara

O Zé da Mouraria, Mouraria

Zé dos Cornos, Mouraria

ETHNIC CUISINE

Boa Bao, Chiado

Cantinho do Aziz, Mouraria

Delícias de Goa, Avenida da Liberdade

Ibo, Cais do Sodré

Nikkei, Belém

Palanca Gigante, Mouraria

Zuari, Santos

DRINK

COFFEE

A Brasileira, Chiado

Botequim, Graça

Café Nicola, Rossio

Comoba, Cais do Sodré

Confeitaria Nacional, Baixa

Copenhagen Coffee Lab, Príncipe Real

Fábrica Coffee Roasters, Avenida da Liberdade

Versailles, Avenidas Novas

The Mill, São Bento

CRAFT BEER

Crafty Corner, Cais do Sodré

Dois Corvos Cervejeira, Marvila

Duque Brewpub, Chiado

Musa, Marvila

Lisbeer, Alfama

Quimera Brewpub, Alcântara

COCKTAILS

A Tabacaria, Cais do Sodré

Cinco Lounge, Príncipe Real

Foxtrot, Príncipe Real

Le Consulat, Chiado

Matiz Pombalina, Santos

O Purista, Chiado

Pavilhão Chinês, Príncipe Real

Pensão Amor, Cais do Sodré

Procópio, Rato

Red Frog, Príncipe Real

The Decadente, Bairro Alto

Ulysses Lisbon Speakeasy, Alfama

OUTDOOR DRINKING

Clube Ferroviário do Portugal, Santa Apolónia

Jardim de Príncipe Real, Príncipe Real

Lost In, Príncipe Real

Lumi at the Lumiares, Bairro Alto

Memmo Alfama, Alfama

Memmo Príncipe Real, Príncipe Real

Park Bar, Bairro Alto

Silk, Chiado

Sky Bar at Tivoli Avenida, Avenida da Liberdade

Topo, Martim Moniz

NIGHTLIFE AND THE PERFORMING ARTS

DANCING

B.Leza, Cais do Sodré

Dock's Club, Alcântara

Europa, Cais do Sodré

Incognito, São Bento

Lux Frágil, Santa Apolónia

Ministerium, Baixa

Titanic Sur Mer, Cais do Sodré

LIVE MUSIC

Damas, Graça

Fábrica Braço da Prata, Marvila

Hot Clube de Portugal, Avenida da Liberdade

Musa, Marvila

MusicBox, Cais do Sodré

Sabotage, Cais de Sodré

THEATER AND PERFORMANCE

Chapitô, Castelo

Teatro Meridional, Marvila

Teatro Nacional de São Carlos, Chiado

Teatro Taborda, Castelo

FOOD AND DRINK IN LISBON

Portuguese food, at its most elemental, is always fresh, simple, honest, and above all, delicious. Plenty of old-school mom-and-pop tascas (simple restaurants) still exist, offering inexpensive food to a largely local clientele, especially away from the most touristy neighborhoods. Now a new generation of innovative chefs is elevating Portuguese traditions and ingredients to fine-dining level. Peruse our Best Bets for more ideas.

SEAFOOD

As the capital of a country that is mostly coastline, Lisbon is packed with places to enjoy simple grilled fish—be prepared to deal with a head and bones—or a seafood feast. Lisbon's *cervejeiras* (breweries) specialize in seafood such as huge, deep-sea *carabinero* shrimp from the Algarve and *bulhão pato* (clams with lemon, olive oil, coriander, and tons of garlic). Prepare to get your hands dirty.

COLONIAL CUISINE

Immigrants from Portugal's former colonies have brought their traditional recipes with them. There are plenty of excellent restaurants, both formal and informal, to try a coconut-laden Mozambican curry or a spicy Goan one.

COFFEE

Lisbon is fueled and socially lubricated by coffee. Catching up with a friend or hammering out a business deal? You meet for coffee. Need a break from work? You meet for coffee. The typical Portuguese coffee is a short, very strong espresso. If you need milk to cut the intensity, ask for a *galão* (café au lait) or a *meia de leite* (latte). A new wave of trendy cafés is serving trendy drinks like nitro cold brew and turmeric lattes.

SWEETS

One of the things Portugal is most famous for is the pastel de nata, a sweet, egg-yolky custard in a pastry shell and sprinkled with cinnamon. It was invented by the Jerónimos monks in Belém and Pasteis de Belém is still one of the best places in town to find one. Many other Portuguese sweets are also made with egg yolks, a tradition said to have begun when people were using egg whites to filter wine and starch clothing.

MADE IN LISBON

Lisbon is an increasingly international melting pot of creative professionals, so what could be a better souvenir than something made locally? Our Best Bets have more ideas.

CLOTHING

There aren't that many Portuguese fashion designers yet, but that's beginning to change. TM Collection by Teresa Martins is a good bet for flowy, drapey women's fashion in natural materials. Alexandra Moura is known for colorful, graphic prints; Fátima Lopez specializes in avant-garde creations; and Storytailors, the alias for João Branco and Luis Sanchez, is known for fanciful fashion (which often is used as wardrobe in theatrical productions).

ACCESSORIES

Cork is everywhere, from handbags to yoga mats. Much of it is cheaply mass produced, but some young designers are trying to use the material for high-quality, high-design products. Inlu is making cork shoes that are a step above what you find in the souvenir shops of Alfama. Cork & Co is known for high-quality wallets and handbags, as is Pelcor, which even makes cork briefcases and umbrellas. Heritage brands include Luvaria Ulisses, which has been making high-quality gloves since 1925, and Pedemeia, which specializes in well-made socks in a rainbow of colors.

HOME DECOR

If you're looking for anything to add to your home (or wardrobe, pantry, or beauty cabinet), A Vida Portuguesa is a must-visit for a variety of Portuguese brands under one roof. Chi Coraçao is known for high-quality, 100% wool blankets and throws, Armazém das Caldas offers a huge array of functional and decorative ceramics, and Cortição & Netos has a massive selection of azulejos, or traditional decorative tiles.

EDIBLES

Lisbon's best-known edible souvenir is tinned fish (which is really quite delicious), and there are plenty of shops where you can find it, including Conserveira de Lisboa and Loja das Conservas. The sweet pasteis de nata can be packed well to travel, especially at bakeries like Manteigaria and Pasteis de Belém. And although the Lisbon wine region isn't as well known as the Douro Valley or the Alentejo, you can pick up some very good Lisbon wines, such as Quinta de Sant'Ana, Casal Santa Maria, and Vale da Capucha.

WHAT TO WATCH AND READ

To learn more about Lisbon, before or after you visit, consider these movies, TV shows, books, magazines, and blogs as a primer to the city's past, present, and ever-changing future.

....

MOVIES

Given Lisbon's beauty and character, it's a wonder Woody Allen never made it here after filming movies in Paris, Rome, and Barcelona. That said, a few filmmakers have produced atmospheric dramas that tell the story of Lisbon.

The 2013 film *Night Train to Lisbon* is based on a 2004 novel of the same name. Told in flashbacks, the story follows a Swiss professor's journey through Lisbon in search of a mysterious woman, and an obscure author who, it turns out, was part of the resistance during the Salazar dictatorship.

Wim Wenders's *Lisbon Story* (1994) tells the story of a film director having trouble finishing a movie about Lisbon. He calls his friend for help, who in turn arrives in Lisbon, falls in love with the city and a Portuguese singer, and takes his camcorder all over to capture hidden Lisbon.

The 1969 James Bond film *At the Service of His Majesty* is set all over and around Lisbon, although it depicts a city of luxury and Salazarist cosmopolitanism rather than reality.

The White City (1983) depicts the poor side of the city as a love story between a sailor and a maid is revealed.

Lisbon and its many monuments figure prominently in the 1990 film *The House of Russia* when the protagonist takes refuge amid the espionage of the Cold War era.

BOOKS

Lisbon is justifiably proud of the work of its literary lions, past and present, and perhaps because of the famous Portuguese melancholia, poets became extremely important figures.

The most internationally famous is Fernando Pessoa, who attributed his prolific writings to a range of alternate selves. His *Book of Disquiet*, a collection of writings found in a trunk after his death in 1935, is considered his posthumous masterpiece. The collection of short aphoristic paragraphs forms an autobiography of one of his alter egos and is part diary, prose poetry, and descriptive narrative. Critics have called it one of the greatest works of the 20th century and argued that it "gives to Lisbon the haunting spell of Joyce's Dublin or Kafka's Prague."

Sixteenth-century poet Luís de Camões was the first great European artist to cross into the southern hemisphere, and his works reflect his years in far-off destinations, as seen through Portuguese eyes. He is most famous as the author of the great Renaissance epic *The Lusiads*, which tells the story of Vasco da Gama's voyage via southern Africa to India. Another fine introduction is *The Collected Lyric Poems of Luís de Camões*, which includes nearly 300 poems.

In 1998 José Saramago became the only Portuguese-speaking author to be awarded the Nobel Prize in Literature. His novel *The Year of the Death of Ricardo Reis* is set in 1936, in the early days of the dictatorship, and marked by visits made by Fernando Pessoa. Another important work is *The History of the Siege of Lisbon*, Saramago's novel about a novel, in which a proofreader willfully adds the word "not," an act that reverses the course of history.

For a good nonfiction overview of the history of Lisbon and Portugal, Martin Page's *The First Global Village: How Portugal Changed the World* is considered the definitive work on the subject.

MAGAZINES AND BLOGS

The English-language edition of *Time Out Lisbon* is a useful guide for visitors, but it's a single edition and is not updated weekly with listings. For that, there's the weekly Portuguese edition, which also exists online, meaning it can be deciphered with Google Translate. The same goes for *Agenda Cultural Lisboa*.

Good English-language blogs and websites include the Lisbon section of *Culinary Backstreets* and *Go Lisbon*, and there is a lot of worthwhile Lisbon content mixed in on blogs like *Julie Dawn Fox in Portugal*, *Salt of Portugal*, and *Portugal Confidential*. *Lisbon Lux* focuses on what's new and noteworthy in the city, with tips for locals and tourists, highlighting the best restaurants, shops, bars and hotels, plus the top attractions in each neighborhood.

LISBON TIMELINE

So much has happened on this plot of land now known as Lisbon and the sea surrounding it. These are just some of the game-changing events that have made the city everything that it is today.

....

Neolithic and pre-Celtic eras: Lisbon's location at the far southwest tip of the European continent has always given it special status as an escape point, an entry point, a strategic military enclave, and a center of foreign trade goods entering from the sea. At the mouth to the Tagus River with the Atlantic Ocean in sight, boats and flotillas, tradesmen, and armadas passed by this hilly territory, with goods or weapons in hand for hundreds of years, hoping to make gain or conquer the area.

800–600 BC: Phoenicians established the first permanent trading settlement in what is now Lisbon, dedicating the territory as Ulissipo, or Olissipo, which likely had origins in the Phoenician "Allis Ubbo," meaning "Enchanting Port." Unsupported folklore attributes the name to Ulysses's founding the city in his own name after leaving Troy to escape the Greeks.

205 BC–AD 409: Over the centuries, Celts, Greeks, Carthaginians, and countless hordes established settlements and trading posts in the valuable area on the water route to the sea. In 205 BC the Roman Empire won the Second Punic War and occupied Lisbon, still known as Olissipo, for more than 600 years. They built magnificent infrastructure, trade flourished, and in the later years it became a center for the dissemination of Christianity.

5th–8th centuries: In AD 409, the port city was overthrown again and loosely held by Germanic barbaric tribes and eventually the Visigothic Kingdom for 300 years. The city was rebranded as Ulixbona.

714–1147: Islamic Moorish invaders, inspired by the Umayyad Caliphate after the death of Muhammad, conquered the whole Iberian Peninsula, including Lisbon, for 433 years. In Lisbon, the language became Arabic, churches were converted to mosques, and Christians and Jews could only continue practicing their religions if they paid a tax. Trade boomed. The city flourished, and the population was estimated to be among the largest in Europe—larger than that of London or Paris at the time.

1147: During the Reconquista, Lisbon was forcibly taken from the Moors by Portuguese Christians and crusaders after a four-month siege of the city. After a treaty, which the Christians ignored, they pillaged Lisbon's wealth from inside the walled fortress the Moors had built.

1179: The pope recognized Portugal as an independent country, with Afonso Henriques as its first king. It was made up of territory north of Lisbon while the Moors still controlled the southern part of present-day Portugal.

1255: Lisbon became the capital of Portugal.

1276: John XXI became the first and only Portuguese-speaking pope, only to die one year later.

1386: The Treaty of Windsor between England and Portugal was signed. It remains the world's oldest diplomatic alliance still in force.

1498–1600: Lisbon became the world's greatest seaport when Vasco da Gama sailed four ships to India from Belém and established trade routes that were more profitable than existing routes between Venice and Egypt. Soon ships reached China, Indonesia, and Japan. Portuguese explorers also created the trade city of Macau. In 1500, they arrived in Brazil. Lisbon's trade was so profitable that many European ports and land routes were abandoned, further strengthening the importance of the city. Global maritime trade (and basically all European trade) was controlled by Lisbon for decades, and it became the richest city in the world.

1748: The stunning Aguas Livres Aqueduct was completed. It is still the highest stone arch in the world, at 213 feet. It is considered one of the greatest engineering feats in the history of Portugal.

1755: An estimated 9.0 earthquake, perhaps Europe's strongest ever, devastated Lisbon. Three shocks hit over the course of several hours, and more than 12,000 buildings were destroyed. When people felt the tremors, they ran to the river to avoid the tumbling buildings. Then a 23-foot tsunami rolled over the low land, killing thousands. The final blow was a citywide inferno that destroyed nearly every structure in the downtown. All told, 60,000 people died, which was 25% of Lisbon's population.

The king appointed Sebastião José de Carvalho e Melo, the first Marquês de Pombal, as prime minister. His efforts were instrumental in rebuilding the city after the earthquake, and many of the new, earthquake-resistant buildings were in a distinctive architectural style known as Pombaline. He also accomplished many economic and social improvements, like abolishing slavery in Portugal and creating several companies and guilds to regulate commercial activity.

1807: The Peninsular War occupation was undertaken by Napoleon's armies and continued for four years.

19th century: Throughout the 1800s, Lisbon was marked by intense class struggle. The poor were taxed, and money was given to the property owners, which eroded society and caused conflict. The elite managed to hang on to most of the power but they lost their monarchy and the political climate was chaotic and approaching anarchy.

1910: The Portuguese Republic was established after a coup d'etat by a group called the Republicans, which was followed by 45 government changes during the next 16 years.

1914: Portugal remained neutral during World War I, but there was heavy internal strife and violence as the class struggle continued.

1926–74: The right-wing (Fascist-Imperialist) Estado Novo (New State) regime ruled as a suppressive government under highly effective dictator António de Oliveira Salazar. It was the longest dictatorship in the history of Western Europe. Although Salazar, an economist, instituted many social programs like schools and health services, his government maintained a tight grip over profitable Portuguese colonies like Angola and Mozambique.

1938: Portugal remained neutral during World War II but became a launch point for elites who wanted to flee the fighting. It was also well known as a hub for international espionage meetings.

1961: Portugal's colonies demanded independence as India annexed Portuguese Goa and rebellion broke out in Angola, Guinea, and Mozambique.

1970: Salazar died.

1974: The Carnation Revolution was a bloodless left-wing coup that ended the Estado Novo and paved the way for democracy and European Union admission. The name is derived from the actions of pacifist Celeste Caeiro, who bought carnations from street vendors and placed them in the muzzles of rifles and on soldiers' uniforms, leading others to follow suit. At this point, Portugal abandoned its colonies.

1974-75: Independence was granted to the Portuguese colonies of Guinea-Bissau, Mozambique, Cape Verde Islands, São Tomé and Príncipe, and Angola. Also, after more than 450 years in power, Portugal withdrew from Portuguese Timor (now East Timor), which was then occupied by Indonesia. All of this resulted in a huge influx of expatriates from former colonies.

1986: Portugal became a member of the European Union.

1998: José Saramago became the first Portuguese (or Portuguese-speaking) author to receive the Nobel Prize in Literature.

2001: Portugal became the only country in the world to decriminalize all drugs. Drug use and drug-related health problems like HIV/AIDS have declined in the years since this law was enacted.

2010: Portugal became the sixth country in Europe and the eighth country in the world to allow same-sex marriage nationwide.

2010–14: The Great Recession hit Portugal especially hard. These years marked the hardest for Portugal, which enacted the most intense austerity policy in Europe. In 2011, Portugal applied to the International Monetary Fund for a bailout, which was completed in 2014. By then, tourism was beginning to take off, solidifying the city's increasingly stable economy. The municipal government also enacted policies that made the city very inviting for international start-ups.

2014: Interior Minister Miguel Macedo resigned in the wake of a corruption inquiry linked to allocation of fast-track residence permits, many of which went to foreigners willing to invest large sums in Portuguese property.

2015: The head of the tax collection authority resigned amid claims that he tried to shield the files of influential figures from scrutiny. Later in the year, following inconclusive parliamentary elections, Socialist leader Antonio Costa formed a center-left government committed to relaxing some austerity measures.

2017: Portugal was cited as the third-safest country in the world, after Iceland and New Zealand, and Lisbon as the safest capital city in Europe.

2018: In a setback for gay rights activists, President Marcelo Rebelo de Sousa vetoed a law that would have made it easier for people to change their gender and name in documents.

BEST LISBON EVENTS

There's always something going on in Lisbon, a food- and music-loving city that loves a good party. These are the standout events, listed by month.

FEBRUARY OR MARCH
Carnival
The Shrove Tuesday festival in Lisbon isn't as elaborate as the ones in other parts of Portugal (let alone Brazil), but there's still a good party to be found, especially in Parque das Nações. During the final night, there's a procession and people don colorful masks and costumes. ⊠ *Parque das Naçoes*

MARCH
Lisbon Half Marathon
More than 35,000 runners from around the world compete in this event, said to be one of the most beautiful half marathons in the world. This is the only time that pedestrians are allowed on Lisbon's iconic Ponte 25 de Abril. The rest of the course follows the waterfront, and fans turn out all along the way to cheer on the runners. ⊠ *Lisbon* ⊕ *maratonaclubedeportugal.com*

APRIL
Peixe em Lisboa
For 11 days, some of the most well-known chefs on the local and international stage, including José Avillez, Henrique Sá Pessoa, Miguel Laffan, David Pasternak (United States), and Diego Gallegos (Spain)

serve tastings of their renditions of Portuguese fish and seafood. ⊠ *Marquês de Pombal* ⊕ *peixemlisboa.com*

APRIL–MAY
Estoril Open
The only Portuguese stop on the ATP World Tour calendar, this tournament draws millions of tennis fans each year. ⊠ *Estoril* ⊕ *millenniumestorilopen.com*

MAY
Festival da Máscara Ibérica
The International Festival of the Iberian Mask is four days of processions, concerts, dances, workshops, and showcases for handicrafts and regional products. It's a celebration of the best of Portuguese and Spanish culture—especially their shared traditions. ⊠ *Belém* ⊕ *fimi.pt*

MAY–JUNE
Lisbon Book Fair
In a tradition that dates from the 1930s, the city's booksellers and publishers set up stalls in Parque Eduardo VII for several weeks, sell their books at reduced prices, host readings and author chats, and generally promote reading. Lisboetas still love to read books, on paper, and turn out in droves, creating a

party-like atmosphere with food and drink vendors. ✉ *Marquês de Pombal* ⊕ *feiradolivrodelisboa.pt*

Alkantara Festival

For a quarter of a century, this festival has been out to champion cutting-edge arts. The programs includes a good deal of dance and other nonlinguistic performances. ✉ *Alvalade* ⊕ *alkantarafestival.pt*

MAY–SEPTEMBER

Out Jazz

Every Sunday evening in the summer, free concerts take place in city parks. The venue changes each month, but it's always someplace beautiful and iconic, such as Monsanto, Jardim de Estrela, or Parque Eduardo VII. ✉ *Lisbon*

JUNE

Santos Populares

Hands-down the biggest, most important festival in Lisbon, and in all of Portugal, is Santos Populares, when the city celebrates its most popular saints by throwing giant street parties. Everyone eats grilled sardines, drinks beer and wine, sings, dances, and generally makes merry. The party goes all month in neighborhoods like Bairro Alto, Alfama, Graça, Santos, and Mouraria, but the main event is June 13, or Santo António's day. Squads from each neighborhood dress up and compete in a procession down Avenida da Liberdade. Also, because Santo António is the patron saint of love, dozens of brides make a procession and take their vows in the Sé Cathedral. ✉ *Lisbon*

JULY

Festival ao Largo

This free outdoor festival celebrates music, singing, theater, and dance in one of the main squares of Chiado. Performers include the National Ballet Company and the Portuguese Symphony Orchestra. ✉ *Chiado* ⊕ *festivalaolargo.pt*

Tall Ships Races

This spectacular event only takes place every four years, with the next in 2020. Sailors race in historic tall ships from another port into Lisbon—originally it was Torbay, England, and most recently it was Antwerp, Belgium. The next regatta will begin in Lisbon and in the days leading up to it, the ships will remain anchored near Lisbon's cruise terminal. See them up close on boat or helicopter tours. ✉ *Alfama* ⊕ *tallshipslisboa.com*

AUGUST

Jazz em Agosto

Internationally renowned contemporary jazz artists take the stage of the open-air amphitheater of the Gulbenkian Foundation for a series of outdoor concerts. ✉ *Avenidas Novas* ⊕ *gulbenkian.pt*

O Sol da Caparica

South of the river at the Parque Urbano in the Costa da Caparica, the O Sol da Caparica is a celebration of sand, surf, and music. The performers include musicians from Portugal, Africa, and Brazil, playing everything from hip-hop and rock to fado and samba. There are also other performance art venues for dance and animated cinema, plus options for skateboarding, surfing, and windsurfing. ⊠ *Costa da Caparica* ⊕ *osoldacaparica-festival.pt*

AUGUST–SEPTEMBER
Lisboa na Rua
This free annual festival takes culture out of the theaters and performance halls and into the city's parks and public squares. The programming includes music, theater, dance, cinema, and magic. ⊠ *Lisbon* ⊕ *egeac.pt*

SEPTEMBER
Festa do Avante!
Since 1976, this festival, named after the newspaper of the Portuguese Communist Party, has taken place during the first weekend in September. Now it's more party than politics (though those certainly do remain), with three days of concerts by well-known Portuguese and international artists and other festivities. Hundreds of thousands of people attend, many of whom camp. There's food, venues for debates, book and music fairs, theater, cinema, and sporting events. ⊠ *Amora* ⊕ *festadoavante.pcp.pt*

Chapéus na Rua
Literally "Hats in the Street," this festival celebrates local buskers of all sorts: musicians, jugglers, acrobats, living statues, and improvisational poets. Along with an opening cabaret show and informal performances, there's a talk about the role that street arts play in society. ⊠ *Intendente*

Festival Santa Casa Alfama
The new name for the annual Grande Festival de Fado, this event brings together the country's premier fado artists for a weekend of more than 40 concerts in 12 venues. ⊠ *Alfama* ⊕ *santacasaalfama.com*

Lisboa Open House
As part of the international Open House movement to invite the pubic into intriguing private spaces, Lisboa Open House unlocks the city's secret spaces and informs visitors about one of Europe's greatest urban environments. Some of the sites were designed by Pritzker Architecture Prize winners. ⊠ *Lisbon* ⊕ *trienaldelisboa.com/ohl*

SEPTEMBER–JUNE
Gulbenkian Music
The city's premier cultural institution puts on the city's most sophisticated concert series in its garden amphitheater. The central pillars are the Gulbenkian Orchestra and Choir, but quite a few international artists also take the stage. ⊠ *São Sebastião* ⊕ *gulbenkian.pt*

OCTOBER
Rock 'n' Roll Lisbon Marathon
Like the half marathon in the spring, this event is famed for its beauty, as well as for its live music throughout the race. Runners start in the near-by beach town of Cascais, follow the coast through towns like Oeiras and Carcavelos, go past the Jerónimos Monastery and through the central Praça do Comércio square, finishing on the Vasco da Gama Bridge. Fans root them on (and enjoy the music) along the way. ✉ *Lisbon* ⊕ *www.runrocknroll.com*

Doclisboa
This long-running film festival champions indie documentary films from around the world. The screenings are at art house Casa do Cinema. ✉ *Bairro Alto* ⊕ *doclisboa.org*

OCTOBER–NOVEMBER
Volvo Ocean Race
Lisbon is the first stop on one of the premier long-distance regattas in the world. The Volvo Ocean Race begins in Alicante, Spain, passes a couple of days in Lisbon, and then continues through some of the most treacherous seas, crossing the Cape of Good Hope, Australia, New Zealand, and Brazil and eventually returning to Europe and the Hague. This is a perfect chance to see the world's most skilled sailors in action on state-of-the-art boats.

NOVEMBER
Web Summit
The largest, most prestigious tech and start-up conference in the world takes place in Lisbon every November. Even if you don't buy a ticket to the conference itself, you can feel the city come alive with entrepreneurial energy. ✉ *Parque das Nações* ⊕ *websummit.com*

Baixa (including Rossio)

GO FOR

Sightseeing

Excellent
transport links

Lots of
restaurants

AMEIXOEIRA

CHARNECA

SANTA MARIA
DOS OLIVAIS

LUMIAR

PARQUE
DAS
NAÇÕES

CARNIDE

SÃO DOMINGOS
DE BENFICA

AVENIDAS
NOVAS

MARVILA

BENFICA

CAMPOLIDE

BEATO

SÃO JOÃO

MARQUÊS DE POMPAL E
AVENIDA DA LIBERDADE

PENHA DE
FRANÇA

ARROIOS

ANJOS

SANTA
ENGRÁCIA

SÃO
MAMEDE

INTENDENTE

CAMPO DE
OURIQUE

ALCÂNTARA

PRÍNCIPE
REAL

MARTIM
MONIZ
ROSSIO

GRAÇA

SÃO
VICENTE

ESTRELA

RESTELO

AJUDA

LAPA

BARRIO

CHIADO

BAIXA

ALFAMA

CAIS DO ALTO

SANTOS

SODRÉ

BELÉM

At the heart of Lisbon's sightseeing action, downtown Lisbon, known as the Baixa, is home to striking Pombaline architecture, sidewalk café-bars, street performers, and a vast array of shops. From the grand Arco da Rua Augusta and the river-facing Praça do Comércio up to bustling Rossio Square, the Baixa is home to some of Lisbon's most distinctive sights. Overseen by the Marquis de Pombal, much of the area was built after the great Lisbon earthquake in 1755, using elegant designs whose strong foundations were designed to withstand any further earthquakes. The first port of call on any visitor's list should be Praça do Comércio, the grandest of the many handsome squares in Lisbon. Here, a statue of King José I on horseback sits proud on a vast plaza flanked by canary-yellow buildings, many of which now operate as bars and restaurants. The Tagus glimmers in the background—tempting sun-baked tourists to sit on the sloped edge of the river and dip their feet in the water or sip cocktails from sunloungers, while street musicians from across the globe provide a lively musical backdrop. From here, a stroll under the Arco da Rua Augusta leads to one of Lisbon's busiest shopping streets. Take the elevator to the top of the arch to get your bearings (and glorious views).—by Lucy Bryson

⊙ Sights

Animatógrafo do Rossio
Built in 1907 as one of Lisbon's grandest cinemas, this beautiful art nouveau building is worth a visit for the ornate tiled facade alone and draws a steady flow of keen photographers and architecture buffs. Many visitors prefer not to step inside—today it hosts peep shows and a sex shop. ⊠ *Rua dos Sapateiros 225–229, Rossio* ☎ *21/395–4959* Ⓜ *Green Line to Rossio.*

Arco da Rua Augusta
Capping the postearthquake restoration of Lisbon's downtown, the Triumphal Arch offers a splendid viewpoint from which to admire the handsome buildings that were constructed in the wake of the devastating quake. Access is via an elevator and then up two narrow, winding flights of stairs. Once at the top, young visitors delight in ringing a giant bell, while the grown-ups can admire views over Praça do Comércio and the river Tejo in one direction, and peek at shoppers, street performers, and sightseers ambling along Rua Augusta in the other. The red-roofed

houses and grand religious buildings that climb up the surrounding hillsides complete the scene. ✉ *Rua Augusta 2, Baixa* 🚋 *€3* Ⓜ *Blue Line to Terreiro do Paço.*

Elevador de Santa Justa

Built in 1902 by Raul Mésnier, who studied under Eiffel, the Santa Justa Elevator, inside a Gothic-style tower, is one of Lisbon's more extraordinary structures. Queues are often frustratingly long in high season, but it's an enjoyable ride up to the top. After stepping outside the elevator compartment at the upper level, you can either take the walkway leading to the Largo do Carmo or climb the staircase to the *miradouro* (viewpoint) at the very top of the structure (147½ feet up) for views of the Baixa district and beyond. The return ticket sold on board includes access to the miradouro, but at €5.15 it is a poor value—a 24-hour Carris public transport card costs €6.30 and is valid on all of Lisbon's lifts as well as buses, trams, and metro. There's an extra €1.50 charge for access to the viewpoint when using the public transport card, but it's included in the price when using a Lisboa Card. ✉ *Rua do Ouro, Baixa* 🚋 *About €6 round trip* Ⓜ *Green/Blue Line to Baixa-Chiado.*

The Fantastic World of Portuguese Sardines (O Mundo Fantastico das Conservas Portuguesas)

If Willy Wonka turned his attention to canned fish, it would probably look something like this flamboyant shop on Rossio Square. A riot of color, complete with a miniature sardine-themed Ferris wheel, it's a gift shop and sightseeing experience all in one. ✉ *Rua Dom Pedro IV 39, Rossío* ☎ *21/134–9044* ⊕ *www.mundofantasticodasardinha.pt* Ⓜ *Green Line to Rossio.*

★ Lisboa Story Centre

This family-friendly interactive museum uses multimedia exhibits to bring Lisbon's history to life. Over the course of an hour, the story is broken down into chapters, with a focus on the golden age of Portuguese maritime adventures. A multilingual audio guide takes visitors through a series of exhibits. Midway through, a small cinema shows a short but dramatic reenactment of the 1755 earthquake and the fiery aftermath. Visitors can buy a ticket that gives access to the Story Centre and Rua Augusta Arch for a discounted price. ✉ *Praço do Comércio 78–81, Baixa* ☎ *21/194–1099*

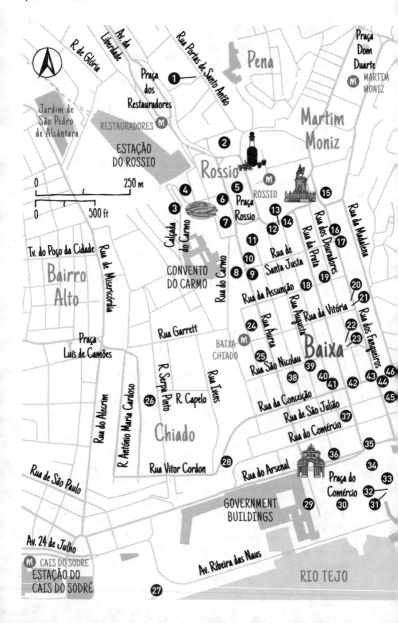

🌐 *lisboastorycentre.pt/en* 🎫 *€7*
Ⓜ *Blue Line to Terreiro do Paço.*

MUDE–Museu do Design e da Moda

The acronym MUDE means "to change" in Portuguese, and it's an apt one for this standout fashion and design museum whose opening in 2009 was a key moment in the regeneration of downtown Lisbon from elegant but stuffy to youthful and forward thinking. Celebrating the connection between high fashion and grand design, it includes well over 1,000 fashion pieces from the likes of Jean Paul Gaultier, Vivienne Westwood, and Yves Saint Laurent, while the world of artistic design is represented by furnishings and homeware pieces from iconic names such as Phillipe Starck and Masanori Umeda. The museum, housed in former bank headquarters, also hosts visiting exhibitions on varying themes from the worlds of couture and design. At this writing, the museum was closed for renovation but MUDE has rotating exhibitions in other locations. ✉ *Rua Augusta 24, Baixa* ☎ *21/888-6117* 🌐 *www.mude.pt* 🕙 *Closed Mon.* Ⓜ *Blue line to Baixa-Chiado or Terreiro do Paço.*

★ Núcleo Arqueologico da Rua dos Correeiros

More than 2,500 years of history has been uncovered at this archaeological treasure trove hidden beneath a bank on one of Lisbon's busiest shopping streets. The buried network of tunnels occupies almost a whole block in Lisbon's historic center and was unearthed in the 1990s during excavation works carried out by Millennium BCP, the bank to which the site belongs. The digs revealed homes and artifacts from the Roman, Visigoth, Islamic, medieval, and Pombaline periods, and much of the space appears to have been used as a major-scale Roman fish-salting factory. It was later used as a Christian burial ground, and there's even a well-preserved skeleton to be seen. Free guided visits (in English or Portuguese) lead visitors through underground walkways, catching a glimpse of how postearthquake foundations were laid for the Pombaline buildings that still stand proud today. Free tours in English leave roughly every two hours on the hour, Monday through Saturday; arrive at least 30 minutes before to book your place, as space is (quite literally) limited. ✉ *Rua dos Correeiros, 21, entrance on Rua Augusta, Baixa* ☎ *21/113-1004* 🕙 *Closed Sun.* Ⓜ *Green/Blue Line to Baixa-Chiado; Blue Line to Terreiro do Paço.*

★ Praça do Comércio

Known to locals as the Terreiro do Paço, after the royal palace (the Paço) that once stood here, the Praça do Comércio is lined with 18th-century buildings now fronted by expansive esplanades that provide a roaring trade in light meals and drinks. Down by the river, steps and slopes—once used by occupants of the royal barges that docked here—lead up from the water, and sunbathers strip down to catch rays here during the summer. The equestrian statue in the center is of Dom José I, king at the time of the earthquake and subsequent rebuilding. In 1908, amid unrest that led to the declaration of a republic, King Carlos and his eldest son, Luís Filipe, were assassinated as they rode through the square in a carriage. On the north side, the Arco Triunfal (Triumphal Arch) was the last structure to be completed, in 1873. ⊠ *Praça do Comércio, Baixa* Ⓜ *Blue Line to Terreiro do Paço.*

★ Rossio

The formal name for this grand public square is Praça Dom Pedro IV, but locals stick to the previous name, Rossio. Built in the 13th century as Lisbon's main public space, it remains a bustling social hub and, traffic noise aside, it's still impressive, and crowds socialize among baroque fountains beneath a statue of Dom Pedro atop a towering column. Visitors can admire the dramatic wave-pattern cobblestones (famously reconstructed on the beach promenades of Rio de Janeiro) and soak up the sense of drama. The square was founded as the largest public space in the city and has seen everything from bullfights and musical performances to public executions. During the Portuguese Inquisition, it was the setting for public autos-da-fé. The site of the gruesome procedures is now occupied by the imposing 19th-century Teatro Nacional (National Theater). On nearby Largo de São Domingos, where thousands were burned, there's a memorial to Jewish victims of the Inquisition. Today, locals come here to relax with a newspaper, have their boots polished by the shoe

While Lisbon's answer to the Parisian Arc de Triomphe is impressive from any angle, the best views are those from the top. Most people just goggle at it from below, but for €3 visitors can take an elevator, before making the final steep ascent on foot. The arch was built to commemorate the rebuilding of the Baixa after the 1755 earthquake. Views take in the grand plaza and glittering river in one direction, while the white domes and red roofs of the city span out in the other.

Share your photo with us!
@FodorsTravel #FodorsOnTheGo

shiners, or sip a *ginjinha* (traditional sour-cherry liqueur) at one of the bars. Tourists come to sip somewhat overpriced coffees and eat snacks at the café-bars that flank the square, and protestors come to loudly but respectfully state their political case. Another suitably grand building houses downtown's main train station, the starting point for trips to Sintra. ⊠ *Praça Dom Pedro IV (Rossio Sq.), Rossío* Ⓜ *Green Line to Rossio.*

Sexiest WC on Earth

Yes, it's a public toilet. And while the name may suggest something untoward, it is in fact good clean fun. Strolling through the entrance on one of Lisbon's grandest piazzas, customers pay a small fee and can take their pick from an array of brightly hued toilet rolls, before making use of the jazzy facilities themselves. You can pick up free stickers on the way out, and there's even a gift shop selling Sexiest WC on Earth souvenirs. ⊠ *Terreiro do Paço 86, Baixa* ☏ *24/983–0257* ⊕ *www.myrenova.com/news/26/the-sexiest-wc-on-earth-lisbon* 🎫 *€1* Ⓜ *Blue Line to Terreiro do Paço.*

Shopping

★AmaTudo

This cute arts-and-crafts store sells traditional and contemporary Portuguese products. Come prepared to spend quite some time browsing the handcrafted ceramics and colorful homeware, beautifully presented in a vintage-chic setting. ⊠ *Rua Madalena 76/78, Baixa* ☏ *91/960–4834* 🕐 *Closed Sun.* Ⓜ *Blue or Green Line to Baixa-Chiado.*

Discoteca Amália

Come here to shop for soulful music by Amália Rodrigues and other leading *fadistas.* You'll know you're close by when you hear fado tunes blasting onto the street. ⊠ *Rua Áurea 272, Baixa* ☏ *21/324–0939* Ⓜ *Green Line to Rossio.*

Garrafeira Napoleão

The helpful staff at this wine store speak English and can recommend vintages. There are also branches in Rua da Conceição and in Chiado, and shoppers can order online. ⊠ *Rua dos Fanqueiros 70, Baixa* ☏ *21/887–2042, 21/886–1108* ⊕ *www.napoleao.eu* Ⓜ *Green/Blue Line to Baixa/Chiado.*

★ GN Conceição

The little sister store of long-established Lisbon wine merchant Garrafeira Nacional is geared to foreign visitors, with clearly presented wares, knowledgeable English-speaking staff, and an efficient shipping service. It's open daily 10–9; you can also order online. The original store, known also for its selection of Portuguese spirits, is at Rua Santa Justa 18. ⊠ *Rua da Conceição 20–26, Baixa* ☏ *21/887–9080* ⊕ *www.garrafei-*

ranacional.com/en/lojas Ⓜ Green/Blue
Line to Baixa-Chiado.

Manuel Tavares

Just off Rossio Square, this enticing
shop, which opened in 1860, stocks
cheeses, preserves, vintage port,
wine, and other fine Portuguese
products. ⊠ Rua da Betesga 1A, Baixa
☏ 21/342–4209 ⊕ www.manuelta-
vares.com Ⓜ Green Line to Rossio.

M. Murteira Antiguidades

Several centuries are represented
at this shop near the cathedral.
It carries furniture, paintings,
sculpture, and religious art from
the 17th and 18th centuries as well
as 20th-century artwork. ⊠ Rua
Augusto Rosa 19–21, Baixa ☏ 21/886–
3851 ⊗ Closed Mon. Ⓜ Blue/Green
Line to Baixa-Chiado.

A Outra Face da Lua

This place is about as unconventional
as Lisbon shopping gets. Prepare to
be completely engaged by the eclectic
mix of vintage clothes, items made
using recycled materials, unique
accessories, music, gadgets, temporary tattoos—you name it, really. Plus
there's a tearoom and bistro. ⊠ Rua
da Assunção 22, Baixa ☏ 21/886–3430
⊕ www.aoutrafacedalua.com
⊗ Closed Sun. Ⓜ Blue/Green Line to
Baixa-Chiado.

Queijaria Nacional

This store is a showcase for
Portugal's wealth of cheeses and
other deli treats. You can sample the
wares while staff explain the product's origins. ⊠ Rua da Conceição 8,
Baixa ☏ 91/208–2450 Ⓜ Blue/Green
Line to Baixa-Chiado.

Toranja

Souvenirs and gifts are fash-
ioned in the best possible taste at
Toranja, whose physical shop (it
first launched online) sells colorful
prints, cushions, handicrafts, and
accessories, all of which manage
to capture the essence of Portugal.
⊠ Rua dos Fanqueiros 180, Baixa
☏ 21/886–2065 ⊕ toranja.com
Ⓜ Green/Blue Line to Baixa-Chiado.

ViniPortugal

Try before you buy at this large
Portuguese wine store at Terreiro
do Paço. Every wine region of the
country is represented, and tasting
sessions are available for a small
fee. ⊠ Terreiro do Paço, Baixa
☏ 21/342–0690 ⊕ www.viniportugal.pt
⊗ Closed Sun. Nov.–Mar. Ⓜ Blue Line
to Terreiro do Paço.

★ W. A. Sarmento

One of the city's oldest goldsmiths
(since 1870), Sarmento produces
characteristic Portuguese gold- and
silver-filigree work. ⊠ Rua Aurea
251, Baixa ☏ 21/342–6774 Ⓜ Blue/
Green Line to Baixa-Chiado.

☕ Coffee and Quick Bites

Bread 4 U

$ | Portuguese. Somewhat more elaborate than the name suggests, this is a cozy bistro-bar-café that has a nice selection of lunch-time set menus. The fresh-baked breads and cakes are perfect with a morning coffee, and there are gluten-free options, too. **Known for:** home baking; good-value lunch deals; excellent seafood dishes and salads. *Average main: €13 ⊠ Rua dos Sapateiros 41, Baixa ☎ 21/139-4632 ⊕ www.bread4you.eu Ⓜ Blue/Green Line to Baixa-Chiado.*

Casa Portuguesa de Pastel do Bacalhau

$ | Portuguese. This downtown pit stop is all about the *pastel de bacalhau* (codfish cake)—a traditional Portuguese snack that here comes with the option of a rich cheese filling. It also serves light lunches and good coffee. **Known for:** location at the heart of the Baixa; good sangria; speedy service. *Average main: €4 ⊠ Rua Augusta 106–108, Baixa ☎ 91/648-6888 ⊕ pasteisdebacalhau.com Ⓜ Blue/Green Line to Baixa-Chiado.*

Chachamoon

$ | Taiwanese. Bubble tea is growing in popularity with hip, young Lisboetas, and Chachamoon is one of the best places to try it. Options run the gamut from simple matcha with milk and tapioca balls to exotic fruity confections. **Known for:** enormous bubble wraps (waffles filled with fruit and ice cream); mochi; dairy-free teas and desserts.

Average main: €8 ⊠ Rua do Crucifixo 112–114, Baixa ☎ 21/347-1779 Ⓜ Green/Blue Line to Baixa-Chiado.

★ Confeitaria Nacional

$ | Café. Serving pasteis de nata and other sweetly delicious treats since 1829, Confeitaira Nacional is the oldest *pastelaria* in Lisbon. The handsome antique decor competes for attention with the glass cabinets packed with mouthwatering cakes, pastries, and some of the best coffee and custard tarts in town. **Known for:** beautiful Pombaline architecture and 1820s decor; delicious cakes and chocolates; tearoom with table service on upper floor. *Average main: €9 ⊠ Praça da Figueira 18B, Baixa ☎ 21/342-4470 ⊕ confeitarianacional. com Ⓜ Green Line to Rossio; Tram 15 to Praça da Figueira.*

Eight—The Health Lounge

$ | Vegetarian. The name comes from the eight healthy-living principles that drive the kitchen at this informal café serving plant-based snacks and meals. The focus is on creating food that tastes good and is good for you. **Known for:** raw, vegan food; smoothies, teas, and juices; fresh-faced clientele and staff. *Average main: €7 ⊠ Praça da Figueira 12A, Baixa ☎ 21/886-2859 ⊕ www.8healthlounge. com ⊙ Closed Sat. Ⓜ Blue/Green Line to Baixa-Chiado; Tram 15E or 25E to Praça Figueira.*

Less Baixa

$$ | European. Sate an appetite for Lisbon's dramatic panoramic views at this chic restaurant-bar, which sits on the top floor of a storied department store. Given a complete overhaul in 2017, the restaurant

HOW TO ORDER COFFEE LIKE A LOCAL

Lisbon's dramatic tourism boom is more evident in the Baixa than anywhere else in the city, with tourists zipping along the streets on Segways and an increasing number of places serving below-par food and drink to a clientele keen to refuel at the first opportunity.

But coffee lovers looking for a caffeine fix needn't opt for a watery Americano (actually called an abatanado). The Portuguese take their coffee every bit as seriously as the Italians and a few words in the local lingo will get you the real deal. Starting with the basics, a café (or bica, pronounced bee-ka) is a small, strong caffeine hit, the Portuguese equivalent of an espresso. For a full cup, ask for a café cheio. For a drop of milk, it's a café pingado. For a double shot, ask for a café duplo.

If you like your coffee milky, a galão is a long coffee with a large splash of milk, while a meia de leite (literally, "half of milk") is the closest thing you'll find to a latte. Don't expect soy or almond milk outside of Starbucks or specialist vegan cafés, though. A garoto is a small cup of coffee topped with foamed milk, while a carioca is a more diluted coffee, made using the leftovers from an espresso. For no caffeine at all, you want a descafeinado.

Coffee almost always comes with two small sachets of white sugar. It's rare to be offered sweetener, but most places will provide it if you ask—the word is adoçante. Whatever you order, your wallet shouldn't suffer—if you're paying more than €1 for a basic coffee, you're in tourist trap territory.

is a sophisticated spot for salads, finger food, and more substantial pan-European dishes. **Known for:** acclaimed chef Miguel Castro e Silva at the helm; sunset cocktails and nibbles; terrace lounge with views over the Baixa. *Average main: €17 ⊠ Pollux, Rua dos Fanqueiros 276, 8th fl., Baixa ☎ 21/320-4373 ⊕ lessrestaurantes.pt/lessbaixa-pollux ☉ Closed Sun. Ⓜ Green Line to Rossio.*

Martinho da Arcada
$$ | Portuguese. Open since the 1700s, this café under the arches overlooking Praça do Comércio is thought to be the oldest in the city. There's a formal dining space inside, but the real appeal is sipping a coffee on the flagstones and watching

Lisbon life go by. **Known for:** grand 18th-century building; rich history of hosting poets and intellectuals; great people-watching opportunities. *Average main: €19 ⊠ Praça do Comercio 3, Baixa ☎ 21/887-9259 ⊕ www.martinhodaarcada.pt Ⓜ Blue/Green Line to Terreiro do Paço.*

MyIced
$ | Café. Lactose-free frozen yogurts and bubble teas are the main draw here, and they're just the thing after a hot day of sightseeing. Grown-up bubble teas come laced with gin or rum. **Known for:** huge range of sugar-free yogurt flavors and toppings; crepes; smoothies and boozy bubble teas. *Average main: €7 ⊠ Rua da Assunção 44, Baixa*

☎ 91/938-2494 ⊕ www.myiced.com/ Ⓜ Blue/Green Line to Baixa-Chiado.

★ Pizzeria al Taglio

$ | Pizza. This small pizzeria in the Baixa has a reputation for serving the best slices in town. Grab one to go or take a seat in the informal dining space. **Known for:** enormous range of pizzas; fresh ingredients and vegetarian options; speedy service. *Average main: €6* ⊠ *Rua da Conceição 44, Baixa* ☎ 21/886-2715 Ⓜ *Blue/ Green Line to Terreiro do Paço.*

¶¶ Dining

Em Alta na Baixa

$$ | Portuguese. On a street filled with tourist traps, contemporary Portuguese restaurant Em Alta na Baixa stands out for its focus on delivering genuinely high-quality food and service. Take a seat outdoors or enjoy the elegant indoor space on chillier days. **Known for:** delicious risottos and pasta dishes; satisfying hamburgers; extensive wine list. *Average main: €19* ⊠ *Rua de São Nicolau 16, Baixa* ☎ 21/887- 0250 ⊕ fullest.pt/en/restaurants/ em-alta-na-baixa Ⓜ *Blue/Green Line to Baixa-Chiado.*

★ Bastardo

$ | Contemporary. The cool, colorful restaurant at Rossio's Internacional Design Hotel is as cheeky and irreverent as its name suggests. Expect the unexpected on the food and drinks menus, both of which take Portuguese culinary traditions on fantastic flights of fancy. **Known for:** innovative, eclectic, and fast-changing menu; playful interior design; funky

separate bar serving potent cocktails. *Average main: €17* ⊠ *Internacional Design Hotel, Rua Betesga 3, Rossío* ☎ 21/324-0993 ⊕ restaurantebastardo. com Ⓜ *Green Line to Rossio.*

Bonjardim

$ | Portuguese. In an alley between Praça dos Restauradores and Rua das Portas de Santo Antão, and known locally as Rei dos Frangos (King of Chickens), Bonjardim specializes in spicy, spit-roasted *peri peri* (hot pepper) chicken. The restaurant and esplanade are crowded at peak times (8–10 pm), but watching the frenzied waiters is a lesson in the service industry. **Known for:** spicy chicken; popularity; efficient waitstaff. *Average main: €9* ⊠ *Travessa de Santo Antão 11–12, Baixa* ☎ 21/342-4389 Ⓜ *Green Line to Rossio.*

Café Nicola

$$ | Portuguese. The distinctive 1930s facade and tables right on Rossio Square make Nicola a memorable spot for a bite to eat while sightseeing in the Baixa. Breakfasts and brunches are good, with lots of strong coffee, eggs, and meaty sausages (or fresh fruit and juices, should you prefer). **Known for:** prime location; historic building; good steaks. *Average main: €18* ⊠ *Praça Dom Pedro IV 24–25 (Rossio Sq.), Rossío* ☎ 21/346-0579 Ⓜ *Green Line to Rossio.*

Can the Can

$$ | Portuguese. The Portuguese take their canned fish seriously. Find out what all the fuss is about at this funky restaurant, where the chefs incorporate canned goods into all manner of dishes—it sounds gimmicky, but the results are delicious. **Known for:** creative menu; prime location on Terreiro do Paço square; good cocktails. *Average main: €19 ⊠ Praça do Comércio 82–83, Baixa ☎ 91/400-7100 ⊕ canthecan.net Ⓜ Blue Line to Terreiro do Paço.*

⭐ Delfina Cantina Portuguesa

$$ | Portuguese. Occupying a corner of one of downtown's finest squares, Delfina Cantina Portuguesa bills itself as a fine Portuguese deli. It's the house restaurant at the chic Alma Lusa boutique hotel, but nonguests are also welcome to enjoy the tapas-style small plates throughout the day and night, as well as more substantial lunches and dinners. **Known for:** great location on flagstones of busy terrace; delicious flour-free chocolate cake; cozy vintage-chic interior. *Average main: €20 ⊠ Praça do Município 21, Baixa ☎ 21/269-7445 ⊕ www.almalusahotels.com Ⓜ Blue/Green Line to Baixa-Chiado; Blue Line to Cais do Sodré.*

MOMA Grill

$ | Portuguese. Slightly off the tourist track, MOMA Grill serves some of the best steaks and grilled fish in the Baixa. They also have good pasta dishes, sides, and small plates. **Known for:** excellent fish dishes; cheerful staff; being a locals' hangout. *Average main: €14 ⊠ Rua dos Correios 16, Baixa ☎ 91/176-2349 ⊗ Closed weekends ▭ No credit cards Ⓜ Blue/Green Line to Baixa-Chiado.*

⭐ Qosqo

$$ | Peruvian. Fans rave that this local favorite serves the best ceviche outside Peru, and it's hard to argue with that. It mixes up excellent pisco sours, too. **Known for:** traditional Peruvian food and decor; attentive service; ceviche served a variety of ways. *Average main: €17 ⊠ Rua dos Bacalhoeiros 26A, Baixa ☎ 91/604-6197 ⊗ Closed Mon. Ⓜ Blue Line to Terreiro do Paço.*

⭐ Taberna na Baixa

$$ | Portuguese. This family-run restaurant is one of an ever-decreasing number of places to enjoy truly traditional Portuguese dishes in the Baixa. The baked cod and pork cheeks are specialties, and there's an extensive Portuguese wine list. **Known for:** daily specials; good range of petiscos (small plates); hearty traditional dishes. *Average main: €17 ⊠ Rua dos Fanqueiros 161–163, Baixa ☎ 21/887-0290 Ⓜ Blue/Green Line to Baixa-Chiado.*

🍸 Bars and Nightlife

⭐ Bebedouro Wine & Food

Wines from the celebrated Douro region of Portugal are the stars of the show at this intimate bar. There's a terrace for outdoor sipping and snacking, with occasional live music performances. ⊠ *Rua de São Nicolau 24, Baixa ☎ 21/886-0376 Ⓜ Green/Blue Line to Baixa-Chiado.*

The George

The only British pub in Lisbon, the George is a convincing homage to the great British boozer, as well as a popular meeting point for Lisboetas and homesick Brits alike. A mutual love of gin could be a factor in the long-standing friendship between the two. ⊠ *Rua do Crucifixo 58–66, Baixa ☎ 21/346-0596 Ⓜ Blue/Green Line to Baixa-Chiado.*

Lisboa Bar

Tucked away behind the ramp up to Rossio's grand old train station, Lisboa Bar has a charmingly old-school exterior but draws a youthful crowd of sangria sippers. ⊠ *Rossio Train Station, Rossío* ⌖ *At back of access ramp* ☎ *21/342–7243* Ⓜ *Green Line to Rossio.*

Ministerium

This slick, modern club above Cantina restaurant takes its name from the government departments that once dominated Lisbon's riverside square. On Saturday, a well-heeled crowd dances to electronica and house music. ⊠ *Praça do Comércio, Ala Nascente 72–73, Baixa* ☎ *21/888–8454* ⊕ *www.ministerium.pt* ☾ *Closed Sun.–Fri.* Ⓜ *Blue Line to Terreiro do Paço.*

Trobadores

Drink mead from a ceramic mug and pretend you're back in medieval times at this offbeat and off-the-tourist-trail tavern. Low rafters, candles, and live folk performances add to the old-world ambience. ⊠ *Rua de São Julião 27, Baixa* ☎ *21/885–0329* Ⓜ *Blue/Green Line to Baixa-Chiado.*

Wine & Pisco

The Portuguese and Peruvian national drinks come together under one roof (or terrace) at one of Rossio's less touristy bars. Drinkers can opt for tasters of different wines or choose pisco cocktails from a range that doesn't begin and end with the pisco sour. ⊠ *Largo do Duque de Cadaval, Baixa* ⌖ *Rossio Train Station square* ☎ *96/434–4296* Ⓜ *Green Line to Rossio.*

🎭 Performing Arts

Quiosque de Ribeiro das Naus

Grab a seat—or a sunlounger—at this riverfront kiosk and listen to live pop, rock, or samba as the sun sets over the Tagus. Musicians gather here on sunny evenings to entertain the totally chillaxed crowds. ⊠ *Av. Ribeira das Naus, Baixa* ☎ *91/827–3697* Ⓜ *Blue Line to Terreiro do Paço.*

★ Teatro Nacional de São Carlos

This grand neoclassical building is home to the Portuguese Symphonic Orchestra and the country's only professional choir. It also hosts major ballet performances. Tickets, and guided tours, can be booked online. ⊠ *Rua Serpa Pinto 9, Baixa* ☎ *21/325–3000* ⊕ *tnsc.pt* Ⓜ *Blue/Green Line to Baixa Chiado.*

Teatro Nacional Dona Maria II

Although Lisbon's principal theater stages plays primarily in Portuguese, there are occasional foreign-language productions. Performances run August through June, and guided tours, held each Monday, are available in English. ⊠ *Praça Dom Pedro IV (Rossio Sq.), Rossío* ☎ *21/325–0835 for ticket office* ⊕ *www.teatro-dmaria.pt* Ⓜ *Green Line to Rossio.*

A Todo Tango!

As the name suggests, this place is all about the tango. Drink, dance, or just watch the showstopping routines onstage. Lessons are available for those itching to join in. ⊠ *Rua dos Fanqueiros 286, 1st fl., Baixa* ☎ *91/252–6890* ⊕ *www.atodotango.pt* Ⓜ *Blue/Green Line to Baixa-Chiado.*

3

Chiado and Bairro Alto

AMEIXOEIRA

CHARNECA

LUMIAR

SANTA MARIA
DOS OLIVAIS

PARQUE
DAS
NAÇÕES

CARNIDE

SÃO DOMINGOS
DE BENFICA

AVENIDAS
NOVAS

MARVILA

BENFICA

CAMPOLIDE

BEATO

SÃO JOÃO

MARQUÉS DE POMPAL E
AVENIDA DA LIBERDADE

ARROIOS

PENHA DE
FRANÇA

ANJOS

SANTA
ENGRÁCIA

INTENDENTE

ALCÂNTARA

CAMPO DE
OURIQUE

SÃO
MAMEDE

PRÍNCIPE
REAL

MARTIM
MONIZ
MOURARIA
ROSSIO

GRAÇA

SÃO
VICENTE

ESTRELA

BAIXA

RESTELO

AJUDA

LAPA

BARRIO
ALTO

CHIADO

ALFAMA

CAIS DO
SODRE

SANTOS

BELÉM

Rising up from Rossio Square downtown, Chiado is Lisbon's most elegant neighborhood, home to belle epoque–style stores and cafés. It's the city's gentrified shopping mecca and where you find the most sophisticated restaurants, many of which have opened in the last few years to join several historic theaters, baroque churches, and old bookstores. At the top, past Camões Square, you reach Bairro Alto (literally "high neighborhood"), the city's first planned neighborhood, laid out in 1513 in a grid of narrow streets. It became the nightlife quarter for hipsters, bohemians, and artists in the 1980s and continues to be the top destination for a big night out, despite competition from the increasing number of bars in the Cais do Sodré district by the river. It still has the biggest variety of restaurants, and groups of all ages still stand outside the bars with drinks in hand. There's a street party atmosphere on Friday and Saturday night, as locals and tourists hop from bar to bar. Although noisy until quite late at night, it's sleepy during the day, when everyone is shopping and having coffee in neighboring Chiado.—*by Mario Fernandes*

 Sights

Convento de São Pedro de Alcântara

This convent from 1670 was never open to the public until 2014, when the last nuns moved out. Although it faces one of the city's most famous viewpoints, it remains an under-the-radar stop. The main church and chapel are free to visit anytime, while the rest of the building can be seen on guided tours on Friday at 3 in English and on Saturday at 3 and 4:30 in Portuguese. To join a tour, you don't need to book in advance, just show up a few minutes before the scheduled time. The baroque church is found between two wings of the convent, and most of its interior dates from 1758, after the devastating 1755 earthquake left it slightly damaged. The older paintings were originally in the colossal convent and palace of Mafra, while the tile panels were added in the late 1700s and illustrate scenes from the life of St. Peter of Alcântara. Another highlight is a cardinal's funerary chapel, covered in inlaid marble. ⊠ *Rua Luísa Todi 1–11, Bairro Alto* ☎ *21/324–0869* 🏷 *Church free, guided tour €3* ⊙ *Historic convent closed Sun.–Thurs.* Ⓜ *Tram 24; Glória funicular.*

Convento do Carmo

The Carmelite Convent—built in 1389 and once Lisbon's largest—was all but ruined by the 1755 earthquake,

GETTING HERE

Chiado and Bairro Alto can be reached by metro or tram. The metro station is Baixa-Chiado, so called because one side exits to the Baixa and the other up a steep escalator to the center of Chiado up the hill. Trams 25 and 28 go through the neighborhood and past Bairro Alto, which can also be reached through the Glória funicular, departing from Restauradores Square.

and its skeletal remains are stark reminders of the quake's devastating impact. Its sacristy houses the **Museu Arqueológico do Carmo** (Carmelite Archaeological Museum), a small collection of ceramic tiles, medieval tombs, ancient coins, mummies, and other city finds. The tree-shaded square outside—accessible via a walkway from the top of the Elevador de Santa Justa—is a great place to dawdle over a coffee. ⊠ *Largo do Carmo, Chiado* ☎ *21/347–8629* ⊕ *www.museuarqueologicodocarmo.pt* ⧌ *€4* ⊙ *Closed Sun.* Ⓜ *Baixa-Chiado or Rossio (then Elevador de Santa Justa)*.

Elevador da Glória

One of the finest approaches to the Bairro Alto is via this funicular railway, inaugurated in 1888 on the western side of Avenida da Liberdade, near Praça dos Restauradores. It runs up the steep hill and takes only about a minute to reach the São Pedro de Alcântara Miradouro, a viewpoint that looks out over the castle and the Alfama. ⊠ *Calçada da Glória, Bairro Alto* ⧌ *€4 round trip (free with Viva Viagem card)* Ⓜ *Restauradores*.

Igreja de Santa Catarina

It's one of Lisbon's richest and most beautiful churches but one of the least visited. Even many travel guides overlook it despite its very central location on the edge of Bairro Alto. The baroque and rococo interior is a monumental mix of gilded wood carving and stucco decoration, added in 1727 to the building, which dates from 1647. The organ is considered a masterpiece of gilded woodwork, while the altar is a highlight of the art commissioned during the wealthy reign of King João V, with sculptures brought from Flanders. Two of Portugal's prominent 18th-century artists (Vieira Lusitano and André Gonçalves) are responsible for the large paintings in golden frames on the side walls. ⊠ *Calçada do Combro 82, Bairro Alto* ☎ *21/346–4443* Ⓜ *Tram 28*.

Igreja e Museu de São Roque

Designed by Filippo Terzi and completed in 1574, this church was one of the earliest Jesuit buildings in the world. While the exterior is somewhat plain and austere, the inside is dazzling, with abundant use of gold and marble. Eight side chapels have statuary and art dating to the early 17th century. The last chapel on the left before the altar is the extraordinary 18th-century Capela de São João Baptista (Chapel of St. John the Baptist); designed and built in Rome, with rare stones

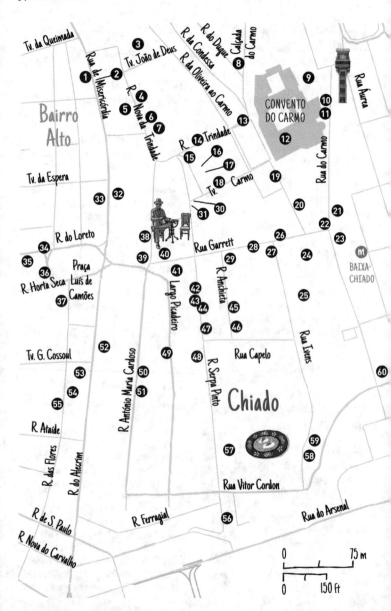

Mourax

ua de Santa Justa

Rua Augusta

Rua dos Fanqueiros

Rua dos Douradores

Rua da Assunção

Rua da Prata

Rua da Vitória

Rua São Nicolau

Rua dos Sapateiros

Baixa

Rua Áurea

Rua da Conceição

Rua de São Julião

Rua do Comércio

SIGHTS

Convento do
Carmo 12

Museu Nacional
de Arte
Contemporânea 57

SHOPPING

A Vida Portuguesa ... 46

Armazens
do Chiado 21

Ás de Espadas 8

Bertrand 29

Cantê 24

Casa dos Ovos
Moles em Lisboa 19

Casa Pereira 26

Claus Porto 1

Eureka 60

Fabrica Features 41

Fábrica Sant'Anna ... 53

The Feeting Room 20

Joalharia do
Carmo 10

Loja da Burel 42

Luvaria Ulisses 11

Maison Nuno Gama . 38

Sapataria do
Carmo 13

Soul Mood 31

Storytailors 56

TM Collection 2

Tous 28

Vista Alegre 39

COFFEE & QUICK BITES

A Brasileira 40

Alcôa 27

Fábulas 25

Landeau 54

Manteigaria 34

Royale Café 16

Santini Chiado 22

Tartine 43

Vertigo Café 18

DINING

Alma 45

Aqui Há Peixe 14

Bairro do Avillez 6

Belcanto 47

Boa Bao 17

Café No Chiado 49

Cervejaria
Trindade 4

Epur 59

Faz Gostos 5

Honorato 30

Largo 44

Mini Bar 50

Palácio Chiado 52

Sea Me 35

Taberna da Rua das
Flores 37

Tágide 58

Tavares 33

BARS & NIGHTLIFE

By the Wine 55

Duque Brewpub 3

Entretanto 23

Le Consulat 36

O Purista 7

Sandeman Chiado 15

Silk 32

Topo Chiado 9

PERFORMING ARTS

Teatro Nacional de
São Carlos 48

Teatro São Luiz 51

and mosaics that resemble oil paintings, the chapel was taken apart, shipped to Lisbon, and reassembled here in 1747. The museum adjoining the church displays a surprisingly engaging collection of clerical vestments and liturgical objects. There is also a stylish café with patio. ✉ *Largo Trindade Coelho, Bairro Alto* ☎ *21/323-5444* ⊕ *www. museudesaoroque.com* 🎫 *Church free, museum €3 (free Sun. until 2 pm)* Ⓜ *Baixa-Chiado or Restauradores and then Glória funicular.*

Miradouro de Santa Catarina

Many call it Miradouro do Adamastor (Adamastor's Viewpoint) due to a rock on the site with a sculpted image of the mythical giant from the seas in the epic poem *The Lusiads*. This is where the most bohemian young locals get together at sunset, drinking and smoking to the sounds of street musicians. It's a place for chilling out, and if you want to enjoy a drink or a meal as the sun goes down, there are several surrounding spots with outdoor seating. ✉ *Rua de Santa Catarina, Bairro Alto* Ⓜ *Baixa-Chiado; Tram 28.*

Miradouro de São Pedro de Alcântara

Arguably Lisbon's most romantic viewpoint, this landscaped promenade is split into two levels, each offering a wonderful view of the castle at the top of a hill. It's a popular spot at night, as the moon shines over the city. A large kiosk surrounded by tables and lounge chairs serves refreshments to those who decide to stay and enjoy the views a little longer. ✉ *Rua de São Pedro de Alcântara, Bairro Alto* Ⓜ *Baixa-Chiado; Tram 24.*

Museu da Farmácia

The Museum of Pharmacy, within an old palace, covers more than 5,000 years of pharmaceutical history, from prehistoric cures to the fantastic world of fictive potions à la Harry Potter. Ancient objects related to pharmaceutical science and art—from Mesopotamian, Egyptian, Roman, and Incan civilizations—are on display in well-lighted showcases, as are those from Europe. Whole pharmacies have been transported here intact from other parts of Portugal, even a traditional 19th-century Chinese drugstore from Portugal's former territory of Macau. There's also a smart bar and restaurant called Pharmacia that serves lunch and dinner as well as afternoon *petiscos* (tasty Portuguese bar snacks). ✉ *Rua Marechal Saldanha 1, Bairro Alto* ☎ *21/340-0680* ⊕ *www.museudafarmacia.pt* 🎫 *€5* Ⓜ *Baixa-Chiado; Tram 28.*

Museu Júlio Pomar

Júlio Pomar was one of Portugal's greatest 20th- and 21st-century artists, and this small museum was also his studio until his death in 2018. The building is a former warehouse, redesigned by Pritzker Prize–winning architect Álvaro Siza Vieira, and it presents temporary exhibitions of Pomar's paintings, drawings, and sculptures spread over two floors. ⊠ *Rua do Vale 7, Bairro Alto* ☎ *21/588-0793* ⊕ *www. ateliermuseujuliopomar.pt* 🎫 *€2* ⊙ *Closed Mon.* Ⓜ *Tram 28.*

Museu Nacional de Arte Contemporânea

Also known as the Museu do Chiado, this museum—housed in a former convent—specializes in Portuguese art from 1850 to the present day, covering various movements: Romanticism, naturalism, surrealism, and modernism. The museum also hosts temporary exhibitions of paintings, sculpture, and multimedia installations, as well as summer jazz concerts in its small walled garden. ⊠ *Rua Serpa Pinto 4, Chiado* ☎ *21/343-2148* ⊕ *www. museuartecontemporanea.gov.pt* 🎫 *€5* ⊙ *Closed Mon.* Ⓜ *Baixa-Chiado.*

 Shopping

Armazéns do Chiado

It calls itself "Lisbon's meeting point" for a reason. This former department store, which reopened as a mall in 1999 after a fire in 1988 almost completely destroyed the building, is where people of all ages meet before a night out on the town. Inside are national and international chain stores, but the main attraction is the food court on the top floor, which offers views of Chiado and the castle. ⊠ *Rua do Carmo 2, Chiado* ☎ *21/321-0600* ⊕ *www.armazensdo-chiado.com* Ⓜ *Baixa-Chiado.*

Ás de Espadas

Stepping into this store is traveling back in time, to when colorful patterns and pleated skirts were the latest styles. Ás de Espadas is a treasure chest filled with vintage wear that looks good in the new millennium and encourages shoppers to show off their individuality. There's everything to complete an outfit, from accessories to shoes, purses, hats, and jewelry. ⊠ *Calçada do Carmo 42, Chiado* ⊙ *Closed Sun.* Ⓜ *Blue or Green Line to Baixa-Chiado.*

Baco Alto

At this Bairro Alto delicatessen, you can taste wines and fine foods from around Portugal before buying. The knowledgeable staff will recommend the right wine for you. ⊠ *Rua do Norte 33, Bairro Alto* ☎ *91/245–6066* Ⓜ *Baixa-Chiado; Tram 28.*

Bertrand

Founded in 1732, this is the world's oldest operating bookstore, and a certificate near the door from Guinness World Records attests to that. Current bestsellers welcome you to the first room, before you continue into the vaulted interior to find different sections divided by theme. It includes a small English-language selection of works by the major Portuguese authors and Lisbon-related books. You can also buy international newspapers and magazines. ⊠ *Rua Garrett 73–75, Chiado* ☎ *21/347–6122* ⊕ *www.bertrand.pt* Ⓜ *Baixa-Chiado.*

Cantê

Exclusivity is guaranteed at this bikini store: it sells only its own inventive designs and stocks no more than eight of each model. Despite the many tropical prints, this is all fashionable beachwear made in Portugal. ⊠ *Rua Garrett 19, Chiado* ☎ *21/014–2912* ⊕ *www.cantelisboa.com* Ⓜ *Baixa-Chiado.*

Casa dos Ovos Moles em Lisboa

Just down the street from Convento do Carmo, this store offers sweets that originated in convents all over Portugal. Nuns used to make a living by selling their confections, often using lots of sugar and eggs.

This store is named after the extra-sweet eggy pastry from the city of Aveiro, but you can buy many other specialties from around the country. ⊠ *Calçada do Sacramento 25, Chiado* ☎ *91/930–3788* ⊕ *www.casadosovosmolesemlisboa.pt* Ⓜ *Baixa-Chiado.*

Casa Pereira

Step into this charming old store with its original 1930s decor to buy exotic coffees, teas, and chocolates, mainly from former Portuguese colonies (Brazil, Cape Verde, and São Tomé in particular). It's also a good place to grab a bottle of port wine. ⊠ *Rua Garrett 38, Chiado* ☎ *21/342–6694* Ⓜ *Baixa-Chiado.*

Claus Porto

This Portuguese brand dates back to 1887, but this is its first flagship store, opened as recently as 2016. It took over the space of a former pharmacy, meeting the increasing demand for its fragrances that are now available in more than 60 countries. There are luxurious soaps, colognes, and scented candles, all beautifully wrapped in retro packages. Photographs on the walls tell the history of the brand. ⊠ *Rua da Misericórdia 135, Chiado* ☎ *91/721–5855* ⊕ *clausporto.com* Ⓜ *Baixa-Chiado.*

Cork & Co

At this store it's all about eco-design and the creation of products made from Portugal's abundant cork forests. On offer are a wide variety of cork furniture and accessories, many of which are now sold and showcased worldwide, including at such design-forward stores as

Milan Triennale and MoMA Design Store in New York. You can be sure that here you're getting the best of Portugal's wonderful world of cork, not to mention a stylish umbrella or a handbag or two. ⊠ *Rua das Salgadeiras 10, Bairro Alto* ☎ *21/609–0231* ⊕ *www.corkandcompany.pt* Ⓜ *Baixa-Chiado; Tram 28.*

Eureka
Portugal is known to produce top-quality shoes, and at this store you can find collections exclusively created by some of the country's leading footwear designers. The attractive, rather futuristic space offers choices for both men and women from a variety of brands, all of them "Made in Portugal." ⊠ *Rua Nova do Almada 26–28, Chiado* ☎ *21/346–8173* ⊕ *www.eurekashoes.com* Ⓜ *Baixa-Chiado.*

A Fábrica dos Chapéus
The young proprietor of this funky store stocks a huge range of hats—more than 1,000—and also makes exclusive designs to order. ⊠ *Rua da Rosa 118, Bairro Alto* ☎ *21/191–4579* ⊕ *www.afabricadoschapeus.com* ⊙ *Closed Sun.* Ⓜ *Baixa-Chiado; Tram 28.*

Fabrica Features
Located above a Benetton megastore, this gallery/store overlooks the busiest part of Chiado, with a particularly Instagram-worthy view of the cobblestone pavement designs from above. When you arrive, you may also be tempted to photograph one of Europe's oldest (and most beautiful) elevators, with its well-preserved art nouveau features from more than a century ago. The collection of bags, stationery, ceramics, and other products designed in Portugal and abroad are worth considering for more than just a photograph. ⊠ *Rua Garrett 83, 4th fl., Chiado* ☎ *21/342–0596* ⊕ *www.fabricafeatures.com* Ⓜ *Baixa-Chiado.*

★ Fábrica Sant'Anna
Established in 1741, this factory uses century-old techniques, including painting and glazing entirely by hand, to create contemporary tile panels and reproductions of antique designs. They're available at this store in Chiado and are on display (and also for sale) at the showroom next to the factory in the Belém district (Calçada da Boa-Hora 96). ⊠ *Rua do Alecrim 95, Chiado* ☎ *21/342–2537* ⊕ *www.fabrica-santanna.com* Ⓜ *Baixa-Chiado.*

The Feeting Room
Originally from the city of Porto, the Feeting Room offers Portuguese footwear and international labels not previously available in the capital. It's more than a shoe store; it also carries a few fashion accessories, home design, and lifestyle pieces, mostly produced in Portugal. ⊠ *Calçada do Sacramento 26, Chiado* ☎ *21/246–4700* ⊕ *www.thefeetingroom.com* Ⓜ *Blue or Green Line to Baixa-Chiado.*

Galeria Graça Brandão
Founded in Porto, this gallery moved to Lisbon and took over an old printing house. It usually presents works by Portuguese and Brazilian artists. ⊠ *Rua dos Caetanos*

26, Bairro Alto ☎ *21/346–9183* ⊕ *www. galeriagracabrandao.com* Ⓜ *Tram 28.*

Joalharia do Carmo

In business since 1924, this is one of Lisbon's oldest and most beautiful shops. Behind its historic art nouveau facade, it displays museum-worthy gold and silver pieces, plus exclusive Portuguese jewelry. It's also the place to look for the traditional handmade filigree from the north of the country. ⊠ *Rua do Carmo 87B, Chiado* ☎ *21/342–3050* ⊗ *Closed Sun.* Ⓜ *Blue or Green Line to Baixa-Chiado.*

★ Loja da Burel

The mountains of Serra da Estrela in central Portugal are in the one of the country's coldest regions, so locals have a centuries-old tradition of using sheep's fleece in a variety of ways. This store has taken that regional product and given it even more uses by creating pieces of modern design, such as handbags, backpacks, blankets, and even chairs. The colorful products come mostly from young Portuguese designers, but they are universally recognized for their innovation, sustainability, and functionality. ⊠ *Rua Serpa Pinto 15B, Chiado* ☎ *21/245–6910* ⊕ *burelfactory.com* Ⓜ *Baixa-Chiado.*

★ Luvaria Ulisses

Lisbon's smallest shop is one of its most charming, selling nothing but custom-made, finely crafted gloves since 1925. It's the last place in Portugal where you can get these exclusive gloves, and it's recognized as one of the best stores of its kind

in Europe. The well-preserved interior fits just about two customers at a time, who go through the process of trying on the different sizes and colors by placing their elbows on a small cushion and letting the fitter make the perfect adjustments. ⊠ *Rua do Carmo 87, Chiado* ☎ *21/342–0295* ⊕ *www.luvariaulisses. com* Ⓜ *Rossio.*

★ Maison Nuno Gama

After several years in the city of Porto, men's fashion designer Nuno Gama moved to Lisbon. In addition to being where he presents his latest collections (of streetwear and sportswear, plus shoes and accessories), the store also doubles as a barbershop. ⊠ *Rua Nova da Trindade, 1, Chiado* ☎ *21/347–9068* ⊕ *nunogama.pt* ⊗ *Closed Sun.* Ⓜ *Yellow Line to Rato; Tram 24 to Príncipe Real.*

Sapataria do Carmo

In business since 1904, this charming old shoe store features an interior that hasn't changed much since the 1950s. Customers still sit on velvet sofas to try on shoes that are stored in vintage boxes, and it still specializes in handmade Portuguese shoes. You can expect top quality at reasonable prices, with some classic and some trendy models, as well as a few exclusive pieces. ⊠ *Largo do Carmo 26, Chiado* ☎ *21/342–3386* ⊕ *www.sapatariado-carmo.com* Ⓜ *Baixa-Chiado.*

Soul Mood

This small, minimalist concept store offers the avant-garde fashions of lesser-known European designers.

It's laid out almost like a gallery, with the curated collections on color-coordinated display. In addition to fashion and accessories, you may find jewelry by local designers like Valentim Quaresma, whose pieces were featured in Lady Gaga's video "G.U.Y." ⊠ *Travessa do Carmo 1, Chiado* ☎ *21/346-3179* ⊕ *www. soulmood.pt* ⊗ *Closed Sun.* Ⓜ *Blue or Green Line to Baixa-Chiado.*

★ Storytailors
For some fairy-tale shopping, browse the racks here filled with fantastical frocks, capes, and more. Madonna is whispered to be among the celeb customers to have done so. ⊠ *Calçada do Ferragial 8, Chiado* ☎ *21/343-2306* ⊕ *www.storytailors.pt* Ⓜ *Baixa-Chiado.*

TM Collection
Teresa Martins named her brand with her initials and has been successful in placing her collections in different concept stores across the country. Her own store in Lisbon is where you can find the latest creations, inspired by her native Portugal but also by India and Nepal, where the designer says she feels "at home." The result is exclusive prints, textures, and styles, using natural fabrics, in fashion and home decor. ⊠ *Rua da Misericórdia 102, Chiado* ☎ *21/347-2293* ⊕ *www. tmcollection.com* ⊗ *Closed Sun.* Ⓜ *Blue or Green Line to Baixa-Chiado.*

Tous
The jewelry on display is now that of the Tous brand, but the Louis XIV–style interior remains that of the original Ourivesaria Aliança, which opened in 1914. It's probably Lisbon's most beautiful store, which tourists can't help photographing. ⊠ *Rua Garrett 50, Chiado* ☎ *21/346-0455* ⊕ *www.tous.com* Ⓜ *Baixa-Chiado.*

★ A Vida Portuguesa
The former storeroom of an old perfumery has become one of Lisbon's most beloved stores. It sells traditional Portuguese brands that have been passed on from generation to generation and that have now become must-haves. Those include luxurious soaps of the Ach. Brito and Claus Porto brands and colorful Bordallo Pinheiro pottery—all displayed in beautifully restored antique glass cases. ⊠ *Rua Anchieta 11, Chiado* ☎ *21/346-5073* ⊕ *www.avidaportuguesa.com* Ⓜ *Baixa-Chiado.*

Vista Alegre
Originally a royal factory founded in 1817, this is now one of Europe's most prestigious porcelain manufacturers. The flagship store in Chiado presents its ever-changing collections, which are often signed by national and international artists. ⊠ *Largo do Chiado 20–23, Chiado* ☎ *21/346-1401* ⊕ *vistaalegre.com* Ⓜ *Baixa-Chiado.*

Príncipe Real and Restauradores

Jardim do Príncipe Real

Jardim de São Pedro de Alcântara

Bairro Alto

R. do Jasmim

Praça do Príncipe Real

Rua Dom Pedro V

R. Eduardo Coelho

Tv. do Arco a Jesus

Rua Academia das Ciências

Rua de O Século

Tv. Conde Soure

Rua Nova do Loureiro

Rua São Boaventura

Rua de São Pedro

R. de São Pedro de Alcântara

R. do Teixeira

Tv. da Boa Hora

Rua da Rosa

Rua Nova de Loureiro

Travessa da Agua da Flor

R. dos Caetanos

Tv. do Poço da Cidade

Tv. da Queima

Tv. dos Fiéis de Deus

R. da Atalaia

R. da Barroca

Tv. da E...

Tv. Mercês

Tv. Convento de Jesus

Rua Vale

R. do Poço dos Negros

Tv. Alcaide

Calçada do Combro

R. Mal. Saldanha

R. de Santa Catarina

Rua da Bica de Duarte Belo

R Chagas

R Horta Seca

Calçada de Silva da Correia de Sá

Rua dos Cordoeiros

Tv. G. Cossoul

R. da Emenda

Rua da Boavista

R. Ataíde

0   100 m

0   200 ft

1 2 3 4 5 6 7 8 9 11 12 13 14 15 16 17 18 19 23 24 25 26 27 28 29 30 31 32 33 34 35 36 37 38 39 40 41 42 43

SIGHTS

Convento de
São Pedro de
Alcântara 6
Elevador da Glória 1
Igreja de
Santa Catarina 31
Igreja e Museu
de São Roque 10
Miradouro de
Santa Catarina 38
Miradouro de São
Pedro de Alcântara.... 2
Museu da
Farmácia 40
Museu
Júlio Pomar 32

SHOPPING

A Fábrica
dos Chapéus 13
Baco Alto 22
Cork & Co 23
Galeria Graça
Brandão 16

COFFEE & QUICK BITES

Madame Petisca 36
The Mill 35
Noobai Café 37

DINING

Agua Pela Barba 41
Alfaia 11
As Salgadeiras 24
Bota Alta 15
Cantinho da Paz 33
Casanostra 29
Cocheira
Alentejana 19
The Decadente 4
Fidalgo 28
The Insólito 3
Lisboa à Noite 21
Lumi 9
O Asiático 7
100 Maneiras 5
Pharmacia 39
Sinal Vermelho 20
Toma Lá Dá Cá 42

BARS & NIGHTLIFE

Artis 18
As Primas 8
Bairru's Bodega 26
The Garden
Rooftop 43
Garrafeira Alfaia 12
Incognito 34
Maria Caxuxa 27
The Old Pharmacy ... 17
Park 30
Portas Largas 14
Purex 25

☕ Coffee and Quick Bites

Alcôa
$ | Portuguese. This pastry shop opened in 1957 in the city of Alcobaça, and six decades later it expanded to the capital. Its rise to fame in Lisbon happened in 2014, when it took the top prize for best custard tart in an annual contest. **Known for:** beautiful interior decorated with contemporary tiles by renowned artist Querubim Lapa; mouthwatering window displays; eggy custard pastries. *Average main: €3* ✉ *Rua Garrett 37, Chiado* ☎ *21/136–7183* Ⓜ *Baixa-Chiado.*

A Brasileira
$ | Portuguese. Lisbon's most famous café dates from 1905 and maintains its beautiful art deco interior, though everyone prefers to sit at the tables outside. The coffee no longer comes exclusively from the former Portuguese colony that gave it its name ("The Brazilian"), but it still serves some of the best in town. **Known for:** statue of poet Fernando Pessoa sitting at a table outside; modernist paintings of major Portuguese artists such as Almada Negreiros; daily specials for lunch or dinner. *Average main: €7* ✉ *Rua Garrett 120–122, Chiado* ☎ *21/346–9541* Ⓜ *Blue or Green Line to Baixa-Chiado.*

Fábulas
$ | Portuguese. You can have coffee and dessert or a full meal here. Although you'll find a few tables outside in a courtyard shared with other cafés and restaurants, sit inside under the two-centuries-old arches on mismatched vintage furniture, which includes Singer sewing machine tables on which you're served your light meals or drinks. **Known for:** weekend brunch; regularly changing art; home-style desserts. *Average main: €13* ✉ *Calçada Nova de São Francisco 14, Chiado* ✥ *Also accessible through courtyard on Rua Garrett 19* ☎ *21/601–8472* ⊕ *www.fabulas.pt* Ⓜ *Baixa-Chiado.*

Landeau
$ | Portuguese. Although Landeau's doesn't claim to be "the best chocolate cake in the world" (as does the star creation of another famous pastry shop in town), ever since the *New York Times* described it as "devilishly good," Landeau's cake has been reason enough to head to Chiado. Here you may buy an entire cake to enjoy at home or sit for a slice with some tea. **Known for:** relaxing, dimly lit interior; reasonably priced drinks to accompany your cake; welcoming staff who will tell you all about the cake. *Average main: €4* ✉ *Rua das Flores 70, Chiado* ☎ *91/181–0801* ⊕ *www.landeau.pt* Ⓜ *Baixa-Chiado.*

Madame Petisca
$ | Portuguese. Overlooking the river and one of the city's most popular viewpoints, this terrace café serves drinks and petiscos throughout the day. It's on the top floor of a hotel, but you'll mostly find young locals, especially for brunch on weekends. **Known for:** reinvented Portuguese petiscos; original desserts; good cocktails. *Average main: €10* ✉ *Rua de Santa Catarina*

17, 3rd fl., Bairro Alto ☎ *91/515–0860* ⊕ *www.madamepetisca.pt* Ⓜ *Baixa-Chiado; Tram 28.*

Manteigaria

$ | Portuguese. The custard tarts of this tiny shop rival those of the famous shop in Belém for the title of the best *pastel de nata* in town. Eat them at the counter or order a box of half a dozen to enjoy later. **Known for:** glassed-in kitchen showing the baking process; art nouveau facade; traditional Portuguese drinks, like ginjinha and port wine. *Average main: €2* ⊠ *Rua do Loreto 2, Chiado* ☎ *21/347–1492* Ⓜ *Blue or Green Line to Baixa-Chiado.*

The Mill

$ | International. This small, Australian-influenced coffee shop has become a popular spot for breakfast or a light meal in the afternoon. Almost everything is produced in-house, including the ceramics. **Known for:** breakfast bowls; exclusive coffee blends; extensive brunch menu. *Average main: €7* ⊠ *Rua do Poço dos Negros 1, Bairro Alto* ⊕ *www.themill.pt* Ⓜ *Tram 28 to R. Poiais S. Bento.*

Noobai Café

$ | Portuguese. With two terraces, this very popular café is located in a corner of the Santa Catarina viewpoint, so expect bird's-eye views over the port and the city. There are daily specials for light meals and refreshing drinks, but it's the weekend brunch that attracts most locals. **Known for:** colorful space with a small play area for kids; small plates of traditional

Portuguese dishes; cocktails. *Average main: €10* ⊠ *Miradouro de Santa Catarina, Bairro Alto* ☎ *21/346–5014* ⊕ *www.noobaicafe.com* Ⓜ *Baixa-Chiado; Tram 28.*

Royale Café

$ | Mediterranean. Having opened in 2005 as a stylish café serving mostly drinks and pastries, Royale has evolved in its decade-plus of life and now presents a sizable menu of creative food. It's mostly Mediterranean inspired and uses seasonal ingredients, attracting young locals. **Known for:** Nordic-style interior; pleasant patio with a vertical garden; Sunday brunch. *Average main: €13* ⊠ *Largo Rafael Bordalo Pinheiro 29, Chiado* ☎ *21/346–9125* ⊕ *www.royalecafe.com* Ⓜ *Baixa-Chiado.*

Santini Chiado

$ | Café. For some of the best ice cream in town, drop into the Lisbon branch of a family concern founded in 1949 in the nearby resort of Cascais. Different flavors are introduced daily, which may include Azorean pineapple, Brazilian açai, or other local and more exotic options. **Known for:** alternative flavors; ice-cream milk shakes; almond tart. *Average main: €5* ⊠ *Rua do Carmo 9, Chiado* ☎ *21/346–8431* ⊕ *www.santini.pt* Ⓜ *Baixa-Chiado.*

Tartine

$ | International. The name is French but this bakery and café is very much Portuguese and offers different types of local bread and pastries. Grab something to go at the counter by the entrance or head upstairs for a light meal and something sweet. **Known for:** Chiado cake specialty; daily brunch menu; small patio. *Average main: €9* ✉ *Rua Serpa Pinto 15A, Chiado* ☎ *21/342–9108* ⊕ *www.tartine.pt* Ⓜ *Blue or Green Line to Baixa-Chiado.*

Vertigo Café
$ | **International.** This vintage café takes you back to the 1930s and '40s through its decor, which includes vintage black-and-white photos on the walls. It's a quiet place to stay with a good book or work on your laptop as you enjoy a cup of tea or a light meal. **Known for:** stained glass and wood-paneled interior; gluten-free chocolate cake; stuffed potatoes. *Average main: €7* ✉ *Travessa do Carmo 4, Chiado* ☎ *21/343–3112* ⊘ *Closed Sun.* Ⓜ *Baixa-Chiado.*

¶¶ Dining

Água Pela Barba
$ | **Seafood.** With a wooden interior inspired by fisherman huts, this restaurant is for those who enjoy the fresh flavors of the sea. The menu lists just half a dozen regular entrées but there are many more small, shared plates. **Known for:** Portuguese wines from all regions; signature Água Pela Barba cocktail; port wine tiramisu. *Average main: €15* ✉ *Rua do Almada 29–31, Bairro Alto* ☎ *21/346–1376* ⊘ *No lunch Mon.* Ⓜ *Tram 28 to Calhariz-Bica.*

Alfaia
$ | **Portuguese.** In this traditional restaurant (it's one of the oldest in Lisbon), courteous staff serve up

Portuguese classics. As is evident from the dining room decoration, wine is a big deal here; indeed, there are 600 bottles on the wine list to choose from. **Known for:** rustic interior; outdoor seating; grilled fish. *Average main: €14* ✉ *Travessa da Queimada 22, Bairro Alto* ☎ *21/346–1232* ⊕ *www.restaurantealfaia.com* Ⓜ *Baixa-Chiado; Tram 28.*

Alma
$$$$ | **Portuguese.** Chef Henrique Sá Pessoa's fine-dining restaurant moved from its original location in Santos to Chiado in 2015, but the name was the only thing that was inherited from the previous space. The decor became darker and minimalist, and the entire menu was changed, adding a slight Asian touch to the contemporary Portuguese cuisine. **Known for:** contemporary decor in a vaulted former stable; some dishes finished by the chef at the table; tasting menu of Portuguese seafood. *Average main: €35* ✉ *Rua Anchieta 15, Chiado* ☎ *21/347–0650* ⊕ *www.almalisboa.pt* ⊘ *Closed Mon.* Ⓜ *Baixa-Chiado.*

★ Aqui Há Peixe
$$$ | **Seafood.** The restaurant's name translates to "There's Fish Here," and make no mistake: it's one of the top places in town to savor the catch of the day. It's an especially good choice for lunch, when the menu always includes a market-based special at a good price. **Known for:** fresh fish from the Lisbon coast; homemade desserts; Brazilian-style picanha (sirloin steak) for those who prefer meat. *Average main: €22* ✉ *Rua da*

Trindade 18A, Chiado ☎ *21/343–2154* ⊕ *www.aquihapeixe.pt* ⊘ *Closed Mon. No lunch weekends* Ⓜ *Baixa-Chiado.*

O Asiático

$$ | **Asian.** This eclectic exploration of Asian food takes you on a journey through the cuisines of Thailand, Vietnam, and Japan, selected with expertise and creativity by chef Kiko Martins. The menu is divided into "hot" and "cold" dishes, and it's recommended that you order several to share at the table. **Known for:** tasteful interior design; pleasant, open-air patio in the back; signature drinks created by the chef. *Average main: €18* ⊠ *Rua da Rosa 317, Bairro Alto* ☎ *21/131–9369* ⊘ *No lunch Mon.–Thurs.* Ⓜ *Baixa-Chiado.*

★ Bairro do Avillez

$$$$ | **Portuguese.** Here you can have different dining experiences depending on where you sit. Distinguished chef José Avillez has divided a large interior into three spaces—a "market," a "tavern," and a "patio"—as a tribute to Lisbon's traditional neighborhoods, serving different types of cuisines in each section. **Known for:** variety of Portuguese cheeses and hams (some of them seen hanging in the open kitchen); seafood platters; signature desserts. *Average main: €30* ⊠ *Rua Nova da Trindade 18, Chiado* ☎ *21/583–0290* Ⓜ *Baixa-Chiado.*

★ Belcanto

$$$$ | **Eclectic.** The name José Avillez (one of Portugal's most renowned young chefs) is synonymous with fine dining in Lisbon, where he oversees several high-end restaurants. To see what all the fuss is about, visit Belcanto, which holds two Michelin stars. **Known for:** molecular gastronomy; witty presentations; huge list of the finest Portuguese wines. *Average main: €50* ⊠ *Largo de São Carlos 10, Chiado* ☎ *21/342–0607* ⊕ *belcanto.pt* ⊘ *Closed Sun. and Mon.* Ⓜ *Baixa-Chiado.*

Boa Bao

$$ | **Asian.** This restaurant takes you on a trip around Asia, with a wide selection of dishes that go from Thailand to Indonesia. In addition to the regular list of choices there are special vegan and gluten-free menus. **Known for:** spicy food; exotic cocktails; lively atmosphere. *Average main: €16* ⊠ *Largo Rafael Bordalo Pinheiro 30, Chiado* ☎ *91/902–3030* ⊕ *www.boabao.pt* Ⓜ *Baixa-Chiado.*

Bota Alta

$ | **Portuguese.** This wood-paneled tavern is one of the Bairro Alto's oldest and most popular—lines form outside by 8 pm. There's little space between the tables, but this only enhances the buzz. **Known for:** walls covered with framed drawings and caricatures; good value; generous portions. *Average main: €12* ⊠ *Travessa da Queimada 37, Bairro Alto* ☎ *21/342–7959* ⊘ *Closed Sun. No lunch Sat.* Ⓜ *Baixa-Chiado; Tram 28.*

Café no Chiado

$$ | **Café.** The tables outside this café and restaurant are some of the best spots to watch the old trams go by throughout the day, from morning to late at night. Less touristy than the historic cafés nearby, it attracts artists from the neighboring theaters who still stop for a drink as they read local and international newspapers. **Known for:** Portuguese cuisine with an international touch; peaceful, shaded terrace; Iberian tapas. *Average main: €17* ⊠ *Largo do Picadeiro 10–12, Chiado* ☎ *21/346–0501* ⊕ *www.cafenochiado. com* Ⓜ *Baixa-Chiado.*

Cantinho da Paz
$ | Indian. This mom-and-pop establishment specializes in the cuisine of former Portuguese colony Goa—otherwise surprisingly hard to find in Lisbon. The dishes reveal Goa's unique mix of Portuguese and Indian influences, and the English-speaking staff can guide you through the menu. **Known for:** spicy food; lobster curry for two; special dishes only available Friday and Saturday, such as crab curry. *Average main: €13* ⊠ *Rua da Paz 4, off Rua dos Poiais de São Bento, Bairro Alto* ☎ *21/390–1963* ☾ *Closed Sun.* Ⓜ *Tram 28.*

Casanostra
$$ | Italian. It was one of the first truly Italian restaurants in Lisbon and is still considered one of the best. On the menu are the favorite dishes of the Italian owner, including meat and fish options, as well as the expected pastas; there are no pizzas on the menu. **Known for:** retro-minimalist interior; Italian desserts; daily specials. *Average main: €15* ⊠ *Travessa do Poço da Cidade 60, Bairro Alto* ☎ *21/342–5931* ⊕ *www.casanostra.pt* Ⓜ *Tram 28 to Pç. Luis Camões.*

Cervejaria Trindade
$$ | Portuguese. The refectory of a 13th-century monastery was turned into a beer hall in 1836 and is now one of the city's most popular traditional restaurants. The spacious, vaulted interior can get quite noisy with the large number of locals and tourists, but for many this is a quintessential Lisbon experience. **Known for:** monumental dining room lined with colorful azulejo tiles; steaks; seafood platters. *Average main: €17* ⊠ *Rua Nova da Trindade 20, Chiado* ☎ *21/342–3506* ⊕ *www.cervejariatrindade.pt* Ⓜ *Baixa-Chiado.*

Cocheira Alentejana
$ | Portuguese. This is a rustic place, both in the decor and in the food, and it hasn't changed a bit over the years. That makes it a favorite among locals, who prefer the good old-fashioned flavors and service, and with tourists who want an authentic Portuguese experience. **Known for:** specialties from the Alentejo region; good-value meals; wine list with Portugal's most popular labels. *Average main: €11* ⊠ *Travessa do Poço da Cidade 19, Bairro Alto* ☎ *21/346–4868* ⊕ *cocheiraalentejana.pt* ☾ *Closed Sun. No lunch Sat.* Ⓜ *Baixa-Chiado, Tram 28.*

The Decadente
$ | Portuguese. No one could have predicted that a restaurant in a hostel would become one of Lisbon's favorites. Locals and tourists enjoy the creative Portuguese cuisine made from seasonal ingre-

dients. **Known for:** weekend brunch; outdoor seating in a backyard; special group menus (reserve at least 48 hours in advance). *Average main: €14 ⊠ Rua São Pedro de Alcântara 81, Bairro Alto ☎ 21/346–1381 ⊕ www.thedecadente.pt Ⓜ Tram 24 to S. Pedro Alcântara.*

Epur

$$$$ | **International.** After many years in the kitchens of some of the top restaurants in Portugal, French chef Vincent Farges opened his own spot in Lisbon, where he presents creative, seasonal tasting menus. His cuisine is inspired by different parts of the world and is accompanied by Portuguese wine. **Known for:** beautiful view over downtown Lisbon; tiled 18th-century interior with modern touches; daily fish or shellfish specials. *Average main: €100 ⊠ Largo da Academia Nacional das Belas Artes 14, Chiado ☎ 21/346–0519 ⊕ www.epur.pt ⊘ Closed Sun. and Mon. Ⓜ Blue or Green Line to Baixa-Chiado.*

Faz Gostos

$$ | **Portuguese.** Formerly a convent and later a factory, this space was redesigned by renowned designer Paulo Lobo and mixes the traditional and the contemporary. The same can be said about the food, with some dishes arriving still in the cooking pot. **Known for:** randomly placed 18th-century tiles covering a stylish modern interior; seafood from the Algarve; wines from the Lisbon region. *Average main: €17 ⊠ Rua Nova da Trindade 11, Chiado ☎ 92/528–6086 ⊕ fazgostoslx.*

com ⊘ *Closed Sun. No lunch Sat.* Ⓜ *Baixa-Chiado.*

Fidalgo

$ | **Portuguese.** Despite the contemporary decor, this is one of Bairro Alto's oldest restaurants and still serves traditional Portuguese cuisine. Locals know here they'll get reliably good food, so it gets packed quite fast; reservations are strongly recommended. **Known for:** steaks; grilled fish; profiteroles with hot chocolate for dessert. *Average main: €14 ⊠ Rua da Barroca 27, Bairro Alto ☎ 21/342–2900 ⊕ www.restaurante-fidalgo.com ⊘ Closed Sun.* Ⓜ *Baixa-Chiado; Tram 28.*

Honorato

$ | **Burger.** Named after the Brazilian chef who came up with the recipes for this restaurant's original burgers, Honorato is a minichain of trendy burger joints. The branch in Chiado is the most popular—it has a lively atmosphere and large windows looking out to one of the neighborhood's main squares. **Known for:** a face sculpted on a wall by famous street artist Vhils; variety of gins and cocktails; home-style fries. *Average main: €11 ⊠ Largo Rafael Bordalo Pinheiro 12, Chiado ☎ 21/347–0100 ⊕ www.honorato.pt* Ⓜ *Blue or Green line to Baixa-Chiado.*

The Insólito

$$ | **International.** Featuring a small terrace overlooking the São Pedro de Alcântara viewpoint and the castle, this rooftop bar and restaurant is one of the most popular spots for meals or drinks with a view. The menu changes regularly but is usually a creative mix of international cuisines. **Known for:** finger food; signature cocktails; charming turn-of-the-century wooden elevator. *Average main: €18 ⊠ Rua de São Pedro Alcântara 83, Bairro Alto* ☎ *21/130–3306* ⊕ *theinsolito.pt* ⊙ *No lunch* Ⓜ *Baixa-Chiado.*

★ Largo
$$$ | Mediterranean. Founded by celebrated Porto chef Miguel Castro e Silva, this upscale restaurant was an immediate hit with the critics when it opened in 2009. And while Castro has moved on, the stylish restaurant retains the flair that won the hearts of Lisbon's fashionable foodies. **Known for:** good-value lunch menu; premium gins; interior by prominent designer Miguel Câncio Martins, which includes tanks with jellyfish. *Average main: €22 ⊠ Rua Serpa Pinto 10A, Chiado* ☎ *21/347–7225* ⊕ *www.largo.pt* ⊙ *Closed Sun.* Ⓜ *Baixa-Chiado.*

★ Lisboa à Noite
$$ | Portuguese. One of Bairro Alto's top restaurants since opening in 2003 serves imaginative cuisine that manages to be both traditional and contemporary, mostly following Portuguese recipes but adding a few international touches. The arched interior was once a stable, and you can still see the ring chains used to tie the horses. **Known for:** beautiful

dining room with blue-and-white tile panels; over a half dozen choices of cod dishes; traditional dessert cart. *Average main: €18 ⊠ Rua das Gáveas 69, Bairro Alto* ☎ *21/346–8557* ⊕ *www.lisboanoite.com* ⊙ *Closed Sun. No lunch* Ⓜ *Baixa-Chiado; Tram 28.*

Lumi
$$ | Portuguese. Serving a mostly Portuguese menu divided into fish and meat options, this restaurant sits at the top of a hotel and looks out onto one of the city's most beautiful vistas. The kitchen uses only seasonal products from local and national producers, so the menu changes regularly. **Known for:** castle views; outdoor seating on a rooftop terrace; special children's menu. *Average main: €19 ⊠ The Lumiares Hotel, Rua do Diário de Notícias 142, Bairro Alto* ☎ *21/016–0210* ▭ *No credit cards* Ⓜ *Tram 24 to S. Pedro Alcântara.*

Mini Bar
$$ | International. Highly lauded chef José Avillez took over this restaurant connected to São Luiz Theater and has turned it into a fun theater-inspired place. He put together a menu of small plates with the greatest hits from his other restaurants and divided it into different "acts." You may choose to just have a drink and enjoy the "opening act," or stay for the entire "show." **Known for:** mixologists performing their art in front of diners; party atmosphere late at night on weekends; theater-themed decor. *Average main: €12 ⊠ Rua António Maria Cardoso 58, Chiado*

☎ 21/130–5393 ⊕ www.minibar.pt
⊘ No lunch Ⓜ Baixa-Chiado; Tram 28.

★ 100 Maneiras

$$$$ | Eclectic. Serbian-born chef Ljubomir Stanisic is inspired by the ingredients he finds daily at the local market to create one of Lisbon's most stimulating, internationally inspired tasting menus. The menu itself changes regularly and is served in a small, all-white dining room with space for just 30 people, so booking ahead is essential. **Known for:** whimsical presentations; good selection of wines; sophisticated yet often lively atmosphere when the chef decides to mingle with diners. *Average main: €60* ✉ Rua do Teixeira 35, Bairro Alto ☎ 91/091–8181 ⊕ www.restaurante100maneiras.com ⊘ No lunch Ⓜ Tram 24.

★ Palácio Chiado

$ | International. The 18th-century Quintela Palace now welcomes diners to a gastronomic experience like no other in the city, creating an elaborate, upscale food court atmosphere. Seven different restaurants occupy the different rooms and corners of the two floors, allowing you to choose among classic dishes of Portuguese cuisine or international or lighter options such as risottos and sandwiches. **Known for:** a grand interior with marble staircase, frescoed walls, stained-glass windows, and stuccoed ceilings; signature cocktails; traditional Portuguese desserts. *Average main: €12* ✉ Rua do Alecrim 70, Chiado

☎ 21/010–1184 ⊕ palaciochiado.pt
Ⓜ Baixa-Chiado.

Pharmacia

$ | Portuguese. Sharing the building of the Pharmacy Museum, this restaurant faces one of the city's most popular viewpoints and is open throughout the day for meals and drinks. The traditional Portuguese cuisine is given a twist by Susana Felicidade, known as a judge on the Portuguese edition of the *Top Chef* television show. **Known for:** small plates to share; decor recreating the atmosphere of an old pharmacy; "therapeutic cocktails". *Average main: €14* ✉ Rua Marechal Saldanha 2, Bairro Alto ☎ 21/346–2146 Ⓜ Baixa-Chiado; Tram 28.

★ As Salgadeiras

$$ | Portuguese. This rustic restaurant was established in a former bakery and has kept the building's original large, brick baking oven and stone arches. It serves well-presented classic Portuguese cuisine and a few original dishes from a menu evenly divided between meat and fish options. **Known for:** variety of cod dishes; chocolate chiffon dessert; excellent service by friendly staff. *Average main: €18* ✉ Rua das Salgadeiras 18, Bairro Alto ☎ 21/342–1157 ⊕ www.as-salgadeiras.com ⊘ No lunch Ⓜ Baixa-Chiado; Tram 28.

Sea Me

$$$ | Seafood. At this so-called modern fish market, you may choose to buy and take home fresh fish, or you can have it prepared on the spot in a variety of ways (from seafood platters to sushi). The cooking has a strong Japanese influence, and a large portion of the menu is devoted to sushi and sashimi. **Known for:** steak sandwiches as dessert; huge list of mostly Portuguese wines; fresh catch of the day displayed on ice. *Average main: €25* ⊠ *Rua do Loreto 21, Chiado* ☎ *21/346–1564* ⊕ *peixari-amoderna.com* Ⓜ *Baixa-Chiado.*

Sinal Vermelho

$ | **Portuguese.** Whether you sit in the traditionally tiled dining room or at one of the few tables outside, you'll have one of the best experiences in town here if you're looking for a classic Portuguese restaurant. On the menu you'll find many of the typical grilled meat and fish dishes, which come well presented on the plate. **Known for:** variety of traditional appetizers; cod dishes; large portions at fair prices. *Average main: €14* ⊠ *Rua das Gáveas 89, Bairro Alto* ☎ *21/346–1252* ⊙ *Closed Sun.* Ⓜ *Baixa-Chiado; Tram 28.*

Taberna da Rua das Flores

$ | **Portuguese.** Following time-tested recipes of traditional Portuguese dishes, this small restaurant has become a mecca for those looking for an old-school experience. Some recipes have fallen out of fashion and even been forgotten by locals, so many dishes are unique to Taberna da Rua das Flores. **Known for:** traditional decor recalling Lisbon's old taverns; freshly baked bread; wines from the Lisbon region. *Average main: €12* ⊠ *Rua das Flores 103, Chiado* ☎ *21/347–9418* ⊙ *Closed Sun.* ▭ *No*

credit cards Ⓜ *Blue or Green Line to Baixa-Chiado.*

Tágide

$$$$ | **Portuguese.** Named after the mythical nymphs that live in the Tagus river, this place is divided into two parts: a restaurant offering refined Portuguese cuisine upstairs and a wine and tapas bar downstairs. Both spaces face the river, so the tables by the windows are some of the most coveted in town. **Known for:** panoramic views of downtown and the river; classical neo-Romantic decor with 18th-century tile panels; list of exclusively Portuguese wines (except for the champagne). *Average main: €28* ⊠ *Largo Academia Nacional de Belas Artes 18–20, Chiado* ☎ *21/340–4010* ⊕ *www.restaurantetagide.com* ⊙ *Closed Sun.* Ⓜ *Blue or Green Line to Baixa-Chiado.*

Tavares

$$$$ | **Portuguese.** Lisbon's oldest restaurant opened in 1784 and still maintains the original baroque and rococo interior that makes it look like a dining room in Versailles. Famous national and international personalities, such as singer Amália Rodrigues, actor Cary Grant, President Eisenhower, and novelist Ernest Hemingway, have dined here over the decades, and although it's no longer on most lists of Lisbon's top dining options, new management in 2018 has been reviving it as a place to try contemporary Portuguese cuisine in historic surroundings. **Known for:** opulent golden and mirrored space;

GOLDEN LISBON

Portugal's golden age of discovery happened through the 15th and 16th centuries, and a century later, the country had a second, literal, golden age.

When gold was discovered in Brazil in the 17th century, Portugal took boatloads of it back (officially 850 tons, but more circulated illegally) and gilded its palaces, churches and cathedrals, and large public buildings. A unique, baroque style of gilded wood carving was born, with some works covering entire interiors, from floor to rafter.

The damage inflicted by the Great Lisbon Earthquake in 1755 means that the most magnificent examples are in Porto, but the capital city still also has a few notable ones, including the two most significant predating the earthquake: Igreja de São Roque is famous for its gem-filled Chapel of St. John the Baptist and has several remarkable golden chapels, like the Chapel of Our Lady of Doctrine; Igreja de Santa Catarina is treasured for its golden organ and sumptuous main altar. Other fine examples include Igreja da Madre de Deus, which is attached to the convent that houses the National Tile Museum, and Convento dos Cardaes in Príncipe Real. If you're lucky to find it open, peek inside Igreja de São Miguel in Alfama.

traditional dishes with a modern twist; refined service. *Average main: €34 ⊠ Rua da Misericórdia 37, Chiado ☎ 21/342–1112 ⊕ restaurantetavares.pt ⊗ Closed Sun. No lunch* Ⓜ *Baixa-Chiado.*

Toma Lá Dá Cá

$ | Portuguese. Locals and tourists who don't show up early often wait for as much as one hour for a table, knowing this is where you can still eat the good old-fashioned Lisbon way. Staff rush from table to table, serving doses of reasonably priced standards like grilled tuna and garlic prawns accompanied by a good house wine. **Known for:** freshgrilled fish; steak with mushroom sauce; delicious cheesecake or strawberry mousse (you have to ask). *Average main: €10 ⊠ Travessa do Sequeiro 38, Bairro Alto ☎ 21/347–*

9243 ⊗ Closed Sun. Ⓜ *Tram 28; Bica funicular.*

🍸 Bars and Nightlife

Artis

Except for a few interruptions over the years, this has consistently been one of Bairro Alto's most popular bars since the 1980s, when it was originally called Bartis. New management in 2009 turned it into a cozy wine bar with wooden furnishings, where everything served is "100% Portuguese." To accompany the wines there's a surprisingly long list of Portuguese petiscos,

so it's also possible to have a full meal here. The most famous choice on the list is its traditional pork sausage, which is flambéed at the table, with the flames causing everyone to grab their phones to snap a photo. ⊠ *Rua do Diário de Notícias 95, Bairro Alto* ☎ *21/342–4795* Ⓜ *Baixa-Chiado; Tram 28.*

Bairru's Bodega

This is one of several wine bars that have sprung up to meet the growing curiosity of foreign visitors about Portugal's *vinhos* (wines), which are sold here by the glass or bottle. Along with regional cheeses, hams, and sausages, you can sample homemade *ginjinha* (sour cherry liqueur) and other liqueurs—all to an exclusively Portuguese soundtrack. It's also known as a lesbian hangout. ⊠ *Rua da Barroca 3, Bairro Alto* Ⓜ *Baixa-Chiado; Tram 28.*

By the Wine

Stepping into this bar is like entering a wine cellar. Hundreds of bottles cover the stone-arch interior, all with labels from the Setúbal region just south of Lisbon. There are also wines from Alentejo and Douro, which can be served by the glass or bottle and accompanied by Iberian petiscos such as cheese and oysters from the Sado River. ⊠ *Rua das Flores 41-43, Chiado* ☎ *21/342–0319* ⊕ *bythewine.pt* Ⓜ *Baixa-Chiado.*

Le Consulat

Part of the former home of the Brazilian consulate was turned into this classy bar with windows opening to a view over Camões Square. It's the place to enjoy post-dinner drinks to the sound of chill-out beats and to admire some art, as it's connected to a gallery of Portuguese and international contemporary art. The drinks menu is quite long, offering Portuguese wines, tea, gins, and cocktails. ⊠ *Praça Luis de Camões 22, Chiado* ☎ *21/242–7470* Ⓜ *Baixa-Chiado.*

Duque Brewpub

A group of friends got together in 2015 and created their own craft beer, which resulted in Lisbon's first brewpub. It's found on a steep street with steps linking downtown to Chiado and Bairro Alto and has tables outside for afternoon or after-dark drinks and snacks. In addition to its own brand, it offers other craft beers from Lisbon and Portugal. ⊠ *Calçada do Duque 49–51, Chiado* ☎ *21/346–9947* ⊕ *www.duque-brewpub.com* Ⓜ *Blue or Green Line to Baixa-Chiado.*

Entretanto

It was one of the city's first rooftop bars and remains one of the spots to be for those who want a drink with a view. Much quieter and relaxing than the competition, it's a place to get 5 o'clock tea or a few snacks to accompany your cocktails. The offerings include a list of oysters and sushi, as well as a wide selection of gins. ⊠ *Rua Nova do Almada, 114, Chiado* ☎ *21/325–6100* Ⓜ *Baixa-Chiado.*

⭐ The Garden Rooftop

Lisbon is packed with rooftop bars, but this 2018 opening tops them all. On the seventh floor of a high-rise overlooking the Tagus, the Garden

Rooftop has a vast wooden terrace complete with sweet-smelling foliage with space for up to 200 revelers, and the 360-degree views over river and city are show-stopping. There's no better place for a sundowner, and luckily a good cocktail and *petiscos* (small plates) list has you covered. Should you feel like staying on, after-dark DJ sets complete the picture. ✉ *Rua do Instituto Industrial 7, 7th fl., Bairro Alto* ☎ *93/513–0230.*

★ Garrafeira Alfaia

This tiny wine store manages to have space for tables (barrels) used for tastings. The wines are accompanied by local cheeses and sausages, and the knowledgeable staff will help you discover the different varieties and qualities of port and other Portuguese wines. ✉ *Rua do Diário de Notícias 125, Bairro Alto* ☎ *21/343–3079* ⊕ *www. garrafeiraalfaia.com* Ⓜ *Baixa-Chiado; Tram 28.*

Incognito

Hidden on a mostly residential street not far from the noisier lanes of Bairro Alto, one of Lisbon's oldest clubs is true to its name—there's no sign at the door and you have to ring a bell to enter. Inside, on the small dance floor, the crowd dances to alternative sounds and pop hits from the present and the past, going all the way back to the 1980s. ✉ *Rua dos Poiais de São Bento 37, Bairro Alto* Ⓜ *Tram 28 to R. Poiais S. Bento.*

Maria Caxuxa

This unique, DJ-driven venue in a former bakery (complete with giant kneading machine) is often packed with young media types. Its toasted sandwiches are perfect for late-night munchies, while the famous shots of strong spirits can ramp up a night on the town. While this is a more spacious bar than others in the neighborhood, almost everyone still prefers to grab a drink and enjoy it outside by the door. ✉ *Rua da Barroca 6–12, Bairro Alto* ⊘ *Closed Sun.* Ⓜ *Baixa-Chiado; Tram 28.*

The Old Pharmacy

The name says it all: this space used to be a pharmacy, but you'd just need to take a peek inside to know that. The medicine cabinets are still there, although they now display bottles of wine. All the wines on offer are from Portugal and poured by the glass, to be accompanied by cheese and meat platters. Other choices change daily, to be enjoyed at the barrel tables. ✉ *Rua do Diário de Notícias 83, Bairro Alto* ☎ *92/023–0989* Ⓜ *Baixa-Chiado; Tram 28.*

Park

On warm evenings (and quite a few cooler ones) this terrace on the roof of a multilevel parking lot heaves with bright young things drinking

in the stunning sunset views and well-mixed cocktails. Surrounded by potted trees, you can also eat a light meal on one of the low wooden tables. Live music and excellent local DJs provide the soundtrack. Weather permitting, it's open from 1 pm to 2 am. ⊠ *Calçada do Combro 58, Bairro Alto* ☎ *21/591–4011* Ⓜ *Tram 28.*

As Primas

This very laid-back bar is known for its cheap drinks and as a lesbian hangout, although everyone drops in to hear the 1980s music on the jukebox. ⊠ *Rua da Atalaia 154–156, Bairro Alto* ☎ *21/342–5925* Ⓜ *Baixa-Chiado; Tram 28.*

Portas Largas

A mixed crowd spills out into the street from this tiled tavern with barn doors, which often offers live Brazilian music. Sangria and caipirinha are the house drinks. Things get crowded after midnight. ⊠ *Rua da Atalaia 105, Bairro Alto* ☎ *21/346–6379* 🕘 *Closed Mon.* Ⓜ *Baixa-Chiado; Tram 28.*

★ Purex

Although not officially a gay bar, this bar is nevertheless mostly gay on most nights, especially on weekends. It's usually quite crowded, both inside and out, as many choose to grab a drink and enjoy it on the street near the door. Part of the rather small interior often becomes a dance floor, as crowds can't help moving to the usual upbeat sounds of pop remixes. ⊠ *Rua das Salgadeiras 28, Bairro Alto* ☎ *21/342–1942* Ⓜ *Baixa-Chiado; Tram 28.*

O Purista

A bar that doubles as a barbershop, or vice versa, this is where Lisbon's coolest guys get pretty with a drink in hand. It's affiliated with Belgium's Affligem beer, but there's also Portuguese beer, gin, whiskey, champagne, port wine, and even fresh juices. The interior is decorated like a classic barbershop and is meant to be a comfortable space for men (and women) to relax at any time of the day. ⊠ *Rua Nova da Trindade 16C, Chiado* ☎ *91/644–2744* Ⓜ *Blue or Green Line to Baixa-Chiado.*

Sandeman Chiado

Unlike most other wine bars in town, this one is open during the day. It has inviting outdoor seating and a tastefully designed interior that tells the story of Sandeman, one of the best-known port wine labels. Naturally, it was founded in the city of Porto, in 1790, but finally revealed itself to the capital in 2016. Since then it has been offering all of its different types of wine and even adds it to the desserts and to a couple of the food options that may accompany the drinking. ⊠ *Largo Rafael Bordalo Pinheiro, Chiado* ☎ *93/785–0068* ⊕ *thesandemanchiado.com* Ⓜ *Baixa-Chiado.*

Silk

Formerly open only to members, this rooftop bar is now open to everyone and offers a good sushi menu together with cocktails and bottles of wine. It's at the top of a small shopping gallery, offering a stunning panoramic view from its terrace and through its glass walls.

GINJINHA CHERRY LIQUEUR

One cannot visit Portugal without trying its delicious, sweet cherry liqueur, ginjinha.

It's made from the ginjinha sour cherry, whose origin is difficult to establish, but it is supposedly derived from the banks of the Caspian River and was gradually dispersed among the Mediterranean countries via trade routes.

The liqueur has a deep, dark red color with an intense flavor and aroma perfumed by the fermented cherries. It's produced and sold in two distinct varieties: the liqueur on its own or the liqueur with actual ginjinha cherries inside, sometimes flavored with vanilla or cinnamon.

The best thing to have with ginjinha is chocolate, and some places serve it in little chocolate cups. Or eat a big slice of chocolate cake with your cordial.

✉ *Rua da Misericórdia 14, 6th fl., Chiado* ☎ *91/300-9193* ⊕ *www.silk-club.com* Ⓜ *Baixa-Chiado.*

Topo Chiado

A large terrace behind Convento do Carmo was redesigned by prominent architect Álvaro Siza Vieira, who turned it into a bar, which is now open throughout the day. It's especially inviting at night, when the neighboring Santa Justa Elevator and the castle ahead are lit up. You may choose to have your cocktails with snacks at the tables or while you relax on the lounge chairs and enjoy the view. ✉ *Terraços do Carmo, Chiado* ✛ *Go up Santa Justa Elevator, or enter through gate to right of facade of Carmo Convent* ☎ *21/342-0626* Ⓜ *Baixa-Chiado.*

 Performing Arts

Teatro Nacional de São Carlos

Lisbon inaugurated what was said to be Europe's biggest opera house in 1755, but it only stood for a few months before it was destroyed in the Great Earthquake of that same year. Its substitute from 1793 is more modest but still built to impress in the style of the grand European opera houses of the time. The exterior is modeled after Milan's La Scala, and the interior was inspired by Naples's San Carlo. Today Teatro Nacional de São Carlos is known for its lavish rococo decorations (check out the luxurious royal box) and for the excellent acoustics. The annual programming includes classic operas and free orchestra concerts on the square outside in the summer. ✉ *Rua Serpa Pinto 9, Chiado* ☎ *21/325-3000* ⊕ *www.tnsc.pt* Ⓜ *Blue or Green Line to Baixa-Chiado.*

Teatro São Luiz
This theater dates from 1894 and became one of Lisbon's most popular movie theaters in 1928. It was the first cinema in the country to show the talkies, but when television reduced the number of moviegoers, it was turned back to a theater once more in 1970. Today you'll find diverse and alternative programming, ranging from classic theater performances to dance, jazz, and lectures. The adjoining restaurant, Mini Bar, is a fun spot for a night of eating and drinking. ⊠ *Rua António Maria Cardoso 38, Chiado* ☎ *21/325–7640* ⊕ *www.teatrosaoluiz.pt* Ⓜ *Baixa-Chiado.*

4

Avenida da Liberdade, Príncipe Real, and Restauradores

AMEIXOEIRA

CHARNECA

LUMIAR

SANTA MARIA DOS OLIVAIS

CARNIDE

PARQUE DAS NAÇÕES

AVENIDAS NOVAS

SÃO DOMINGOS DE BENFICA

MARVILA

BENFICA

CAMPOLIDE

BEATO

MARQUÊS DE POMPAL E AVENIDA DA LIBERDADE

ARROIOS

SÃO JOÃO

PENHA DE FRANÇA

ANJOS

SÃO MAMEDE

INTENDENTE

SANTA ENGRÁCIA

CAMPO DE OURIQUE

PRÍNCIPE REAL

MARTIM MONIZ

GRAÇA

ESTRELA

ROSSIO

SÃO VICENTE

ALCÂNTARA

LAPA

BARRIO ALTO

BAIXA

CHIADO

ALFAMA

RESTELO

AJUDA

CAIS DO SODRÉ

SANTOS

BELÉM

Sightseeing ★★★☆☆ | Shopping ★★★★★ | Dining ★★★★☆ | Nightlife ★★★☆☆

Tree-lined Avenida da Liberdade was modeled after Paris's Champs-Élysées and is covered with some of Lisbon's most beautifully designed cobblestone pavements. It's home to most of the city's luxury stores, and down its central lanes are several food kiosks open throughout the day, each with its own specialty (from smoothies to seafood). Like the Parisian boulevard, it ends at a square with a traffic circle, Praça Marquês de Pombal, named after the man who oversaw downtown Lisbon's reconstruction following the Great Earthquake of 1755 and whose statue stands at the center, overlooking the city. Behind him is Lisbon's Central Park (Parque Eduardo VII), laid out in the 19th century and home to a beautiful greenhouse garden.—*by Mario Fernandes*

At the other end of the avenue is Restauradores Square, with an obelisk commemorating the restoration of the Portuguese crown in 1640, ending 60 years of the Iberian Union, when Portugal and Spain shared the same king. Surrounding it are a number of attractive buildings, most notably Foz Palace, built in 1777 with an interior inspired by the Palace of Versailles and home to a tourist office.

Rising up the hill to the west of the Avenida is romantic Príncipe Real, a neighborhood of stately mansions, trendy restaurants, concept stores, antiques traders, and green spaces for a break. It's also known as Lisbon's "gayborhood," with discreet LGBT bars and clubs on quiet residential streets.

 Sights

Avenida da Liberdade

"Liberty Avenue" was laid out in 1879 as an elegant Parisian-style boulevard modeled on the Champs-Élysées. It has since lost some of its allure: many of the late 19th-century mansions and art deco buildings that once graced it have been demolished; others have been turned into soulless office blocks. There are, however, still some notable survivors of the original boulevard, now turned into luxury hotels and international fashion outlets. It's worth a leisurely stroll up the 1½-km (1-mile) length of the avenue, past ponds, fountains, and statues, from Restauradores Square to Parque Eduardo VII, at least once, if only to cool off with a drink in one of the *quiosques* (refreshment kiosks) beneath the trees and to admire the iconic designs of the cobblestone pavements. ⊠ *Av. da Liberdade, Avenida da Liberdade* Ⓜ *Blue Line to Avenida*.

Casa-Museu Medeiros e Almeida

One of Lisbon's lesser-known but extraordinary museums, this is the former residence of collector António de Medeiros e Almeida. Every room of his late 19th-century mansion is filled with works of art, ranging from paintings to ceramics, sculptures, and furniture. Highlights include paintings by Rubens and Tiepolo, a Rembrandt portrait, a silver tea set used by Napoleon, fountains originally from the Palace of Versailles, and what's said to be the world's most notable private collection of clocks. ⊠ *Rua Rosa Araújo 41, Avenida da Liberdade* ☎ *21/354–7892* ⊕ *www.casa-museu-medeirosealmeida.pt* 🖃 *From €5* 🕙 *Closed Sun.* Ⓜ *Blue or Yellow Line to Marquês de Pombal.*

Convento dos Cardaes

One of Lisbon's hidden treasures, the exterior of this 17th-century convent belies the riches inside. Still inhabited by Dominican nuns, it opens for visits in the afternoon, starting in the beautiful church lined with Portuguese and Dutch tile panels. They're found below paintings framed by gilded wood carvings, which, together with the gold-and-marble altar, make it one of Lisbon's most notable examples of Portuguese baroque. ⊠ *Rua do Século 123, Príncipe Real* ☎ *21/342–7525* ⊕ *www.conventodoscardaes.com* 🕙 *Closed Sun.* Ⓜ *Yellow Line to Rato.*

Jardim Botânico

Lisbon's main botanical garden was first laid out in 1874 to teach students about botany. Hidden behind the small **Museu de História**

Natural about 2 km (1 mile) north of the Bairro Alto, the garden had been looking somewhat neglected but was cleaned up in 2018 and makes a restful stop, with 10 acres of paths, benches, and nearly 15,000 species of subtropical plants. ⊠ *Rua da Escola Politécnica 58, Príncipe Real* ☎ *21/392–1808 garden, 21/392–1800 Natural History Museum* ⊕ *www.mnhnc.ul.pt* 🖃 *From €3* Ⓜ *Yellow Line to Rato.*

Jardim do Torel

Also known as Miradouro do Torel, this garden-viewpoint is accessed through a gate at the top of a hill above Avenida da Liberdade. Unlike the other famous viewpoints in the city, it gets very few visitors, except for young couples and older folks of the neighborhood, who sit in the shade admiring the view, walk their dogs, or stop for coffee. The café is found down a few steps that lead to an 18th-century fountain

0
400 m

0
800 ft

SÃO SEBASTIÃO Ⓜ

São Sebastião da Pedreira

Rua Latino Coelho

Rua Tomás Ribeiro

Av. António Augusto de Aguiar

Avenida Sidónio Pais

Pereira de Melo

PICOAS
Ⓜ

Av. Fontes

R. Sousa Martins

Campolide

❶

Jardim Amália Rodrigues

❷

Av. Miguel Torga

Rua Marquês de Fronteira

Rua Castilho

Rua Rodrigo da Fonseca

Rua da Artilharia 1

Av Conselheiro Fernando de Sousa

Parque Eduardo VII

❸

PARQUE
Ⓜ

Avenida da Liberdade

Av. Eng. Duarte Pacheco

R. Carlos Alberto da Mota Pinto

Rua das Amoreiras

R. Seara Nova

Rua São Filipe de Neri

❹ R. Joaquim António de Aguiar

Praça Marquês de Pombal

❺ Ⓜ MARQUÊS DE POMBAL

Rua Braancamp

❼

Rua Alexandre Herculano

❽

❾

Av. da Liberdade

AVENIDA

Rua Silva Carvalho

Rua Dom João V

Rua do Sol ao Rato

RATO
Ⓜ

Rua do Salitre

❿ ⓫ ⓬

Rua Barata Salgueiro

⓯

⓭
⓮

AVENIDA
Ⓜ

㊽

㊼ ㊾
㊿

Santa Isabel

Avenida Álvares Cabral

⓱

Príncipe Real and Restauradores

Jardim Botânico

⓰

㊹ ㊻

Praça da Alegria
㊸

Cemitério dos Ingleses

Horta Biológica do CNN

Rua de São Bento

R. da Imprensa Nacional

⓲ ⓳

⓴ ㉑

㉒ ㉓

R. de São Marçal

㉔

㉚ ㉛

㉙

㉜

㉝ ㉞

Jardim do Príncipe Real
㉘

㉖ ㉗

㉕

Rua das Trin...

㊱ ㊳ ㊴
㊲ ㊵

㊶ ㊷

㉟

Estrela

Jardim da Estrela

and a terrace. That fountain often becomes a pool used by local children in the summer, when the terrace becomes a small "urban beach." ✉ *Travessa do Torel, Avenida da Liberdade* Ⓜ *Lavra funicular.*

Museu Nacional do Desporto

An annex of Foz Palace became the National Sports Museum in 2012, and since then it has presented small temporary exhibitions of its collection, which is made up of donated memorabilia from the country's sports heroes. You may see cleats worn by Cristiano Ronaldo, shirts worn by Olympic runner Rosa Mota, the golden shoe awarded to soccer legend Eusébio, or the sneakers worn by Nelson Évora at the 2008 Olympics when he won the gold medal. ✉ *Praça dos Restauradores, Avenida da Liberdade* ☎ *21/395–8629* ☉ *Closed Sun. and Mon.* Ⓜ *Blue Line to Restauradores.*

Palácio Foz

Scheduled to be become the National Music Museum sometime in 2020, this sumptuous palace facing Restauradores Square is open for guided tours. Originally built in 1777, it features a Louis XIV–style interior inspired by the Palace of Versailles. In the basement is a former restaurant from the early 1900s, with an intriguing mix of esoteric symbols and neo-Gothic architecture. ✉ *Praça dos Restauradores, Avenida da Liberdade* ☎ *21/322–1200* Ⓜ *Blue Line to Restauradores.*

WORTH A TRIP

Palácio dos Marqueses de Fronteira
Way off the beaten path and far from the city center, this palace by the modern district of Benfica and on the edge of Monsanto Park is one of Lisbon's most beautiful buildings. Built in 1670, it's known for some of the finest examples of Portuguese tile panels, both inside the palace and outside around the garden. It's tricky to reach by public transportation, but a taxi from the Jardim Zoológico metro stop, about a mile away, will be quick and inexpensive. ✉ Largo de São Domingo de Benfica 1, Benfica ☎ 21/778–2023 ⊕ www.fronteira-alorna.pt ☎ From €4 ☉ Closed Sun. (gardens open all day, palace only in morning) Ⓜ Blue Line to Jardim Zoológico (then 20-min walk, taxi, or Bus 770).

⭐ Parque Eduardo VII

Formerly Parque da Liberdade, this park was renamed in 1903 when England's Edward VII visited Portugal and celebrated the centuries-old Anglo-Portuguese Alliance. Its large central promenade has manicured lawns featuring traditional Portuguese cobblestone pavement with geometric designs, and at the top, you have a view of the city center. The **Estufa Fria** is a sprawling 1930s greenhouse garden whose various habitats are arranged around a pretty pool. It's a beautifully kept, romantic oasis in the middle of the city. If you visit in June, you may catch the city's annual book fair, which takes over almost the entire park. ✉ *Praça*

Marquês de Pombal, Avenida da Liberdade ⊠ Park free, Estufa Fria €4 (free Sun. until 2) Ⓜ *Blue Line to Parque or Marquês de Pombal.*

Praça dos Restauradores

This square, which is adjacent to Rossio Train Station, marks the beginning of modern Lisbon. Here the broad, tree-lined Avenida da Liberdade starts its north-westerly ascent. *Restauradores* means "restorers," and the square commemorates the 1640 uprising against Spanish rule that restored Portuguese independence after a 60-year hiatus; an obelisk (1886) commemorates the event. Note the elegant 18th-century Foz Palace on the square's west side. Before World War I, it contained a casino; today it houses a national tourist office, the tourist police, the National Sports Museum and a shop selling reproductions from the country's state museums. The only building to rival the palace is the restored Éden building, just to the south. This art deco masterpiece of Portuguese architect Cassiano Branco now contains a hotel. You'll also see the Glória funicular, which goes up the hill from here to Bairro Alto and its famous viewpoint. ⊠ *Avenida da Liberdade* Ⓜ *Blue Line to Restauradores.*

Praça Marquês de Pombal

Dominating the center of Marquês de Pombal Square is a statue of the marquis himself, the man responsible for the design of the "new" Lisbon that emerged from the ruins of the 1755 earthquake. On the statue's base are representations of both the earthquake and the tidal wave that engulfed the city; a female figure with outstretched arms signifies the joy at the emergence of the refashioned city. The square is effectively a large roundabout and a useful orientation point, since it stands at the northern end of Avenida da Liberdade with Parque Eduardo VII just behind, and the metro station here is an interchange between two lines. ⊠ *Avenida da Liberdade* Ⓜ *Blue or Yellow Line to Marquês de Pombal.*

 Shopping

El Corte Inglés

Even though this is a Spanish chain, it sells expected big-name brands from Portugal and beyond in fashion, accessories, cosmetics, home decor, and more. On the top floor is a food hall where some of the city's top chefs present varied menus ranging from contemporary Portuguese cuisine to creative vegetarian options. ⊠ *Av. António Augusto de Aguiar 31, Avenida da Liberdade* ☎ *21/371–1700* ⊕ *www.elcorteingles.pt* Ⓜ *Blue or Red Line to São Sebastião.*

★ Embaixada

Shopping doesn't get any more stylish than at this grand 18th-century mansion, which has been transformed into a gallery showcasing some of the best of Portuguese design and even a few international brands. The bar and restaurant in the inner Moorish-style courtyard is an attractive place for a meal or drink. ✉ *Praça do Príncipe Real 26, Príncipe Real* ☎ *96/530–9154* ⊕ *www.embaixadalx. pt* Ⓜ *Yellow line to Rato.*

★ Fashion Clinic

Dozens of luxury labels (from Christian Louboutin to Stella McCartney to YSL) are represented at this store, which is a favorite of Lisbon's fashionistas. In addition to finding the perfect outfit for their most glamorous nights out, they can choose from a large selection of handbags and shoes, elegantly displayed in the well-designed space. ✉ *Tivoli Forum, Av. da Liberdade 180, Avenida da Liberdade* ☎ *21/354–9040* ⊕ *www.fashionclinic. com* Ⓜ *Blue Line to Avenida.*

Fly London

Despite the name, this is the flagship store of one of Portugal's most successful footwear brands, known for its funky yet comfortable styles. It's been around for close to 20 years and now sells clothes and accessories. ✉ *Av. da Liberdade 230, Avenida da Liberdade* ☎ *91/059–4564* ⊕ *www.flylondon.com* Ⓜ *Blue Line to Avenida.*

J. Andrade Antiguidades

Museum curators are among the regulars poring over the unusual objects, paintings, sculptures, and furniture to be found in this store, run by two brothers since 1985. It's open Saturday by appointment only. ✉ *Rua da Escola Politécnica 39, Príncipe Real* ☎ *21/342–4964* ⊕ *www. jandrade-antiguidades.com* ⊙ *Closed Sun.* Ⓜ *Yellow line to Rato.*

Luis Onofre

Famous women like Michelle Obama, Naomi Watts, and Paris Hilton have worn Portuguese designer Luis Onofre's shoes, and it's here that you can try on his latest creations. Next to the luxurious footwear that he now mostly exports worldwide are his collections of bags and clutches. ✉ *Av. da Liberdade 247, Avenida da Liberdade* ☎ *21/131–3629* ⊕ *luisonofre.com* ⊙ *Closed Sun.* Ⓜ *Blue or Yellow Line to Marquês de Pombal.*

Maria João Bahia

Designer Maria João Bahia has been creating jewelry since 1985 and after two successful decades she opened this store, where she presents her exclusive jewels together with silverware, crystals, and handbags, all created by her. ✉ *Av. da Liberdade 102, Avenida da Liberdade* ☎ *21/324–0018* ⊕ *mariajoaobahia.pt* ⊙ *Closed Sun.* Ⓜ *Blue Line to Avenida.*

★ Pelcor

This award-winning brand designs pieces using Portugal's most exported material—cork. Everything from handbags to shoes and even umbrellas is made of that eco-friendly material. Pelcor's wares are now sold at stores all over the world, but it's here that you can find the entire collection and exclusive pieces. ✉ *Pátio do Tijolo 16, Príncipe Real* ☎ *21/886–4205* ⊕ *www.pelcor.pt* ⊙ *Closed Sun.* Ⓜ *Yellow Line to Rato; Tram 24 to Príncipe Real.*

ART AT YOUR FEET

When Lisbon rose from the ashes of the Great Earthquake of 1755, it was paved with much of the rubble resulting from the disaster.

Small basalt and limestone pieces were creatively put together, forming imaginative patterns inspired by Roman mosaics. The first artistic pavement was created for the redesigned Rossio Square, and its wave patterns were then reproduced in other parts of Portugal and the colonies, most famously in Rio de Janeiro's boardwalks. Other iconic examples are the abstract and floral designs that cover Avenida da Liberdade, creating a carpet effect when seen from above (from any of the hotels that line the avenue, for example). Dark cobblestones also form

letters and numbers describing many of the statues and monuments down the avenue, and when you reach Restauradores Square you find a more modern, abstract design, created by prominent artist and architect João Abel Manta.

In a corner of the same square, outside the Avenida Palace Hotel, notice the monument paying tribute to the pavers/artists who've created these designs around the city over the years. It's made up of two sculptures of men working on a pavement illustrating the barge with two ravens that's the official symbol of Lisbon. For more contemporary examples of cobblestone designs, head to the Parque das Nações district, where there are sea monsters surrounding the Oceanarium.

Solar

One of Lisbon's best-known antiques shops, Solar specializes in azulejo panels and also stocks 16th- to 18th-century Portuguese furniture and paintings, most of them salvaged from old mansions, churches, and palaces. ⊠ *Rua Dom Pedro V 68–70, Príncipe Real* ☎ *21/346–5522* ⊕ *solar.com.pt* ⊘ *Closed Sun. Closed Sat. in July and Aug.* Ⓜ *Yellow line to Rato.*

 Coffee and Quick Bites

Bettina & Niccolo Corallo

$ | International. Coffee addicts and chocolate lovers stop at this small store across from the Príncipe Real garden, drawn by the scent of the beans that arrive straight

from a family plantation in the former Portuguese colony of São Tomé and Príncipe in Africa. **Known for:** chocolate sorbets; variety of coffee; 100% cocoa bars. *Average main: €3* ⊠ *Rua da Escola Politécnica 4, Príncipe Real* ☎ *21/386–2158* ⊘ *Closed Sun.* Ⓜ *Yellow Line to Rato; Tram 24 to Príncipe Real.*

Copenhagen Coffee Lab

$ | International. The roasted coffee beans come from Copenhagen, as did the inspiration for the minimalist decor. The Coffee Lab has become a favorite among Lisbon's coffee lovers, both for the different types on the menu and the welcoming and relaxed atmosphere. **Known for:** filter coffees; breakfast plates; organic hot chocolate. *Average main: €7* ⊠ *Rua Nova da Piedade 10,*

Príncipe Real ☎ *21/604-7980* ⊕ *www.copenhagencoffeelab.com* Ⓜ *Yellow Line to Rato.*

DeliDelux Avenida

$$ | International. The initial branch on the riverfront in Alfama was one of the first popular weekend brunch spots in town, and here it serves healthy light meals throughout the day, starting with breakfast. It's also a gourmet store, offering Portuguese and imported products. **Known for:** brunch menus; variety of international teas; outdoor seating with a view of Avenida da Liberdade. *Average main: €16* ⊠ *Rua Alexandre Herculano 15A, Avenida da Liberdade* ☎ *21/314-1474* ⊕ *www.delidelux.pt* Ⓜ *Blue Line to Avenida.*

Delta Q

$ | International. The flagship store of this Portuguese coffee brand faces Avenida da Liberdade and offers more than its coffee. Come here for a light meal, brunch, or a cocktail in the wood-clad interior or at the tables outside. **Known for:** organic coffee; reasonably priced menus; refreshing teas. *Average main: €10* ⊠ *Av. da Liberdade 144-156, Avenida da Liberdade* ☎ *21/342-7351* Ⓜ *Blue Line to Avenida.*

Fábrica Coffee Roasters

$ | International. Hidden just a few feet from the Lavra funicular, this was one of the first places in the city to offer specialty coffee, roasted and ground on the premises. Sandwiches and pastries are also available. **Known for:** inviting terrace; industrial and vintage-style interior; craft beer. *Average main: €4* ⊠ *Rua das Portas de Santo Antão 136, Avenida da Liberdade* ☎ *21/139-9261* ⊕ *www.fabricacoffeeroasters.com* Ⓜ *Blue Line to Avenida.*

Il Matriciano

$$ | Italian. Recognized as one of the most authentic Italian restaurants in Lisbon, Il Matriciano faces the São Bento Palace and is owned by a couple from Rome. Diners are greeted like family and presented with a menu made from ingredients brought in twice a month from Italy. **Known for:** cheese from Italy's different regions; rustic-style interior; fruit-shaped artisanal Italian ice cream. *Average main: €16* ⊠ *Rua de São Bento 107, São Bento* ☎ *21/395-2639* ⊙ *Closed Sun.* Ⓜ *Tram 28 to Rua de São Bento/Calçada da Estrela.*

In Bocca al Lupo

$$ | Pizza. With almost three dozen choices on the menu, this is the place for alternative pizza toppings, including practically the only vegan option in town. The pizzas come straight out of a wood oven, which is right in the dining room, and are topped with Portuguese and Italian ingredients. **Known for:** 100% organic pizzas; craft beer; cocktails. *Average main: €16* ⊠ *Rua Manuel Bernardes 5A, Príncipe Real* ☎ *21/390-0582* ⊕ *www.inboccaallupo.pt* ⊙ *No lunch. Closed Tues.* Ⓜ *Yellow Line to Rato.*

★ Lost In

$ | International. A curious Indian-inspired decor welcomes you to this café/bar/restaurant, but your attention immediately goes to the view of Avenida da Liberdade. Despite the decor, the menu lists international dishes. **Known for:** colorful terrace; weekday happy hours; large selection of petiscos (small plates). *Average main: €14* ⊠ *Rua Dom Pedro V 56 D, Príncipe Real* ☎ *91/775–9282* ✆ *Closed Sun.* Ⓜ *Yellow Line to Rato; Tram 24 to Príncipe Real.*

Nannarella

$ | Italian. An Italian family opened this small ice-cream shop around the corner from the Parliament building (and just a short walk from the Príncipe Real garden), and it immediately drew locals who don't mind waiting in line to try the variety of flavors. They're served in a cup or cone, with or without whipped cream on top. **Known for:** sgroppino (lemon sorbet cocktail); ice-cream cakes; flavors that change daily. *Average main: €3* ⊠ *Rua Nova da Piedade 64, Príncipe Real* ☎ *92/687–8553* ⊕ *www.nannarella.pt* Ⓜ *Tram 28 to Rua de São Bento/Calçada da Estrela.*

🍴 Dining

Avenida SushiCafé

$$$ | Japanese. Open for almost a decade, Avenida was one of the first restaurants to offer a more creative variety of sushi. It opens up onto a terrace that quickly fills at lunchtime but is also popular at night. **Known for:** stylishly designed interior; special lunch menu; a mix of Japanese cuisine and international flavors. *Average main: €25* ⊠ *Rua Barata Salgueiro 28, Avenida*

Before it was Avenida da Liberdade, Lisbon's main boulevard was the Passeio Público (Public Promenade). It was enclosed by a wall and accessed through a gate, which opened to a lake where the obelisk in Restauradores Square now stands. Despite the name, it wasn't exactly public, as it was for the almost exclusive use of the higher classes, especially those living in the mansions and palaces in the surrounding area. Foz Palace in Restauradores Square was one of those, but most others have since disappeared. It was especially popular on weekends, when people wore their Sunday best for parades of carriages and horseback riding. Surviving features from that time are the sculptures representing the Tagus and Douro Rivers by a couple of the ponds on Avenida da Liberdade and an elegant bandstand that's now in Jardim da Estrela.

da Liberdade ☎ *21/192–8158* ⊕ *www. gruposushicafe.pt* ✆ *Closed Sun.* Ⓜ *Blue Line to Avenida.*

Casa do Alentejo

$ | Portuguese. Originally a social club for the people from the region of Alentejo, this restaurant is found on the upper floor of a Moorish-style building from the 1800s. The beautiful Louis XVI–style ballroom is for special events and for when there's not enough space at the two separate dining rooms covered in blue-and-white tile panels. **Known for:** carne de porco à alentejana (pork with clams); traditional açorda (bread and egg soup); regional sweets. *Average main: €14 ⊠ Rua Portas de Santo Antão 58, Avenida da Liberdade ☎ 21/340-5140 ⊕ www.casadoalentejo.com.pt Ⓜ Blue Line to Avenida.*

A Cevicheria

$$ | **Latin American.** This trendy spot draws the attention of passersby as much for the number of people drinking at the door as for the gigantic octopus hanging from the ceiling inside. Chef Kiko Martins, who is behind a handful of restaurants in town, was influenced by Peruvian cuisine but incorporates Portuguese and global flavors.
Known for: creative ceviche; Latin American–inspired desserts; pisco sours. *Average main: €20 ⊠ Rua Dom Pedro V 129, Príncipe Real ☎ 21/803-8815 Ⓜ Yellow Line to Rato; Tram 24 to Príncipe Real.*

★ Cervejaria Liberdade

$$$$ | **Seafood.** Lisbon's seafood restaurants and beer halls tend to be noisy, informal places, but those looking for the flavors of the sea in a less casual, more sophisticated atmosphere should head to this restaurant facing Avenida da Liberdade. You still find the traditional dishes listed on the menu, but they're served with flair by an attentive staff. **Known for:** oysters and prawns from Algarve; steak tartare; 70% cocoa mousse for dessert.
Average main: €28 ⊠ Av. da Liberdade 185, Avenida da Liberdade ☎ 21/319-8620 Ⓜ Blue Line to Avenida.

Comida de Santo

$ | **Brazilian.** Excellent northeastern Brazilian food is served in a funky, brightly painted dining room to a suitably lively soundtrack that keeps this tiny place buzzing until late at night. Enjoy classic Bahian dishes, sip a caipirinha, and finish your meal with a traditional dessert made with tropical fruits.
Known for: colorful jungle-inspired interior; traditional feijoada à brasileira (black bean and pork stew); moqueca de peixe (fish stew). *Average main: €14 ⊠ Calçada Engenheiro Miguel Pais 39, Príncipe Real ☎ 21/396-3339 ⊕ www.comidadesanto.pt ⊗ Closed Tues. No lunch in Aug. Ⓜ Yellow line to Rato.*

★ Delícias de Goa

$ | **Indian.** Goa is a the former Portuguese colony in India, and this restaurant is just a short walk from Avenida da Liberdade. Delícias de Goa shows how five centuries of Portuguese rule created a unique cuisine, mixing the spicy Indian flavors with Portuguese staples such as shellfish and pork.
Known for: colorful, traditionally Goan interior; Goan-style feijoada (Portuguese bean stew) available only on Wednesday; bebinca (traditional Indo-Portuguese dessert). *Average main: €13 ⊠ Rua do Conde de Redondo 2D, Avenida da Liberdade ☎ 96/149-1521 ⊕ www.deliciasdegoa.com ⊗ Closed Mon. No dinner Sun. Ⓜ Blue Line to Avenida.*

★ Eleven

$$$$ | **Mediterranean.** Sitting at the top of Parque Eduardo VII, this was the first modern restaurant to bring a new wave of Michelin stars to Lisbon. Its à la carte and tasting menus change every season and attract businesspeople for lunch and couples at dinnertime. **Known for:** view over Avenida da Liberdade; refined Mediterranean cuisine (mainly from Portugal and Spain); fish from the Portuguese coast. *Average main: €50* ⊠ *Rua Marquês de Fronteira, Jardim Amália Rodrigues, Avenida da Liberdade* ☎ *21/386-2211* ⊕ *www.restauranteleven.com* ⊘ *Closed Sun.* Ⓜ *Blue Line to Parque.*

Gambrinus

$$$$ | **Seafood.** On a busy street that's full of fish restaurants, Gambrinus stands out from the competition, with more than 70 years of experience in serving super fresh fish and shellfish. In a series of somber, dark-paneled dining rooms, or even sitting at the bar, you're led through the intricacies of the day's seafood specials by waiters who know their stuff. **Known for:** elaborate stained-glass windows; good seafood and steak; attentive waitstaff. *Average main: €34* ⊠ *Rua das Portas de Santo Antão 23–25, Restauradores* ☎ *21/342-1466* ⊕ *www.gambrinuslisboa.com* Ⓜ *Blue Line to Restauradores; Green Line to Rossio; Tram 15E or 25E to Praça da Figueira.*

Guilty

$$ | **International.** Unlike the name states, Guilty shamelessly serves delicious, decadently large portions with no apology. The business lunch crowd appreciates the fast service, and evenings see a hipper clientele who come for the pasta, pizza, and burgers and stay late, when a live DJ spins and the restaurant becomes a bar. **Known for:** supersize hamburgers; special lunch menus; cocktails. *Average main: €19* ⊠ *Rua Barata Salgueiro 28A, Avenida da Liberdade* ☎ *21/191-3590* ⊕ *restaurantesolivier.com/en/guilty* Ⓜ *Blue Line to Avenida.*

★ Jardim dos Sentidos

$ | **Vegetarian.** A short walk up the hill from Avenida da Liberdade leads to this restaurant that many say is the best vegetarian spot in town. It has an inviting patio in the back and a colorful dining room where you can have a variety of dishes inspired by world cuisines, from Mexico to India, Thailand, and Morocco. **Known for:** good-value lunch buffet; Zen massage-and-dinner combos; vegan desserts. *Average main: €11* ⊠ *Rua da Mãe de Água 3, Avenida da Liberdade* ☎ *21/342-3670* ⊕ *jardimdosentidos.com* ⊘ *Closed Sun.* Ⓜ *Blue Line to Avenida.*

★ JNcQUOI

$$$$ | **International.** A room inside the Tivoli Theater, designed in the 1920s, is now this upscale restaurant featuring a classy decor that somehow includes a life-size skeleton of a dinosaur. It's actually a three-in-one (a restaurant, bar, and gourmet store), open throughout the day. **Known for:** international cuisine but with classics from Portugal, France, and Italy; French "Ladurée" desserts; attracting the local elite. *Average main: €40* ⊠ *Av. da Liberdade 182–184, Avenida da Liberdade* ☎ *21/936-9900* ⊕ *www.jncquoi.com* Ⓜ *Blue Line to Avenida.*

K.O.B.

$$$$ | International. Local celebrity restaurateur Olivier has several spots in town, and this one is all about meat. The name is an acronym for "Knowledge of Beef," and there are cuts from different origins, from Portugal to Argentina. **Known for:** Black Angus dishes; long list of Portuguese wines; classic and original cocktails. *Average main: €35* ⊠ *Rua do Salitre 169, Príncipe Real* ☎ *93/400–0949* ⊕ *restaurantesolivier.com/en/kob* ⊘ *No lunch on weekends* Ⓜ *Yellow Line to Rato.*

La Paparrucha

$$$$ | Argentine. Although inspiration for this restaurant's menu comes from Argentina, you'll also find fish dishes borrowed from traditional Portuguese cuisine. A meat-heavy menu has long made this a favorite among Lisbon's carnivores, but there are now also a couple of vegetarian options on the menu, too. **Known for:** panoramic views; lunchtime buffets on weekdays; kids' menu, which makes it especially family-friendly. *Average main:* ⊠ *Rua D. Pedro V 18–20, Príncipe Real* ☎ *21/342–5333* ⊕ *www.lapaparrucha.com* Ⓜ *Tram 24.*

Less/Gin Lovers

$ | International. The Moorish-style courtyard of Ribeiro da Cunha Palace (now the Embaixada shopping gallery) was turned into a restaurant serving contemporary Portuguese and international cuisine by top chef Miguel Castro e Silva. It shares the space with a trendy bar that's open throughout the day. **Known for:** variety of gin; huge cocktail list; reasonably priced tasting menu. *Average main: €12* ⊠ *Praça do Príncipe Real 26, Príncipe Real* ☎ *21/347–1341* Ⓜ *Yellow Line to Rato; Tram 24 to Príncipe Real.*

O Churrasco

$$ | Portuguese. On a street lined with tourist traps, O Churrasco is the local favorite and deservedly so. The restaurant serves top notch peri peri grilled chicken, grilled meats, and fish. **Known for:** good location in prime sightseeing territory; skewer kebabs; spicy chicken. *Average main: €17* ⊠ *Rua das Portas de Santo Antão 83–85, Restauradores* ☎ *21/342–3059* Ⓜ *Blue Line to Restauradores; Green Line to Rossio.*

★ Pinóquio

$$$ | Portuguese. Although it's quite spacious and comfortable inside, most people choose to sit at one of the many tables outside facing Restauradores Square. Waiters rush from table to table, mostly serving seafood and grilled fish and meats. **Known for:** friendly and professional staff; excellent seafood; popularity with locals and visitors. *Average main: €22* ⊠ *Praça dos Restauradores 79, Avenida da Liberdade* ☎ *21/346–5106* ⊕ *www.restaurantepinoquio.pt* Ⓜ *Blue Line to Restauradores.*

Ribadouro

$$ | Seafood. One of Lisbon's best-known seafood spots, Ribadouro is a smarter-than-average beer hall that offers the works: take your pick of lobster, mantis shrimp, crayfish, tiger shrimp, whelks, oysters, and clams, or combine the lot in a vast seafood platter. Evenings and weekends are busy, so arrive before 8 or make reservations. **Known for:** fish tanks where you can see what will end up at the tables; grilled steaks as alternatives to the seafood; late-night dinners. *Average main: €20 ⊠ Av. da Liberdade 155, Avenida da Liberdade ☎ 21/354–9411 ⊕ www. cervejariaribadouro.pt Ⓜ Blue line to Avenida.*

★ Sítio Valverde

$$ | **Portuguese.** This restaurant facing the courtyard of the Valverde Hotel focuses on contemporary Portuguese cuisine reinterpreted by the chef. Its brunch and afternoon tea is popular among locals who work nearby and those looking for a more intimate spot. **Known for:** different menus for different times of the day; sophisticated vintage decor; signature cocktails. *Average main: €20 ⊠ Av. da Liberdade 164, Avenida da Liberdade ☎ 21/094–0300 Ⓜ Blue Line to Avenida.*

★ Solar dos Presuntos

$$$$ | **Portuguese.** Photographs and caricatures of celebrities who've visited (from Cristiano Ronaldo to Adele) cover the walls of this split-level restaurant. It's one of the city's most popular and oldest (in business since 1947), so reservations are a must. **Known for:** specialties from northern Portugal; lobster rice; seasonal lamprey dishes. *Average main: €26 ⊠ Rua das Portas de Santo Antão 150, Avenida da Liberdade ☎ 21/342–4253 ⊕ www. solardospresuntos.com ⊗ Closed Sun. Ⓜ Blue Line to Avenida.*

Tapisco

$$ | **Portuguese.** This restaurant is a gastronomic trip through Portugal and Spain, serving traditional Iberian specialties with the touch of local celebrity chef Henrique Sá Pessoa. Dishes are beautifully presented and meant to be shared in a relaxing and informal environment. **Known for:** Iberian hams; modern riffs on traditional dishes; vermouth cocktails. *Average main: €18 ⊠ Rua D. Pedro V 81, Príncipe Real ☎ 21/342–0681 ⊕ tapisco.pt Ⓜ Yellow Line to Rato; Tram 24 to Príncipe Real.*

Terra

$$ | **Vegetarian.** Countering the common local view that vegetarians must suffer for their convictions, Terra offers a meatless buffet feast. The cheaper lunchtime deal includes drink and dessert, and at dinner, dishes change daily and include adaptations of Portuguese classics. **Known for:** open-air dining in the garden; organic wines; large tea selection. *Average main: €16 ⊠ Rua da Palmeira 15, Príncipe Real ☎ 21/342–1407 ⊕ www.restaurante-terra.pt ⊗ Closed Mon. Ⓜ Yellow line to Rato.*

Os Tibetanos

$ | **Vegetarian.** Delicious meat-free dishes (think mango-and-tofu curry, seitan steak, and spinach-filled Tibetan *momo* dumplings) ensure that there's always a line for a table in this restaurant's dining room or on the pleasant patio. It's part of a Buddhist center: a small shop stocks books and crafts, incense, homeopathic medicines, and other natural products, while yoga and meditation classes take place upstairs. **Known for:** good-value lunch menu; food inspired by world cuisines, mostly from Asia; colorful interior. *Average main: €11* ⊠ *Rua do Salitre 117, Avenida da Liberdade* ☎ *21/314-2038* ⊕ *tibetanos.com* ▭ *No credit cards* ⊘ *No lunch on public holidays* Ⓜ *Blue Line to Avenida.*

Varanda

$$$$ | **Portuguese.** The main restaurant at the Ritz is rare among hotel eateries in staying consistently at the top of its game. Frenchman Pascal Meynard keeps a tight grip on the reins here, overseeing a seasonally changing tasting menu (dinner only) and a wide à la carte choice of Portuguese and international dishes. **Known for:** Lisbon's best lunch buffet; rich weekend brunch; creative desserts. *Average main: €45* ⊠ *Four Seasons Hotel Ritz Lisbon, Rua Rodrigo de Fonseca 88, Avenida da Liberdade* ☎ *21/381-1400* Ⓜ *Blue or Yellow Line to Marquês de Pombal.*

★ Zero Zero

$ | **Italian.** One of the trendiest spots in town, this restaurant serves pizzas prepared in a rotating oak-wood oven. It has an attractive wood-and-marble interior, but you'll want to sit outside on the terrace facing the Botanical Garden. **Known for:** whole-wheat pizzas; ingredients imported directly from Italy; prosecco cocktails. *Average main: €15* ⊠ *Rua da Escola Politécnica 32, Príncipe Real* ☎ *21/342-0091* ⊕ *www.pizzeriazerozero.pt* Ⓜ *Yellow Line to Rato; Tram 24 to Rua Escola Politécnica.*

For a view over Avenida da Liberdade and toward Príncipe Real, head up the hill to Jardim do Torel. This "secret" garden is one of Lisbon's quietest viewpoints, unknown to most tourists and even many locals. It can be reached by taking Lisbon's oldest funicular (the Elevador do Lavra, in operation since 1884), hidden around the corner from the Avenida.

 Share your photo with us!
@FodorsTravel #FodorsOnTheGo

🍸 Bars and Nightlife

Ático

From this bar on the rooftop of the NH Collection Lisboa Liberdade Hotel you can look over Avenida da Liberdade and see the castle at the top of the hill. It's found next to a pool that's open to everyone (for a fee if you're not staying at the hotel), and on warmer days it attracts a mix of locals and hotel guests enjoying cocktails with the views. ⊠ *Av. da Liberdade 180B, Avenida da Liberdade* ☎ *21/351-4060* Ⓜ *Blue Line to Avenida.*

★ Cinco Lounge
Widely recognized as Lisbon's best cocktail bar, here you can have a variety of original drinks in a cool, relaxed atmosphere. The creativity and innovation comes from the British owner, who mixed cocktails in his homeland (as well as in New York and Australia) before deciding to move to Lisbon and open his own place. ⊠ *Rua Ruben Leitão 17A, Príncipe Real* ☎ *91/466-8242* ⊕ *www.cincolounge.com* Ⓜ *Yellow line to Rato.*

Construction
A popular gay venue since it opened in 2012, this club promises weekend nights of fun to the sound of thumping house music. The scaffolding that decorates the interior by the dance floor explains the name of the place. ⊠ *Rua Cecilio de Sousa 84, Príncipe Real* ⊗ *Closed Sun.–Thurs.* Ⓜ *Yellow line to Rato.*

Finalmente
Open for more than 40 years, this is one place where you can still catch drag shows in the city. Its biggest star is "Deborah Kristall," who starred in the Portuguese movie *To Die Like a Man* in 2009. On Monday nights new talents take to the stage, but on weekends you'll find the small space filled with mostly gay men and a few of their straight friends, starting at midnight. ⊠ *Rua da Palmeira 38, Príncipe Real* ☎ *21/347-9923* ⊕ *www.finalmenteclub.com* Ⓜ *Yellow line to Rato.*

Foxtrot
In business since the 1970s, this bar feels like it could have opened in the early 20th century thanks to the art deco interior. Inspired by English pubs and Prohibition-era speakeasies, you must ring a bell to enter the dimly lit rooms. There's a cozy fireplace for chilly evenings and a pleasant, open-air patio for warmer nights. In addition to a long list of creative cocktails, Foxtrot serves small bites and larger plates, perfect for late-night snacking. ⊠ *Travessa Santa Teresa 28, Príncipe Real* ☎ *21/395-2697* ⊕ *www.barfoxtrot.pt.*

★ Hot Clube de Portugal
Europe's oldest jazz club started in a tiny basement in 1948, and despite moving to another building nearby, it remains the place for live jazz performances. Hot Clube features local and international acts and has almost daily performances. ⊠ *Praça da Alegria 47–49, Avenida da Liberdade* ☎ *21/346-0305* ⊕ *www.hcp.pt* ⊗ *Closed Sun. and Mon.* Ⓜ *Blue Line to Avenida.*

★ Pavilhão Chinês
For a quiet drink in an intriguing setting, you can't beat this spot. It's filled to the brim with fascinating junk collected over the years—from old toys to statues—and it has two snooker tables. Once famous for its tea selection, it's now more of a cocktail bar than a tearoom, but expect a classic atmosphere and service, not party crowds. ⊠ *Rua Dom Pedro V 89, Príncipe Real* ☎ *21/342-4729* Ⓜ *Yellow line to Rato.*

★ Red Frog

Inspired by 1920s speakeasies, this cocktail bar by Avenida da Liberdade is one of the city's top spots for a relaxing night of drinks. The name comes from the frog you see by the bell at the door, which you must ring to enter. A soft soundtrack of jazz, soul, and swing plays in the vintage-styled interior and there's a wall that leads to a secret room that can be booked for private events. ✉ *Rua do Salitre 5A, Avenida da Liberdade* ☎ *21/583-1120* ⊕ *www.redfrog.pt* Ⓜ *Blue Line to Avenida.*

★ Sky Bar Lisboa

The largest rooftop bar in town sits at the top of the Tivoli Avenida Liberdade Hotel. It looks over Avenida da Liberdade and the castle and serves predinner drinks and late-night cocktails to a mix of locals and visitors staying at the hotel. ✉ *Av. da Liberdade 185, Avenida da Liberdade* ☎ *21/319-8641* ⊕ *www.skybarrooftop. com* Ⓜ *Blue Line to Avenida.*

★ Trumps

Lisbon's oldest and biggest gay club has attracted the city's trendiest crowds of all sexual orientations since it opened in the 1980s. Today, those you find on the two separate dance floors (one playing pop hits, another house music) are mostly gay men and a few lesbians. It often hosts theme parties, especially in the summer. ✉ *Rua da Imprensa Nacional 104B, Príncipe Real* ☎ *91/593-8266* ⊕ *www.trumps.pt* ⊘ *Closed Sun.– Thurs.* Ⓜ *Yellow line to Rato.*

 **Performing Arts**

Cinema São Jorge

This movie theater from 1950 is now the stage for most of the city's annual film festivals. A renovation in 2001 kept the original interior and facade and brought its three screening rooms back into operation. The popular independent film festival IndieLisboa happens here in the spring, the gay and lesbian film festival QueerLisboa every September, and the documentary, the Italian, and the French film festivals are scheduled at other times throughout the year. From its balcony on the top floor you have a view of Avenida da Liberdade's famous pavement designs. ✉ *Av. da Liberdade 175, Avenida da Liberdade* ☎ *21/310-3400* ⊕ *www.cinemasao-jorge.pt* Ⓜ *Blue Line to Avenida.*

Cinemateca Portuguesa

Lisbon's cinema museum screens classic films from all over the world, usually in the original language and often with Portuguese or English subtitles. Arrive early to explore the space and check out the treasures displayed around the building, like the first Lumiére projector used in the country. Be sure to take a peek at the beautiful Moorish-style atrium. End your visit at the café and grab a drink on the pleasant terrace. ✉ *Rua Barata Salgueiro 39, Avenida da Liberdade* ☎ *21/359-6200, 21/359-6262 for ticket office* ⊕ *www. cinemateca.pt* Ⓜ *Blue Line to Avenida.*

AMEIXOEIRA

CHARNECA

LUMIAR

SANTA MARIA DOS OLIVAIS

CARNIDE

PARQUE DAS NAÇÕES

AVENIDAS NOVAS

MARVILA

SÃO DOMINGOS DE BENFICA

BENFICA

CAMPOLIDE

BEATO

SÃO JOÃO

MARQUÊS DE POMPAL E AVENIDA DA LIBERDADE

ARROIOS

PENHA DE FRANÇA

ANJOS

SANTA ENGRÁCIA

SÃO MAMEDE

INTENDENTE

CAMPO DE OURIQUE

PRINCIPE REAL

MARTIM MONIZ

GRAÇA

SÃO VICENTE

ESTRELA

MOURARIA

ALCÂNTARA

ROSSIO

LAPA

BARRIO ALTO

BAIXA

CHIADO

ALFAMA

RESTELO

AJUDA

CAIS DO SODRÉ

SANTOS

BELÉM

Sightseeing ★★★★★ | Shopping ★★★☆☆ | Dining ★★★★☆ | Nightlife ★★★★☆

B efore there was Lisbon, there was Alfama. It's the oldest part of the city, and it remains a charming warren of narrow, hilly streets and alleyways. The neighborhood miraculously survived the devastating earthquake of 1755 that destroyed much of Lisbon, so its historic architecture is largely intact (or decaying in a glorious way). Now it's a must-stop on every visitor's itinerary, and one of the best places to buy souvenirs, listen to traditional fado music, savor the stunning views, or simply allow yourself to get lost. It's also home to major landmarks including Castelo São Jorge and the 12th-century Sé Cathedral, the oldest in the city. Although the streets can be quite hilly, Alfama is best seen by foot, slowly, so as to allow its charms to unfold.—*by Ann Abel*

👁 Sights

Casa dos Bicos

This Italianate dwelling is one of Alfama's most distinctive buildings. It was built in 1523 for Bras de Albuquerque, the son of Afonso, who became the viceroy of India and conquered Goa and Malacca. The name translates as House of Points, and it's not hard to see why—it has a striking facade studded with pointed white stones in diamond shapes. The top two floors were destroyed in the 1755 earthquake, and restoration did not begin until the early 1980s. Since 2012 the building has housed the José Saramago Foundation, a cultural institute set up in memory of the only Portuguese-language winner of the Nobel Prize in Literature, with two floors dedicated to his life and works. ⊠ *Rua dos Bacalhoeiros, Alfama* ☎ *21/880–2040* ⊕ *www.josesaramago.org* 🎫 *€3* ⊘ *Closed Sun.* Ⓜ *Blue Line to Terreiro do Paço.*

⭐ Castelo de São Jorge

Although St. George's Castle was constructed by the Moors, the site had previously been fortified by Romans and Visigoths. To your left as you pass through the main entrance is a statue of Dom Afonso Henriques, whose forces in 1147 besieged the castle and drove the Moors from Lisbon. The ramparts offer panoramic views of the city's layout as far as the towering 25 de Abril suspension bridge. Be careful of the uneven footing. Remnants of a palace that was a residence of the kings of Portugal until the 16th century house a snack bar, a small museum showcasing archeological finds, and

beyond them a stately restaurant, the Casa do Leão, offering dining with spectacular sunset views. From the *periscópio* (periscope) in the Torre de Ulísses, in the castle's keep, you can spy on visitors going about their business below. Beyond the keep, traces of pre-Roman and Moorish houses are visible thanks to recent archaeological digs, as well as the remains of a palace founded in the 15th century. The castle's outer walls encompass a small neighborhood, Castelo, the medieval church of Santa Cruz, restaurants, and souvenir shops. ⊠ *Rua de Santa Cruz do Castelo, Alfama* ☎ *21/880–0620* ⊕ *www.castelodesaojorge.pt* 🎫 *€9* Ⓜ *Blue or Green Line to Baixa-Chiado.*

Igrega do Santo António

This church, constructed in 1767, sits on the site where Lisbon's patron saint, Santo António, was born. Although it's fairly compact, the interior is stunning, with ornately painted walls, abundant natural light, and stone carvings. The altarpiece on the side of the nave's gospel is thought to be from the 16th century, representing Saint Anthony (known as the "effigy of the Saint"), and locals still come to express their devotion. ⊠ *Largo de Santo António da Sé, Alfama* ☎ *21/886–9145* ⊕ *stoantoniolisboa. com* Ⓜ *Blue Line to Terreiro do Paço.*

Miradouro de Santa Luzia

$ | Café. Hop off Tram 28 at the Miradouro de Santa Luzia, a terrace-garden viewpoint that takes in Alfama and the Rio Tejo. Here, as at most of the parks and *miradouros* (viewpoints) in Lisbon, there is a small café-bar kiosk with outdoor seats from which you can watch ships on the river. *Average main: €5* ⊠ *Largo de Santa Luzia, Alfama* ☎ *91/522–5592* ▭ *No credit cards* Ⓜ *Blue Line to Terreiro do Paço.*

Museu do Teatro Romano

This small museum close to the cathedral displays some of the few visible traces of Roman Lisbon. The space was once a Roman amphitheater with capacity for 5,000 spectators and was built by Emperor Augustus in the 1st century BC. It fell into disrepair during the Middle Ages and lay buried and forgotten until reconstruction of the area began in the 18th century. Columns and other interesting artifacts are on display here, and multilingual touch-screen videos outline the history of the amphitheater and Lisbon's Roman history. ⊠ *Rua de São Mamede 3A, Alfama* ✛ *Entrances are on Rua de São Mamede and on main road opposite cathedral* ☎ *21/817–2450* ⊕ *www. museudelisboa.pt/equipamentos/ teatro-romano* 🎫 *€3 (free Sun. and national holidays until 2)* ☾ *Closed Mon.* Ⓜ *Blue Line to Terreiro do Paço.*

GETTING HERE

Alfama is the tourist heart of Lisbon, an easy walk from Praça do Comércio and other major sites. The famous 28 tram runs right through the heart of it, but the area can also be accessed by taking the metro to Terreiro do Paço or Santa Apolónia or by taking the 759 bus.

Rua Leite de Vasconcelos

Rua C

Rua da Verónica

PALÁCIO DOS
MARQUESES DO
LAVRADIO

São Vicente

Jardim
Botto Machado

54

Campo de Sta. Clara

PANTEÃO
NACIONAL

de S. Vicente

Rua do Paraíso

MUSEU
MILITAR

51

48 49 50

52

53

Rua do
Vigário

6

47

R. Museu da Artilharia

R. Jardim do Tabaco

RIO TEJO

0   150 M

0   500 ft

SIGHTS

Casa dos Bicos.........15

Castelo de
São Jorge....................4

Igreja do Santo
António 11

Miradouro de
Santa Luzia...............30

Museu do Teatro
Romano 24

Museu-Escola de
Artes Decorativas 28

Museu Militar..........52

Sé de Lisboa.............17

SHOPPING

A Arte da Terra 23

Chi Coração.............25

Conserveira
de Lisboa 9

Cortição & Netos 1

Feira da Ladra.........54

Loja dos
Descobrimentos.......14

O Passeio da D.
Sardinha e do Sr.
Bacalhau..................51

Porto Alfama 37

Teresa Pavão............20

COFFEE & QUICK BITES

Café da Garagem 3

Gelateiro d'Alfama.....5

Palacete
Chafariz D'el Rei......33

Pois Café 19

Portas do Sol............29

Prima Basilco...........44

DINING

A Travesso
do Fado 39

Barração
de Alfama 38

Bica do Sapato 53

Boi-Cavalo................45

Cantina Zé Avillez 12

Le Petit Café.............27

Leopold 6

Memmo Alfama
Wine Bar & Terrace.31

Mestre André 43

Santo António de
Alfama 35

Solar dos Bicos 16

Taberna Moderna 13

Trigo Latino..............34

BARS & NIGHTLIFE

A Baiuca....................36

Bela Vinhos e
Petiscos 50

Casa de Linhares.....22

Clube de Fado 21

The CorkScrew
Wine Bar 47

Duetos da Sé 18

Mesa de Frades 48

Museu do Fado.........40

Outro Lado................10

Parreirinha
de Alfama 41

Páteo de Alfama.......32

Santiago
Alquimista 26

Sr. Fado 49

Tejo Bar 46

Ulysses Lisbon
Speakeasy 42

Wine Bar
do Castelo.................7

PERFORMING ARTS

Chapitô 8

Teatro Taborda 2

Museu-Escola de Artes Decorativas

In the 17th-century Azurara Palace, the Museum-School of Decorative Arts has objects that date from the 15th through 19th centuries. Look for brightly colored Arraiolos—traditional, hand-embroidered Portuguese carpets based on Arabic designs—as well as silverwork, ceramics, paintings, and jewelry. With so many rich items to preserve, the museum has become a major center for restoration. Crafts such as bookbinding, carving, and cabinetmaking are all undertaken here by highly trained staff; there are regular workshops open to the public (for a fee) to learn crafts like tile painting and paper marbling.
⊠ *Fundação Ricardo do Espírito Santo, Largo das Portas do Sol 2, Alfama* ☎ *21/881-4600 weekdays, 21/888-1991 weekends* ⊕ *www.fress. pt* 🎫 *€4* ⊙ *Closed Tues.* Ⓜ *Green Line to Martim Moniz.*

Museu Militar

The spirit of heroism is palpable in the huge Corinthian-style barracks and arsenal complex of the Military Museum, which houses one of the largest artillery collections in the world. Visitors can ogle a 20-ton bronze cannon and admire Vasco da Gama's sword in a room dedicated to the explorer and his voyages of discovery. As you clatter through endless, echoing rooms of weapons, uniforms, and armor, you may be lucky enough to be followed—at a respectful distance—by a guide who can convey exactly how that bayonet was jabbed or that gruesome flail swung. In this beautifully ornate building there is also a collection of 18th- to 20th-century art. The museum is on the eastern edge of Alfama, at the foot of the hill and opposite the Santa Apolónia station.
⊠ *Largo do Museu da Artilharia, Alfama* ☎ *21/884-2300* ⊕ *www.exer- cito.pt/sites/MusMilLisboa/Paginas/ default.aspx* 🎫 *€3* ⊙ *Closed Mon.* Ⓜ *Blue Line to Santa Apolónia.*

★ **Sé de Lisboa** *(Lisbon Cathedral)* Lisbon's austere Romanesque cathedral, Sé (which stands for *Sedes Episcopalis*), was founded in 1150 to commemorate the defeat of the Moors three years earlier. To rub salt in the wound, the conquerors built the sanctuary on the spot where Moorish Lisbon's main mosque once stood. Note the fine rose window, and be sure to visit the 13th-century cloister and the treasure-filled sacristy, which contains the relics of the martyr St. Vincent, among other things. According to legend, the relics were carried from the Algarve to Lisbon in a ship piloted by ravens; the saint became Lisbon's official patron. The cathedral was originally built in the Romanesque style of the time but has undergone several rebuilds and refurbishments over the years, and today its rather eclectic architecture includes Gothic, baroque, and neoclassical adornments. ▰TIP→ Visitors are expected to dress respectfully.
⊠ *Largo da Sé, Alfama* ☎ *21/887-6628* ⊕ *www.patriarcado-lisboa.pt/site* 🎫 *Cathedral free, cloisters €3* Ⓜ *Blue Line to Terreiro do Paço.*

Shopping

★ A Arte da Terra

Opposite the Sé in the old cathedral stables, A Arte da Terra uses old stone mangers as display cases for handiwork, traditional and modern, from around the country. As well as linen, felt hats, wool blankets, embroidery, and toys, you can pick up fado and folk CDs and an amazing range of representations of Santo António, the city's favorite saint. ⊠ Rua Augusto Rosa 40, Alfama ☎ 21/274–5975 ⊕ www.aartedaterra. pt/en Ⓜ Blue Line to Terreira do Paço.

Chi Coração

Part of the name means "heart," and that's exactly what the family behind this wool shop has put into their business. Since the 1960s, they have been saving and restoring old mills and tools used for wool production, and recreating typical Portuguese designs. The top-quality products range from blankets to coats for women and men as well as children's puppets. ⊠ Rua Augusto Rosa 22–24, Alfama ☎ 21/346–1082 ⊕ chicoracao.com Ⓜ Blue Line to Terreiro do Paço.

★ Conserveira de Lisboa

There's a feast for the eyes at this shop, whose walls are lined with colorful tins of sardines and other seafood, as well as fruit preserves and other delicacies. Staff serve from behind an antique wooden counter. ⊠ Rua dos Bacalhoeiros 34, Alfama ☎ 21/886–4009 ⊕ www. conserveiradelisboa.pt ⊙ Closed Sun. Ⓜ Blue Line to Terreiro do Paço.

Cortição & Netos

This company, founded by Joaquim José Cortiço in 1979, gathers, stores, and sells countless azulejos from discontinued lines of Portuguese factories. In this simply styled shop, the tiles are curated as they should be—as miniature works of art. The store's revenue is used to fund the family's ongoing commitment to preserving the ceramic tradition. ⊠ Calçada de Santo André 66, Alfama ☎ 91/970–3705 ⊙ Closed Sun. and at lunchtime (1–2) Ⓜ Green Line to Martim Moniz.

★ Feira da Ladra

One of Lisbon's main shopping attractions is this flea market held on Tuesday morning and all day Saturday. It's fun to browse, and you never know what sort of treasure you'll come across. ⊠ Campo de Santa Clara, Lisbon Ⓜ Blue Line to Santa Apolónia.

Loja dos Descobrimentos

You can often see artists at work in this shop specializing in hand-painted tiles. What's more, they ship worldwide, and you can even order online so there's no need to haul any breakables home in your bags. ✉ Rua dos Bacalhoeiros 12A, Alfama ☎ 21/886-5563 ⊕ www.loja-descobri-mentos.com Ⓜ Blue Line to Terreiro do Paço.

O Passeio da D. Sardinha e do Sr. Bacalhau

This tidy, family-owned shop sells all sorts of locally made souvenirs. The wares are nothing unexpected—lots of cork and items shaped like sardines—but the quality is high and the prices fair. ✉ Rua dos Remédios 169, Alfama ☎ 91/739-3675 ⊕ alfa-mashop.blogspot.com Ⓜ Blue Line to Santa Apolónia.

Porto Alfama

This is a good place to pick up gifts and souvenirs of the edible (and drinkable) sort: the shelves display jars of conserves and preserves, Portuguese port and table wines, and tinned fish in old-school pack-aging that's almost worth buying for the artwork alone. There are a few tables at which you can sit and sample some of the wines and fish as well. ✉ Rua de São Pedro 26, Alfama ✛ Close to Museu do Fado ☎ 21/887-2265 ⊕ portoalfama.com 🕙 Closed Sun., Tues., and Wed. Ⓜ Blue Line to Terreiro do Paço.

★ Teresa Pavão

Occupying a onetime historic bakery next to the Sé Cathedral, this space is half atelier and half showroom

for Portuguese ceramicist Teresa Pavão. Her work has been exhibited worldwide and locally, including at the well-regarded MUDE (Museu do Design e da Moda). Now, instead of bread (and bread bags) it is a place to buy subtle and sublime decora-tive and practical ceramics made from white clay that is polished or glazed or joined with other mate-rials like bone, wood, iron, silver, and gold, as well as bags made from rare fabrics. ✉ Rua de São João da Praça 120, Alfama ☎ 21/887-2743 ⊕ teresapavao.com Ⓜ Blue Line to Terreiro do Paço.

☕ Coffee and Quick Bites

Café da Garagem

$ | Café. The food at the café at the Teatro Taborda performing arts space (also known as Teatro da Garagem) is nothing unusual—standard sandwiches, salads, and the like—but they have the loveliest views of the city. It's decorated with theatrical objects and sometimes hosts jazz concerts, poetry sessions, and recitals. Known for: city views; cozy vibe; Instagram potential. *Average main: €6* ✉ *Costa do Castelo 75, Alfama* 🕾 *21/885-4190* ⊕ *teatrodagaragem.com* ⊘ *Closed Mon.* 🚫 *No credit cards* Ⓜ *Green Line to Martim Moniz.*

Gelateiro d'Alfama

$ | International. This compact ice-cream shop serves only a few flavors, but they are well made, ever changing, and often interesting (*pastel de nata*, anyone?) and come in a variety of cones, on top of warm waffles, or inside crepes. Known for: Oreo ice cream and milk shakes; pastel de nata (a Portuguese egg tart pastry) ice cream; cozy and cute vibe. *Average main: €4* ✉ *Rua das Escolas Gerais 124, Alfama* 🕾 *96/865-6226* 🚫 *No credit cards* Ⓜ *Blue Line to Terreiro do Paço.*

Palacete Chafariz D'el Rei

$$ | International. Palacete Chafariz D'el Rei, one of the most eye-catching buildings in Alfama, also houses one of its best refined hideaways. The tearoom in this lavish palace-turned-hotel is open to the public, and it's a great place to duck into for a spot of tea—the real deal, from Gorreana in Portugal's Azores islands, Europe's only tea plantation—or a brunch fit for royalty with cheeses, fruits, eggs, cakes, and homemade marmalades. Known for: location in the Palacete Chafariz D'el Rei; afternoon tea; weekend brunch. *Average main: €20* ✉ *Palacete Chafariz D'el Rei, Travessa Chafariz del Rei 6, Alfama* 🕾 *21/888-6150* ⊘ *chafarizdelrei.com* Ⓜ *Blue Line to Terreiro do Paço.*

Pois Café

$ | International. Foreigners and Portuguese laugh at the word *pois*, which is a sort of indecipherable interjection that peppers many conversations. (The closest meaning might be "yeah, I get it.") Just as the word fills conversational gaps, coffee fills the gaps in daily life. Hence this café, which opened a decade ago in a homey "third space" (between work and home), with magazines for browsing, free Wi-Fi for surfing, and, of course, top-quality coffee and cakes (and more substantial meals) for fuel. Known for: laid-back vibe; secondhand library and book exchange; great location. *Average main: €9* ✉ *Rua São João da Praça 93–95, Alfama* 🕾 *21/886-2497* Ⓜ *Blue Line to Terreiro do Paço.*

Portas do Sol

$ | International. Unlike many of the city's overlooks and terraces, where the mass-produced sandwiches and cheap wine are something of an afterthought, Portas do Sol (meaning "doors to the sun") actually serves food and drinks that match the stunning river and city views. Don't expect Michelin-star cuisine, but you could do far worse than a couscous or caprese salad and fresh-squeezed juice. **Known for:** appealing indoor area for rainy days and chilly nights; above-average kiosk food; spectacular views. *Average main: €9* ⌧ *Largo das Portas do Sol, Beco de Santa Helena, Alfama* ☎ *21/885-1299* ⊕ *portasdosol. pt* Ⓜ *Blue Line to Terreiro do Paço.*

Prima Basilico

$ | Pizza. Run by an Italian family, this small restaurant does only three things but it does them really well: square slices of thick Italian-style pizza, foccacia, and calzones. The mozzarella, Parmesan, and sausages are imported from Italy, but Portuguese ingredients are used whenever possible; it's counter service, so you can take your pizza to go or sit at one of the few tables inside. **Known for:** authentic recipes; good variety of meat and vegetarian options; Italian limoncello. *Average main: €3* ⌧ *Rua dos Remédios 37, Alfama* ☎ *21/888-5287* ⊕ *primobasilico.com* ▭ *No credit cards* Ⓜ *Blue Line to Santa Apolónia.*

🍴 Dining

Barração de Alfama

$ | Portuguese. Unfussy, authentic fish and seafood dishes have put this cozy restaurant on the local (and visiting) food lovers' radar. Expect staples like grilled octopus, seafood rice, and, of course, grilled sardines in the summer months; there's also plenty of meat for those who prefer it. **Known for:** extensive list of Portuguese wines; traditional cooking techniques; integrity of ingredients. *Average main: €13* ⌧ *Rua de São Pedro 16, Alfama* ☎ *21/886-6359* 🕑 *Closed Mon.* Ⓜ *Blue Line to Santa Apolónia.*

Boi-Cavalo

$$$$ | Eclectic. Known as a wild child among the relentlessly traditional neighborhood dining spots, you'll hear indie rock instead of fado at Boi-Cavalo and experience a menu that features unusual Portuguese products like lamb tartare and heart of cauliflower, instead of the typical grilled fish and meats. The chef, a onetime design student, is using his kitchen as a lab for experiments with these oddball products, pairing them with Asian and other international influences; the short, creative tasting menu changes weekly. **Known for:** creative tasting menus; intimate environment; celebration of forgotten Portuguese ingredients. *Average main: €35* ⌧ *Rua do Vigário 70B, Alfama* ☎ *21/887-1653* ⊕ *boi-cavalo. pt* 🕑 *Closed Mon.* Ⓜ *Blue Line to Santa Apolónia.*

★ Cantinha Zé Avillez

$$ | Portuguese. José Avillez (of the Michelin two-star Belcanto) has been opening new restaurants at a brisk pace. At this spot, one of his newest, the cooking and service are as impeccable as always with a menu that emphasizes Portuguese classics like grilled octopus and steaks with fried eggs on top and a relaxed vibe in the dining areas. **Known for:** classic Portuguese cuisine; Portugal's biggest celebrity chef at the helm; creative desserts. *Average main: €18* ✉ *Rua dos Arameiros 15, Alfama* ✛ *On Campo das Cebolas* ☎ *21/580-7625* ⊕ *cantinazeavillez.pt* Ⓜ *Blue Line to Terreiro do Paço.*

★ Leopold
$$$$ | International. The couple that owns and runs this tiny restaurant made quite a stir a few years ago when they opened with just four tables and no stove. They have since moved their restaurant to the boutique Palácio Belmonte hotel, slightly expanded their seating capacity, and properly outfitted their kitchen; even with the new appliances, chef Tiago Feio still employs a thoughtful minimalism in his ever-changing tasting menus. **Known for:** good selection of wines from small producers, including natural wines; creative cuisine; minimalist decor. *Average main: €40* ✉ *Palácio Belmonte, Patéo Dom Fradique 12, Alfama* ✛ *In courtyard of hotel* ☎ *21/886-1697* ⊙ *Closed Mon. and Tues.* Ⓜ *Green line to Martim Moniz.*

★ Memmo Alfama Wine Bar & Terrace
$$ | Portuguese. The terrace bar and restaurant at the casual-chic Memmo Alfama hotel has some of the neighborhood's best views, with tables and chairs arranged around a small infinity pool. Tapas-style small plates are the items to order here, and the selection of Portuguese cheeses, served with a basket of breads and crispbreads, is a good place to start. **Known for:** sunset views; Portuguese petiscos; great selection of local wines

by the glass. *Average main: €20* ✉ *Memmo Alfama Hotel, Travessa das Merceeiras 27, Alfama* ☎ *21/049-5660* ⊕ *www.memmohotels.com/alfama/wine-bar-amp-outdoor-pool.html* Ⓜ *Blue Line to Terreiro do Paço.*

Mestre André
$ | Portuguese. For more than three decades, this restaurant has aimed to serve home-style Portuguese food in an environment that's meant to make guests feel at home—nothing is cutting edge, but everything is fresh and made with love. The dining room is small and cozy, but the menu is long and varied—and it hits all the Portuguese classics: octopus salad, *amêijoas à bulhão pato* (clams with coriander, lemon, and garlic), roasted chorizo, and various cuts of meat. **Known for:** seafood cataplanas (pans used to prepare Portuguese seafood dishes); lemon mousse; welcoming atmosphere. *Average main: €14* ✉ *Calçadinha de Santo Estevão 6, Alfama* ☎ *21/886-6232* ⊕ *restaurantemestreandre.com* ⊙ *Closed Mon.* Ⓜ *Blue Line to Santa Apolónia.*

Le Petit Café
$$ | Portuguese. Don't let the name of this restaurant fool you: this is not a casual, French café, but rather a sophisticated restaurant that serves a menu that is largely Portuguese—there's plenty of codfish, octopus, and grilled Portuguese meats—but also includes Italian appetizers and pastas (and the occasional head-scratcher like chicken samosas). **Known for:** romantic atmosphere; eclectic wine list; good pasta. *Average main: €16* ✉ *Largo São*

Martinho 6, Alfama ☎ 21/888–1304 ⊕ lepetitcaferesto.wixsite.com/lepetit-cafe Ⓜ Blue Line to Terreiro do Paço.

Santo António de Alfama
$$ | Portuguese. The motto here is "We don't have sardines or fado," but the fact that it's still busy despite the absence of these tourist favorites is a testament to the great food and atmosphere. The simple but sophisticated dining room is hung with black-and-white photos of famous artists, the terrace is lovely in summertime, and the kitchen turns out a varied menu that emphasizes authentic Portuguese dishes such as *morcela com grelos* (blood sausage and turnip leaves) and flavorful fresh fish. **Known for:** late-night service (until 2); an absence of tourist clichés; long history. *Average main: €19* ⊠ *Beco de São Miguel 7, Alfama* ☎ 21/888–1328 ⊕ *www.siteantonio.com* Ⓜ *Blue Line to Terreiro do Paço.*

Solar dos Bicos
$ | Portuguese. This charming restaurant with its stone arches and beautiful azulejos offers typical Portuguese cuisine at very reasonable prices. Grilled fish and seafood are the main attraction, but there are also plenty of no-nonsense meat dishes. **Known for:** good people-watching outdoors; friendly service; large portions. *Average main: €12* ⊠ *Rua dos Bacalhoeiros 8A, Alfama* ☎ 21/886–9447 ⊕ *www.solardosbicos. pt* ⊙ *Closed Mon.* Ⓜ *Blue Line to Terreiro do Paço.*

Taberna Moderna
$$$ | Portuguese. This restaurant embodies every idea visitors have about Portugal: big blue doors welcome guests to an informal dining space where good food is ready at hand and everyone is relaxing with a cocktail—there are 80 gins on the list. That said, food is hardly an afterthought as the kitchen turns out all sorts of delicious shareable dishes like black rice with cuttlefish or simply braised tuna. **Known for:** reputation as one of the city's best places to go for a G&T; delicious shareable dishes; old-school Portuguese vibe. *Average main: €21* ⊠ *Rua dos Bacalhoeiros 18, Alfama* ☎ 21/886–5039 ⊕ *tabernamoderna.com* ⊙ *Closed Sun. No lunch Mon.* Ⓜ *Blue Line to Terreiro do Paço.*

A Travesso do Fado
$ | Portuguese. Yes, this restaurant is located right by the Museu do Fado, and yes, there is occasional live fado performed, but it's not a typical fado house, as it consistently turns out excellent, shareable plates of *petiscos* (snacks), such as codfish croquettes and tempura green beans. The dining room is simple and attractive, with menu items written on chalkboards and accents of pink on the tables, and there's an inviting courtyard out front. **Known for:** soulful food; fado on Wednesday; great location. *Average main: €12* ⊠ *Largo do Chafariz de Dentro 1, Alfama* ☎ 21/887–0144 ⊙ *Closed Mon. and Tues.* Ⓜ *Blue Line to Terreiro do Paço.*

UNDERSTANDING FADO

The traditional music of Portugal, fado has its roots in Alfama and other port districts of Lisbon in the 1820s.

It's known for being soulful and melancholy, the embodiment of the Portuguese concept of saudade (loosely translated as "longing.") Lisbon's most beloved fadista, Amália Rodrigues, performed regularly in Alfama. A few years ago the city commissioned street artist Alexandre Farto, who signs his work with the name Vhils (and has been called Lisbon's answer to Banksy), to create a mural in Amália's image, as a memorial to her.

The music is still very much alive and well in large concert halls and small restaurants—Sr. Fado, Parreirinha de Alfama, and A Baiuca are among the standouts. Although fado is always performed in Portuguese, you don't have to speak the language to feel the emotion in classic fado songs like "Uma Casa Portuguesa" and "Ai Mouraria," which are celebrations of Portuguese life and particular neighborhoods. In fact, you shouldn't say anything as it's considered disrespectful to talk during a fado performance.

Trigo Latino

$ | Mediterranean. With its partially green walls, red chairs, black-and-white tiled floors, and colorful artwork on the walls, this onetime grain warehouse stands apart from many other restaurants in the area. It's an inviting place to enjoy the mostly Portuguese and Mediterranean-influenced menu, with dishes like a local sea bass fillet stuffed with mushrooms and beetroot risotto flavored with truffles. **Known for:** playful vibe; eclectic and creative menu items; great gin cocktails. *Average main: €14* ⊠ *Largo Terreiro do Trigo 1, Alfama* ☎ *21/882-1282* ⊘ *Closed Mon.* Ⓜ *Blue Line to Terreiro do Paço.*

🍸 Bars and Nightlife

★ A Baiuca

At the family-run A Baiuca, the quality of both food and singing varies, but a great atmosphere is guaranteed. It's a fado *vadio* ("vaga-bond" fado) spot, which means enthusiasm alone will get you onto the stage, and the night often ends with local amateurs lined up outside, raring to perform. (You can just drop in after dinner if you want a few drinks.) ⊠ *Rua de São Miguel 20, Alfama* ☎ *21/886-7284* Ⓜ *Blue Line to Terreiro do Paço.*

Bela Vinhos e Petiscos

This homey fado tavern is also known for the high quality of its typical Portuguese dishes that are meant to be shared, such as tempura green beans, cod with chickpeas, and octopus salad. The fado shows are performed

Thursday–Sunday, and reservations are recommended. ✉ *Rua dos Remédios 190, Alfama* ☎ *92/607–7511* Ⓜ *Blue Line to Santa Apolónia.*

Casa de Linhares

Some of the biggest names in modern-day fado—Jorge Fernando, Fábia Rebordão, Vânia Duarte, and André Baptista—are in residence in this establishment. The dark, candle-lit dining room is located in the remains of a Renaissance building that was once owned by the counts of Linhares and was damaged in the 1755 earthquake; the atmospheric location matches the melancholy and strong emotion of the music. ✉ *Beco dos Armazéns do Linho 2, Alfama* ☎ *21/823–9660* ⊕ *casadelinhares.com* Ⓜ *Blue Line to Terreiro do Paço.*

Clube de Fado

Locals and tourists flock to this spot to hear established performers, such as owner Mário Pacheco, and rising singing stars. Dinners are pricey, but music fans arriving from around 10:30 pm can skip the food and concentrate on the fado. ✉ *Rua S. João de Praça 86–94, Alfama* ☎ *21/885–2704* ⊕ *www.clube-de-fado. com* Ⓜ *Blue Line to Terreiro do Paço.*

The CorkScrew Wine Bar

As the name implies, this is a pretty straightforward wine bar—a wide array of Portuguese vintages are complimented with local cheese, charcuterie, and even main dishes. But you don't come here for the cod; you come for a glass of a unique varietal you've never tried in a cozy room whose walls are covered with drawings of musicians and shelves of wine bottles, which are both available for sale. ✉ *Rua dos Remédios 95, Alfama* ☎ *21/595–1774* ⊕ *www.thecorkscrew.pt/en_GB* Ⓜ *Blue Line to Santa Apolónia.*

Duetos da Sé

Nightly fado performances are the draw at this traditional establishment near the Sé Cathedral. As the name implies, they are done in pairs, usually a singer and guitarist but sometimes a singer and a pianist or even two singers. There are no surprises on the menu, just good-quality Portuguese snacks and main dishes. There's also a gallery space showcasing works of various visual artists that's worth checking out. ✉ *Travessa do Almargem 1B, Alfama* ☎ *21/885–0041* ⊕ *duetosdase. com* Ⓜ *Blue Line to Terreiro do Paço.*

★ Mesa de Frades

All the rage among local fado lovers, this place is housed in a tiny, azulejo-lined former chapel. The food quality varies, but the music and atmosphere are always top rate; in any case, you can slip in at the end of the night, order a drink or two, and enjoy the show. ✉ *Rua dos Remédios 139A, Alfama* ☎ *91/702–9436* Ⓜ *Blue Line to Santa Apolónia.*

Museu do Fado

Prominent fadistas, both traditional singers and next-generation artists who are expanding the boundaries of the form, perform most nights in the modern café attached to the city-run Museu do Fado; it becomes more of a restaurant in the evening. Since this is a popular spot, reservations are essential. ✉ *Largo do Chafariz de Dentro 1, Alfama* ☎ *21/887-0144* ⊕ *www.museudofado. pt* Ⓜ *Blue Line to Terreiro do Paço.*

Outro Lado
Craft beer is a recent arrival in Lisbon, and this is still one of the few places to find a good selection of artisanal brews. All of Portugal's major breweries are represented, as are a number from Belgium, the United States, and around the world. If you want to try a beer (or cider or barley wine) from Warsaw or Tallinn in Lisbon, this is your place. ✉ *Beco do Arco Escuro 1, Alfama* Ⓜ *Blue Line to Terreiro do Paço.*

★ Parreirinha de Alfama
This little club has been owned by fado legend Argentina Santos since the 1960s, and though she no longer sings, she sits by the door most nights, and the place hires many other highly rated singers. Food plays second fiddle to the music, but you could do worse than fresh grilled fish and a bottle of wine as the singers work their magic. ✉ *Beco do Espírito Santo 1, Alfama* ☎ *21/886-8209* ⊕ *www.parreirinha-dealfama.com* Ⓜ *Blue Line to Santa Apolónia.*

Páteo de Alfama
There is more entertainment than authenticity in the 30-minute fado shows at this restaurant. Although the performers are first-rate and include a number of the genre's current famous names, there is a theme that traces the evolution of fado from the 19th century to the present, and folklore shows feature

dancers in old-fashioned costumes. ✉ *Rua São João da Praça 18, Alfama* ☎ *21/882-2174* ⊕ *pateodealfama. pt* 🎫 *€15* Ⓜ *Blue Line to Terreiro do Paço.*

Santiago Alquimista
This former factory near the castle is now a popular live music venue that draws a young crowd to see local and international musicians. Opened in 1989, it still packs people in to fill the tables around the stage and on the mezzanine and balconies above it. When there isn't a concert, there may be DJ sets, plays, or movie screenings. ✉ *Rua de Santiago 19, Alfama* ☎ *21/443-2995* Ⓜ *Blue Line to Terreiro do Paço.*

Sr. Fado
This long-running fado house is owned and run by fado singer Ana Marina and fado violist Duarte Santos, who had the idea of serving guests home-cooked Portuguese food before they or other performers take the stage. The menu is limited to a choice of a *cataplana* (copper cooking pan) of seafood or pork, but it's hard to quibble with that when you realize that it's Ana in the kitchen and Duarte and their daughter, Nadia, serving guests. ✉ *Rua dos Remédios, Alfama* ☎ *21/887-4298* ⊕ *sr-fado.com* Ⓜ *Blue Line to Santa Apolónia.*

Tejo Bar
This tiny, somewhat divey music bar has a cozy living-room vibe. Its hard-to-find location makes it more popular with local music lovers than with tourists. The concerts tend to be informal, often more like jam

sessions (not just fado) among local and touring musicians who head here after their own performances; things really start rolling around midnight. ⊠ *Beco do Vigário 1A, Alfama* ☎ *96/975-6148* Ⓜ *Blue Line to Santa Apolónia.*

Ulysses Lisbon Speakeasy
Something of a rarity in Lisbon, this tiny, eight-stool bar serves only classic and speakeasy cocktails, Portuguese wines, craft beer, and other lovely things to sip (nothing to eat). The owner has assembled one of the largest collections of bourbon in Lisbon, including the full range of hard-to-find Pappy Van Winkle and the Buffalo Trace antique collection. ⊠ *Rua da Regueira 16A, Alfama* ☎ *92/769-6684* Ⓜ *Blue Line to Terreiro do Paço.*

Wine Bar do Castelo
This is a great place to flop down after visiting the Castelo de São Jorge. It has a good selection of wines to sample, plus authentic Portuguese snacks, particularly local cheese and charcuterie. ⊠ *Rua Bartolomeu de Gusmão 11–13, Alfama* ☎ *21/887-9093* ⊕ *www.winebardo-castelo.blogspot.pt* Ⓜ *Green Line to Martim Moniz.*

 Performing Arts

Chapitô
A good way to hurdle the language barrier is to see a show at this theater, where contemporary clowning, circus acts, and physical theater, often with a mix of languages, is the order of the day. There's also a bustling esplanade, the pleasant Chapitô à Mesa restaurant with fine views of the city and river, and the bohemian downstairs Bartô bar with a mix of live music and DJs. ⊠ *Costa do Castelo 1–7, Alfama* ☎ *21/885-5550* ⊕ *www.chapito.org* Ⓜ *Blue Line to Terreiro do Paço.*

Teatro Taborda
The resident company at this historic theater has spent three decades exploring and performing new, historic, and experimental works. Although Portuguese is the primary language, many performances incorporate dance and multimedia elements that make them entertaining to visitors. ⊠ *Costa do Castelo 75, Alfama* ☎ *21/885-4190* ⊕ *teatrodagaragem.com* Ⓜ *Green Line to Martim Moniz.*

Graça, São Vicente, Beato, and Marvila

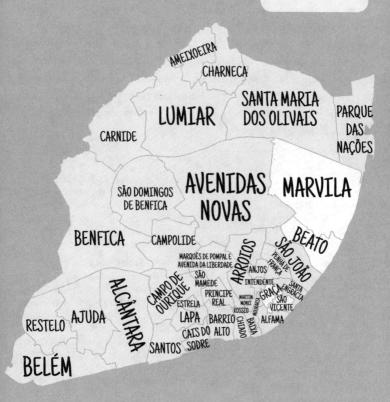

AMEIXOEIRA

CHARNECA

SANTA MARIA DOS OLIVAIS

LUMIAR

PARQUE DAS NAÇÕES

CARNIDE

AVENIDAS NOVAS

MARVILA

SÃO DOMINGOS DE BENFICA

BEATO

BENFICA

CAMPOLIDE

SÃO JOÃO

ARROIOS

PENHA DE FRANÇA

MARQUÊS DE POMPAL E AVENIDA DA LIBERDADE

ANJOS

SANTA ENGRÁCIA

SÃO MAMEDE

INTENDENTE

CAMPO DE OURIQUE

PRINCIPE REAL

GRAÇA

ESTRELA

MARTIM MONIZ

SÃO VICENTE

ALCÂNTARA

AJUDA

LAPA

MOURARIA

ROSSIO

ALFAMA

RESTELO

BARRIO ALTO

BAIXA

CHIADO

CAIS DO SODRE

SANTOS

BELÉM

E ast of the tourist center, Graça and São Vicente are traditional, fairly sedate neighborhoods where life is lived calmly. There are also a number of very fine classically Portuguese restaurants. Given its perch higher up the hill from Alfama, Graça has a number of miradouros (viewpoints) with dramatic sunset views over the city. Farther east, between the former eastern frontier of the historic city and the contemporary Parque das Nações, the previously overlooked districts of Beato and Marvila have begun to be spiffed up by young, creative Lisboetas opening restaurants, galleries, and craft breweries and turning derelict factories into multiconcept performing and visual arts venues. They are adding to the emerging neighborhoods' dynamism, along with the trendy restaurants and throbbing nightclubs that have hugged the edge of the Tejo River for years.—by Ann Abel

👁 Sights

Galaria Baginski

This art gallery in Beato represents a roster of emerging and established artists with a particular focus on Europe, Latin America, and Africa. The gallery is being increasingly recognized internationally by artists, curators, critics, and other lovers of contemporary art. Exhibitions encompass photography, installation art, drawing, painting, and other mediums. ✉ Rua Capitão Leitão 51–53, Lisbon ☎ 21/397–0719 ⊕ baginski.com.pt ⊘ Closed Sun. and Mon. Ⓜ Blue Line to Santa Apolónia.

★ Galeria Filomena Soares

Housed in a large former warehouse not far from the Museu Nacional do Azulejo, this gallery is owned by, and bears the name of, one of Europe's leading female art dealers. Her roster includes leading local and international artists, such as Ângela Ferreira and Shirin Neshat. ✉ Rua da Manutenção 80, Lisbon ☎ 21/862–4122 ⊕ www.gfilomenasoares.com Ⓜ Blue Line to Santa Apolónia.

Galeria Francisco Fino

After five years as a nomadic gallery, presenting exhibitions in other museums and commercial establishments, this art space opened in its permanent home, in Marvila, in 2017. It continues to show the work of artists such as Fernanda Gomes, David Maljković, and Tris Vonna-Michell, among many others. Their genres range from video art to sculpture installations, meaning there's always something thought-provoking to see. ✉ Rua Capitão Leitão 76, Lisbon ☎ 21/584–2211 ⊕ franciscofino.com ⊘ Closed Sun. and Mon. Ⓜ Blue Line to Santa Apolónia.

Mosteiro de São Vicente de Fora

The Italianate facade of the twin-towered St. Vincent's Monastery heralds an airy church with a barrel-vault ceiling, the work of accomplished Italian architect Filippo Terzi (1520–97), finally completed in 1704. Its superbly tiled cloister depicts the fall of Lisbon to the Moors. The monastery also serves as the pantheon of the Bragança dynasty, which ruled Portugal from the restoration of independence from Spain in 1640 to the declaration of the republic in 1910. It's worth the admission fee to climb up to the rooftop terrace for a look over Alfama, the dome of the nearby Santa Engrácia, and the river. ⊠ *Largo de São Vicente, Lisbon* 🕾 *21/888–5652* 🎫 *€5* ⊘ *Closed Mon.* Ⓜ *Blue Line to Santa Apolónia.*

★ Museu Nacional do Azulejo

A tile museum might not sound thrilling, but this magnificent museum dedicated to Lisbon's eye-catching azulejos is one of the city's top tourist attractions—and with good reason. Housed in the 16th-century Madre de Deus convent and cloister, it displays a range of individual glazed tiles and elaborate pictorial panels. The 118-foot-long *Panorama of Lisbon* (1730) is a detailed study of the city and its waterfront and is reputedly the country's longest azulejo piece. The richly furnished convent church contains some sights of its own: of note are the gilt baroque decoration and lively azulejo works depicting the life of St. Anthony. There are also a little café-bar and a gift shop that sells tile reproductions. ⊠ *Rua da Madre de Deus 4, Lisbon* 🕾 *21/810–0340* ⊕ *www.museudoazulejo.gov.pt* 🎫 *€5* ⊘ *Closed Mon.* Ⓜ *Blue Line to Santa Apolónia.*

Panteão de Santa Engrácia

The large domed edifice immediately behind and below São Vicente is the former church of Santa Engrácia. It took 285 years to build, hence the Portuguese phrase "a job like Santa Engrácia." Today the building doubles as Portugal's Panteão Nacional (National Pantheon), housing the tombs of the country's former presidents as well as cenotaphs dedicated to its most famous explorers and writers. A more recent arrival is fado diva Amália Rodrigues, whose tomb is invariably piled high with flowers from admirers. ⊠ *Campo de Santa Clara, Lisbon* 🕾 *21/885–4820* 🎫 *€4* ⊘ *Closed Mon.* Ⓜ *Blue Line to Santa Apolónia.*

GETTING HERE

Graça and the neighborhoods beyond are not the easiest places to reach (which is one reason they're so pleasant to relax in). The famous 28 tram goes to the heart of Graça, but to explore the neighborhoods farther to the east, you will need a bit more patience. The closest metro stop is Santa Apolónia, and most of this area is a reasonable walk from there. Uber and taxis are good options for reaching the general vicinity, but you can also take the 759, 942, or 718 bus to Beato.

★ Underdogs Gallery

One of Lisbon's most important contemporary art galleries, Underdogs, founded in 2010, works with some of the most renowned urban-inspired contemporary artists from around the world. Not only are there several solo and group shows in the warehouse-type space, but the founders are out to create opportunities for local, international, well-known, and up-and-coming artists to make art that is in the city and for the city—meaning street art. They had a hand in some of the city's most iconic murals, including pieces by local hero Vhils and American artist Shepard Fairey, and they periodically lead group tours to admire the city's prevalent public art. ⊠ *Rua Fernando Palha 56, Lisbon* ☎ *21/868-0462* ⊕ *www.under-dogs.net* ⊘ *Closed Sun. and Mon.* Ⓜ *Blue Line to Santa Apolónia.*

 Shopping

Armazém das Caldas

This shop, which occupies a permanent space adjacent to the Feira da Ladra market, specializes in ceramics from various Portuguese factories and artisans' workshops in and around the town of Caldas da Rainha, Portugal's intellectual hub for pottery. Crockery, tableware, and decorative pieces take the form of pumpkins, cabbages, swallows, roosters, frogs, lizards, sardines, and hanging codfish. Prices are more than fair. ⊠ *Campo de Santa Clara 112, Lisbon* ✛ *Near Feira da Ladra market* ⊘ *Closed Sun.,*

Mon., and Wed. Ⓜ *Blue line to Santa Apolónia.*

Collectors–Vintage Department

The popular Príncipe Real furniture-and-curiosity shop Vintage Department spun off a sibling shop in newly cool Marvila in 2018. This location has the same eclectic mix of midcentury furnishings, taxidermied birds, and retro lighting, plus a large array of collectible art. ⊠ *Rua Pereira Henriques, Armazém 6, Lisbon* ☎ *91/177-8837* Ⓜ *Blue Line to Santa Apolónia.*

Garbags

This stylish little boutique specializes in messenger bags, backpacks, wallets, and small cases that are upcycled from materials that would normally be found in the trash. Everything is handmade in Lisbon using materials donated by local businesses or individuals. ⊠ *Calçada da Graça 16–16A, Lisbon* ☎ *93/798-1772* ⊕ *www.garbags.eu* Ⓜ *Blue Line to Santa Apolónia.*

 Coffee and Quick Bites

Le Bar à Crêpes

$ | French. A slice of Brittany in Lisbon, this French-owned café specializes in buckwheat crepes, or *galettes bretonnes*, with sweet or savory fillings and cheeky names borrowed from singers, actors, directors, musicians, writers, designers, and stylists. The owners are usually around, loving their work. **Known for:** authentic French flavors; friendly waitstaff; gluten-free options. *Average main: €6*

✉ *Largo da Graça 18–19, Lisbon*
☎ *91/150–0259* ⊘ *Closed Sun.* ⊟ *No credit cards* Ⓜ *Blue Line to Santa Apolónia.*

Estaminé
$ | Brazilian. Everything is made with love at this tiny, Brazilian-owned café, from the collection of art on the walls (much of which is for sale) to the fresh juices and French-press coffee, and the simple snacks like cheese and charcuterie boards, bruschetta, and toasts with tapenade. There are just two tables, with four seats each, so reservations are advised for lunch or dinner. **Known for:** juices made with Brazilian fruits, like maracujá and cupuaçu; French-press coffee; Brazilian cheese bread. *Average main: €8* ✉ *Calçada do Monte 86A, Lisbon* ☎ *91/058–4194* ⊘ *Closed Tues. and Wed.* ⊟ *No credit cards* Ⓜ *Blue Line to Santa Apolónia.*

Focaccia in Giro
$ | Italian. Focaccia sandwiches, made according to traditional Italian recipes but with high-quality Portuguese ingredients, are the draw at this small shop in the Feira da Ladra market. An orange food truck can often be spotted around the city serving the same delicious treats. **Known for:** authentic Italian flavors; organic Portuguese ingredients; easy snacks while on the go. *Average main: €5* ✉ *Campo de Santa Clara 141, Lisbon* ☎ *21/598–2367* ⊘ *Closed Mon.* ⊟ *No credit cards* Ⓜ *Blue Line to Santa Apolónia.*

Miradouro da Senhora do Monte
$ | Eclectic. Even higher than Miradouro Sophia de Mello Breyner Andresen, this viewpoint has, of course, spectacular views. There's no permanent café, but there are generally trucks serving coffee, adult beverages, and snacks, which are often more interesting than the standard kiosk fare. **Known for:** city views; peaceful atmosphere; food and drink trucks. *Average main: €5* ✉ *Largo Monte, Lisbon* ⊕ *At top of hill* ☎ *92/755–2901* ⊟ *No credit cards.*

Miradouro Sophia de Mello Breyner Andresen
$ | Café. Perhaps the best place in the city to watch the sunset, the menu here is like at every other kiosk in the city, but there's friendly table service and great people-watching. The spectacular views that stretch from the castle to the river make this a popular hangout from sunrise to sunset. **Known for:** city views; speedy service; lively scene. *Average main: €5* ✉ *Calçada da Graça, Lisbon* ⊕ *Next to church* ☎ *92/004–9951* ⊟ *No credit cards* Ⓜ *Green Line to Martim Moniz.*

Pastelaria Centro Ideal da Graça
$ | Bakery. The cakes and pastries in this shop, from the classic *pasteis de nata* (custard tarts) to croissants and Christmas miniatures, are known for their high-quality and made-daily freshness. Of course, there is strong Portuguese coffee to go with them. **Known for:** pasteis de nata; strong Portuguese coffee; Christmas cakes. *Average main: €1* ✉ *Largo da Graça 5/7, Lisbon*

☎ 21/886–1673 ▭ No credit cards
Ⓜ Blue Line to Santa Apolónia.

🍴 Dining

Bica do Sapato
$$$ | Eclectic. A favorite among fashionable locals, this riverfront restaurant is known for its stylish interior: international furniture designers Knoll, Eero Saarinen, and Mies van der Rohe all feature. The menu features modern Portuguese fare and nouvelle cuisine, with a couple vegetarian options, and September–June, there's Sunday brunch; the upstairs sushi bar (dinner only) offers a range of classic Japanese and fusion dishes. **Known for:** river views; excellent cocktails; superb soundtrack. *Average main: €24* ✉ *Av. Infante Dom Henrique, Armazém B, Santa Apolónia* ☎ *21/881–0320, 91/761–5065* ⊕ *www. bicadosapato.com* ⊘ *No dinner Sun. No lunch Mon.* Ⓜ *Blue Line to Santa Apolónia.*

Bistrô e Brechó Gato Pardo
$ | Eclectic. With its green walls, vintage furniture, and broken-in leather chairs and couches, this restaurant feels more someone's living room than a public establishment. The menu hopscotches around Europe, with Swiss-inspired sweet and savory crepes, Italian-inflected pasta dishes, salads, and Portuguese classics. **Known for:** eclectic vibe; cat theme; cheerful service. *Average main: €10* ✉ *Rua de São Vicente 10, Lisbon* ☎ *93/469–6871* ⊘ *Closed Wed. and Thurs.* Ⓜ *Blue Line to Santa Apolónia.*

A Casa do Bacalhau
$$ | Portuguese. The 90-seat dining room here sits below a vaulted brick ceiling that dates from the 18th century. Likewise, many of the dishes were resurrected from archival recipes. **Known for:** extensive wine list; mix of classic and contemporary cod dishes; historic site. *Average main: €18* ✉ *Rua do Grilo 54, Lisbon* ☎ *21/862–0000* Ⓜ *Blue Line to Santa Apolónia.*

★ Cais da Pedra
$ | Burger. Celebrity chef Henrique Sá Pessoa (of the Michelin-starred Alma) is behind this unpreten-

tious waterfront restaurant. The cooking is as high quality as one might expect, but the food is simple: hamburgers (including the salmon and vegetarian variety), salads, and a few of Pessoa's classics, such as Alentejo pork cheeks and prawn curry. **Known for:** waterfront terrace; good cocktails and burgers; weekend brunch. *Average main: €14* ⊠ *Av. Infante Dom Henrique, Armazém B, Shop 9, Santa Apolónia* ☎ *21/887-1651* ⊕ *caisdapedra.pt* Ⓜ *Blue Line to Santa Apolónia.*

Casanova
$ | Pizza. An institution on the riverfront for almost 20 years, Casanova serves a full range of authentic Italian fare, but most people come for the pizzas. Before she opened the restaurant, the Italian owner spent months training with some of her country's most respected *pizzaiolos.* **Known for:** wood-fired pizzas; burrata from Puglia; riverside terrace. *Average main: €11* ⊠ *Cais da Pedra, Av. Infante Dom Henrique, Armazém B, Shop 7, Santa Apolónia* ☎ *21/887-7532* ⊕ *pizzeriacasanova.pt* Ⓜ *Blue Line to Santa Apolónia.*

Cozinha Urbana
$ | Asian. At this stylish little dining room in the Tings hotel, the menu is varied. Much of it is based on Asian street food: pad Thai, dumplings, wasabi peanuts, and so on, but there are also a variety of very good burgers and salads. **Known for:** Asian snacks; good music; friendly service. *Average main: €10* ⊠ *Tings hotel, Rua Senhora do Monte 37, Lisbon* ☎ *21/886-0160* ⊕ *cozinhaurbana.com* ⊗ *Closed Mon.* Ⓜ *Green Line to Martim Moniz.*

DeliDelux
$$ | International. This old car warehouse was reborn in 2005 as Lisbon's first gourmet shop, with products from five continents, plus a stylish restaurant and café alongside the river. Now the restaurant gets equal billing, and the top-quality menu of tapas, sandwiches, and salads is equally wide-ranging, with ingredients like kalamata olives, foie gras, Italian pastas and tomatoes, and buffalo mozzarella, along with Portuguese classics such as *pica-pau* (quick-fried beef with pickles) and octopus salad. **Known for:** lavish daily brunch; eggs Benedict; terrace overlooking the river. *Average main: €17* ⊠ *Cais da Pedra, Av. Infante Dom Henrique, Armazém B, Shop 8, Santa Apolónia* ☎ *21/886-2070* ⊕ *delidelux.pt* Ⓜ *Blue Line to Santa Apolónia.*

Faz Figura
$$$ | Portuguese. For more than 40 years, this riverfront restaurant has been successfully experimenting with creative takes on traditional Portuguese gastronomy. There are also spot-on pastas and risottos on the menu, as well as dishes that defy categorization, such as lamb lollipops with orange gel and vegetable spaghetti, and cod marinated in port wine with potatoes. **Known for:** killer views; cool scene; great variety of wines by the glass. *Average main: €24* ⊠ *Rua do Paraíso 15B, Lisbon* ☎ *21/886-8981* ⊗ *Closed*

for lunch Mon. Ⓜ *Blue Line to Santa Apolónia.*

Graça 77

$ | **Vegetarian.** In a space that was part of a water reservoir from the 12th century, this cozy restaurant now serves a mostly vegetarian and vegan menu (the one exception: codfish sausage, of course) of meal-size salads, satisfying seasonal specials like asparagus and a portobello stuffed with tofu and mushrooms, and meat-free takes on the traditional Portuguese *petiscos* (snacks). The space also holds art exhibitions and gatherings and serves a great Sunday brunch. **Known for:** vegan pancakes; meat-free croquettes; biological wines. *Average main: €12* ⊠ *Largo da Graça 77, Lisbon* ☎ *21/134–8839* ⊗ *Closed Wed.* ▭ *No credit cards* Ⓜ *Green Line to Martim Moniz.*

Maça Verde

$ | **Portuguese.** Before the World Expo in Lisbon in 1998, this place was called Green Apple (in English) and was just another snack bar selling hamburgers. After Expo, owners Zé Carlos and Dona Laura translated the name and the menu back into Portuguese. **Known for:** honest cooking; historic vibe; light-filled dining room. *Average main: €9* ⊠ *Rua dos Caminhos de Ferro 84, Lisbon* ☎ *96/551–2266* ⊕ *restaurante-maca-verde.business. site* ⊗ *Closed Sun.* Ⓜ *Blue Line to Santa Apolónia.*

Maritíma de Xabregas

$ | **Portuguese.** This typical restaurant opened in 1966, and not all that much has changed since then; it's a wonderful journey back in time. The menu hits all the Portuguese classics, including fire-grilled steaks, *bulhão pato* (clams steamed in wine and garlic), and a full-on *cozida à portuguêsa* (a stew with all the meats you can think of), but the main reason to go is the impeccably fresh fish and seafood. **Known for:** cod with eggs and potatoes; grilled entrecote; old-world ambience. *Average main: €15* ⊠ *Rua Manutenção 40, Lisbon* ☎ *21/868–2235* ⊕ *restaurantemaritimadexabregas.com.pt* ⊗ *Closed Sat.* Ⓜ *Blue Line to Santa Apolónia.*

Parreirinha de São Vicente

$ | **Portuguese.** The food at this spot around the corner from the Feira da Ladra flea market is well seasoned and mostly comes in portions large enough for two. The brothers who run the place are from the northern Beiras region, and many of the dishes are meat-rich examples of its traditions, but there is plenty of seafood on the menu. **Known for:** typical, hearty food; local vibe; friendly and efficient service. *Average main: €12* ⊠ *Calçada de São Vicente 54–58, Lisbon* ☎ *21/886–8893* ▭ *No credit cards* Ⓜ *Blue Line to Santa Apolónia.*

★ O Pitéu

$ | **Portuguese.** This charming, sometimes boisterous restaurant is about as old-world Portuguese as it gets, with massive portions of grilled meat, seafood, and fish in a no-nonsense, brightly lit room with typical azulejos on the walls and crimson cloths (beneath white papers) on the tables. Most of the tables seat six or more, which should tell you something about its popularity with neighborhood families. **Known for:** fish fillets; fresh ingredients; good wine cellar. *Average main: €15* ⊠ *Largo da Graça 95–96, Lisbon* ☎ *21/887–1067* ⊕ *restauranteopiteu.pt* ⊘ *Closed Sun.* ⊟ *No credit cards* Ⓜ *Green line to Martim Moniz.*

Restaurante Ti'Ascenção
$ | Portuguese. The menu is short and contains few surprises, but the traditional Portuguese gastronomy is celebrated well here. Unlike many traditional restaurants, where vegetables can be hard to come by, this one serves shareable sides like grilled mushrooms and beetroot salad. **Known for:** porco Iberico; desserts flavored with wine; classic ambience. *Average main: €13* ⊠ *Rua do Sol à Graça 61A, Lisbon* ☎ *92/735–5005* ⊕ *tiascencao.business.site* ⊘ *Closed Sun.* ⊟ *No credit cards* Ⓜ *Green Line to Martim Moniz.*

Santa Clara dos Cogumelos
$$ | Eclectic. An Italian living in Lisbon had the odd but surprisingly successful idea of opening a restaurant that would serve only mushroom-based dinners; then he had the even better idea of locating it inside the Feira da Ladra market. The chefs here have certainly managed to find a lot of ways to use mushrooms: in ceviche, pâté,

or croquettes, standing in for the meat in traditional Portuguese pica-pau, and even in ice cream. **Known for:** shiitakes bulhão pato; porcini and black trumpet risotto with walnuts; Thai-style coconut soup with Pleurotus. *Average main: €16* ⊠ *Mercado de Santa Clara, Campo de Santa Clara 7, Lisbon* ☎ *21/887–0661* ⊕ *santaclaracogumelos.wixsite.com/ santaclaracogumelos* Ⓜ *Blue line to Santa Apolónia.*

Via Graça
$$$ | Portuguese. This hilltop restaurant has "date night" (or at least "big splurge") written all over it. The city views are so spectacular that what lands on the plate is almost an afterthought. **Known for:** sunset views; customized menus (with advance notice); romantic mood. *Average main: €22* ⊠ *Rua Damasceno Monteiro 9B, Lisbon* ☎ *21/887–0830* ⊕ *restaurantevia-graca.com* ⊘ *Closed for lunch weekends* Ⓜ *Green Line to Martim Moniz.*

¶ Bars and Nightlife

★ Botequim

This homey bar is as inviting as it gets, with mismatched chairs, assorted books on the shelves, and sometimes a guitar waiting to be picked up. It serves bottles from Lisbon's major craft breweries (Nusa and Dois Corvos), Portuguese wines, competent cocktails, and a handful of typical Portuguese snacks, as well as some atypical ones like seitan *prego* (typically a small beef sandwich) on coconut bread. ✉ *Largo da Graça 79–80, Lisbon* ☎ *21/888-8511* Ⓜ *Green Line to Martim Moniz.*

Clube Ferroviário do Portugal

This warehouse near the Santa Apolónia train station has many personalities. It's home to several neighborhood sporting clubs, training studios, and indoor workshop venues, but it's the large rooftop terrace, with unobstructed views of the Tagus River, that is most popular. After sunset, there can be a diverse range of entertainment, such as street performers, small concerts, televised football matches, and alfresco cinema. ✉ *Rua de Santa Apolónia 59–63, Santa Apolónia* ☎ *21/815-3196* ⊕ *clubeferroviario.pt/espacos/#main* Ⓜ *Blue Line to Santa Apolónia.*

★ Damas

A former bakery, this restaurant, bar, and concert venue has maintained its original interior features like the kitchen's stainless steel work surfaces where bakers would roll and knead dough into rolls and loaves. It's a cool vibe, and the food and drinks are good, but the real emphasis is on providing musicians with a place to perform. An eclectic range and local and international bands and DJs take the stage around 11 on most nights. ✉ *Rua da Voz do Operário 60, Lisbon* ☎ *96/496-4416* Ⓜ *Blue Line to Santa Apolónia.*

★ Dois Carvos Cervejeira

One of Lisbon's first craft breweries and its first taproom, Dois Corvos is a brewer-owned outfit that is known for its range of beers, from dependable session beers and IPAs to big barrel-aged stouts, experimental ales, and mixed fermentations. The family behind it didn't want to make a taproom so much as an extension of the brewery, where you can quaff with other beer lovers and brewers, among the working fermenters and other equipment. All the core beers are on tap, along with seasonal experiments and a guest tap for other breweries. ✉ *Rua Capitão Leitão 94, Lisbon* ☎ *21/138-4366* Ⓜ *Blue Line to Santa Apolónia.*

EKA Palace

This multicultural, multigenre art space occupies the second floor of a palace and has eight studios to view art, dancing, music, martial arts, or whatever else is going on. It also has a cool little bar, lots of places to hang out with creative types, a pretty terrace, and regular shows by local bands and DJs. ✉ *Calçada de Dom Gastão 12, Door 8, Lisbon* ☎ *96/930-0402* Ⓜ *Blue Line to Santa Apolónia.*

Graça do Vinho

There are just a handful of barstools and tables at this quaint, colorful wine bar, where bottles and jugs line the walls and chairs hang as art from the ceiling (don't ask). The menu includes a number of notable Portuguese wines, many of which are available by the glass, plus cheese and charcuterie boards. ⊠ Calçada da Graça 10A/B, Lisbon ☎ 21/011–8041 Ⓜ Green Line to Martim Moniz.

Lux Frágil

Lisbon's most famous club is dotted with designer furniture and has two dance floors favored by big-name local and foreign DJs—plus a rooftop terrace with great river views. A young, stylish crowd comes to dance until dawn. ■TIP→ The doormen are selective and there can be a long line so be prepared. ⊠ Av. Infante Dom Henrique, Armazém A, Santa Apolónia ☎ 21/882–0890 ⊕ www.luxfragil.com 🎟 From €12 Ⓜ Blue Line to Santa Apolónia.

★ Musa

Near friendly rival brewery Dois Corvos, Musa is also making a range of terrific small-batch artisanal beer using traditional methods and archival recipes. The taproom here is less a cathedral of hops and more a place to have a good time. The equipment is visible, and the bartenders are more than happy to tell you all about it, but it's also a place with music blasting and dinner roasting: there are frequent concerts by emerging artists in various genres and a full menu of better-than-it-has-to-be, beer-

friendly food, like chicken wings, banh mi, and authentic Mexican tamales. ⊠ Rua do Açucar 83, Lisbon ☎ 21/387–7777 ⊕ cervejamusa.com Ⓜ Blue Line to Santa Apolónia.

O Vinhaça

This barely marked hole-in-the-wall looks more like a Portuguese grandma's kitchen than a typical restaurant, with copper pots hanging on the walls and tableware stored in a vintage china cabinet. There's a good selection of Portuguese wine and craft beers, and the tapas-style snacks are just as traditional: shrimp with garlic, sardines, cod with spinach, and beef on a stone slab. ⊠ Rua do Salvador, 53, Lisbon ☎ 96/804–7184 ⊕ Closed Mon. Ⓜ Blue Line to Santa Apolónia.

🎭 Performing Arts

★ Fábrica Braço de Prata

In a former armaments factory, this multiconcept cultural space encompasses art exhibition rooms, a bookstore, shops, cinema, theater, conferences, film screenings, and concerts ranging from jazz to rock, funk, and world music. At one point it was an illegal, underground venue, and now, even though everything is aboveboard, it's still a half-abandoned building with 12 mutant rooms that different

artists take over from time to time. Once there was circus tent where concerts, fairs, performances, and aerial acrobatics took place—hopefully it's coming back. ✉ *Rua Fábrica de Material de Guerra 1, Lisbon* ☎ *96/859-9969* ⊕ *bracodeprata.com* Ⓜ *Blue Line to Santa Apolónia.*

Teatro Meridional
This experimental theater company is one of the most highly regarded in Portugal. While many of the productions are dramas performed in Portuguese, the programming also includes adaptations of major theatrical works (Shakespeare et al.), opera, dance, and other performances in which the spoken word isn't the main form of communication. ✉ *Rua do Açúcar 64, Beco da Mitra - Poço do Bispo, Lisbon* ☎ *91/999-1213* ⊕ *teatromeridional. net* Ⓜ *Blue Line to Santa Apolónia.*

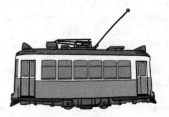

7 | Alcântara, Cais do Sodré, and Santos

GO FOR

Cool nightlife

Bohemian vibe

Vibrant street art

Sightseeing ★★★☆☆ | Shopping ★★★☆☆ | Dining ★★★★☆ | Nightlife ★★★★★

Cool kids flock to this triangle of neighborhoods to hang out at the many independent bars, cafés, and boutique stores. Alcântara is synonymous with Lisbon's rebirth as Europe's Capital of Cool, thanks in large part to the funky revamped warehouses at LX Factory—now a miniature village packed with boho-chic bars, boutiques, and bookshops. Nearby Village Underground is a colorful collection of coworking spaces, art installations, and late-night party spots. A stroll along the banks of the Tagus takes visitors to Santos, where rooftop bars, tapas restaurants, and sushi joints sit side by side with family homes—residents grill sardines on the cobblestone streets and washing flaps from the windows. Nightlife steps it up a level in nearby Cais do Sodré, where partiers pack the famous Pink Street until dawn, and there's a chance to sample food from across Portugal at the hugely popular Mercado da Ribeira. A stroll along the riverfront takes you from one neighborhood to the next, or you can jump on a train to save time and energy; each of these hipster hotspots is on the railway line to Cascais.—*by Lucy Bryson*

 Sights

Docas de Santa Amaro

Here, in the lee of the huge Ponte 25 de Abril, the old wharves have been made over so that you can now walk along the landscaped riverfront all the way to Belém (a 30-minute stroll). At Docas de Santo Amaro, known to locals simply as Docas (docks), a line of swanky restaurants and clubs now inhabit the shells of former warehouses. On the terrace in front of the marina, the party goes on until late into the night. ⊠ *Alcântara* Ⓜ *Tram 15E or 18E to Cais Rocha.*

★ **LX Factory**

A former industrial area that's been transformed into a symbol of Lisbon's creative spirit, LX is a colorful collection of bars, boutiques, cafés, and coworking spaces. An organic food market attracts hungry shoppers each Sunday and a lively rooftop bar-restaurant—Rio Maravilha—offers drinking and dining with fabulous views across the river. ⊠ *Rua Rodrigues de Faria 103, Alcântara* ☎ *21/314–3399* ⊕ *www.lxfactory.com* Ⓜ *Train to Alcântara Terra; Tram 15E or 18E to Calvário.*

Museu da Carris

This museum celebrating Lisbon's public transport past and present is right next door to creative hub Village Underground and donated the distinctive double-decker buses that now house Village Underground's café. It's well worth taking the opportunity to climb aboard a classic tram that trundles from one converted warehouse to another, allowing visitors to admire vintage buses, streetcars, uniforms, and other artifacts from Lisbon's public transport history. A gift shop sells cute miniature buses and trams. ⊠ *Rua 1 de Maio 101–103, Alcântara* 🕾 *21/361-3087* ⊕ *museu. carris.pt* 🎟 *€4* ☉ *Closed Sun.* Ⓜ *Tram 15E or 18E to Estação Santo Amaro.*

Museu da Marioneta *(Puppet Museum)*

Portugal has a rich history of using puppets—from cute to creepy—to tell stories, and this fascinating museum is an opportunity to see the marionettes and masks up close. The only one if its kind in Portugal, the Marionette Museum has expanded in recent years to include an impressive collection of African and Asian puppets alongside the Portuguese exhibits. The location, inside a former convent, adds an extra dash of drama to the proceedings, and there's a chance to get hands-on with some of the puppets. ⊠ *Convento das Bernardas, Rua da Esperança 146, Santos* 🕾 *21/394-2810* ⊕ *www.museudamarioneta.pt* ☉ *Closed Mon.*

GETTING HERE

Trains, metros, buses, and ferries arrive at and depart from Cais do Sodré, making it one of the best spots in the city for transportation. It's also flat, so walking is a breeze. Trains from Cais do Sodré stop at Alcântara and Santos on their way to Belém and the beaches of the Estoril coast. A second train station, Alcântara Terra, has connections to the Algarve, while a bus terminal nearby serves destinations south of the river Tagus. Santos has no metro stop, and parts of the neighborhood are hilly, with some narrow streets difficult to reach by car—something to bear in mind in the heat of summer or if you're laden down with luggage.

Museu Nacional de Arte Antiga

Portugal's National Ancient Art Museum is housed in an opulent 17th-century palace, built at the behest of the count of Alvor and later occupied by the brother of the Marquis de Pombal. Try not to spend too much time gaping at the dramatic painted ceilings, stucco detailing, and baroque doorways or you'll miss the collection of more than 40,000 works, including the unsettling 1501 triptych *Temptation of Saint Anthony* by Hieronymous Bosch, one of the most important pieces in the country. A café set in lovely gardens is the perfect place for a postviewing drink or bite to eat. ⊠ *Rua das Janelas Verdes, Alcântara* 🕾 *21/391-2800* ⊕ *www.museudeart-eantiga.pt* 🎟 *€6* ☉ *Closed Mon.* Ⓜ *Tram 15E or 18E to Cais Rocha.*

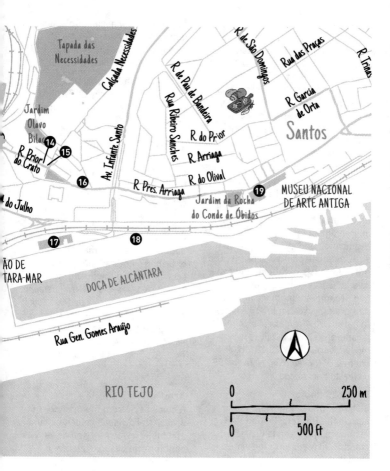

Museu do Oriente

Housed in a former *bacalhau* (salted cod) cold store with impressive bas-reliefs on its facade, the Museu do Oriente opened in 2008 and has become one of Lisbon's most important cultural institutions. Funded by the Fundação Oriente (a legacy of colonial Macau and its gaming revenues), this dockside giant seeks both to tell the story of the centuries-long Portuguese presence in Asia and to provide a showcase for Asian cultures. Highlights of the permanent collections include unique maps and charts from the golden age of Portuguese maritime exploration and stunning Chinese and Japanese painted screens. The museum hosts excellent, inexpensive concerts in its cozy auditorium and organizes a plethora of cooking and crafts workshops. ⊠ *Av. Brasília 352, Doca de Alcântara (Norte), Alcântara* ☎ *21/585-2000* ⊕ *www. museudooriente.pt/* 🎫 *€6, Fri. 6–10 pm free* 🕐 *Closed Mon.* Ⓜ *Tram 15E or 18E to Cais Rocha.*

Ponte 25 de Abril

Lisbon's first suspension bridge across the Rio Tejo, linking the Alcântara and Almada districts, stands 230 feet above the water and stretches almost 2½ km (1½ miles). Reminiscent of San Francisco's Golden Gate Bridge, it's somewhat smaller but still a spectacular sight from any direction, although most gasps are reserved for the view from the top downward. Overlooking the bridge from a hill on the south bank is the **Cristo Rei** (Christ the King) statue, which is smaller and stiffer than Rio de Janeiro's more famous Redeemer. ⊠ *Ponte 25 de Abril, Alcântara* Ⓜ *Tram 15E to Estação de Santo Amaro.*

★ Village Underground

Together with nearby LX Factory, Village Underground is a colorful symbol of Lisbon's rebirth as Europe's Capital of Cool. Beneath the river-spanning 25 de Abril Bridge, shipping containers and double-decker buses have been transformed into spaces for eating, drinking, and working (the coworking spaces are popular with the city's creative class). DJ sets, vibrant murals, and that famous double-decker bus make it one of Lisbon's hottest hangouts for scenesters and the Instagram brigade. ⊠ *Museu da Carris, Estação de Santo Amaro, Rua 1 de Maio 103, Alcântara* ☎ *21/583-2469* ⊕ *www. vu.lisboa.com* Ⓜ *Tram 15E or 18E to Alcântara–Av. 24 Julho.*

 Shopping

ArteFaB

A block back from the main tourist drag, ArteFaB sells colorful, chunky, and funky jewelry as well as vintage clothing and bespoke pieces. If you've bought something elsewhere that doesn't fit, staff can alter it for you here. ⊠ *Rua de São Paulo 63–65, Cais do Sodré* ☎ *21/347-7379* ⊕ *www. wix.com/artefab/shop* 🕐 *Closed Sun.* Ⓜ *Green Line to Cais do Sodré; Tram 25E to Rua de São Paulo/Bica.*

Garrafeira Estado D'Alma

There's a staggering array of national and imported wines, spirits, and liqueurs at this off-the-tourist-track bottle shop. It's handily midway between Alcântara's two train stations (Alcântara Mar and Alcântara Terra) and a perfect place to stock up on boozy goodies. For an inexpensive treat, try the Licor ZimbroMel, which combines two distinctive flavors of Portugal, juniper and honey, to dangerously delicious effect. ⊠ *Rua João de Oliveira Miguens 3B, Alcântara* ☎ *21/362–1639* ⊕ *garrafeiraestadodalma.pt* ⊗ *Closed Sun.* Ⓜ *Tram 15E or 18E to Alcântara–Av. 24 de Julho.*

★ Gleba

Sourdough loaves made with love by talented and passionate young baker Diogo Amorim attract carb-craving Lisboetas from across the city. Amorim learned his trade in the kitchens of the near-legendary, triple-Michelin-starred Fat Duck in Bray, United Kingdom, and here he perfects the art, using flour prepared in an on-site stone mill. ⊠ *Prior do Crato 16, Alcântara* ☎ *96/606–4697 to order bread, 93/517–3026 information* ⊕ *www.gleba-nossa.pt* Ⓜ *Tram 15E or 18E to Alcântara–Av. 24 de Julho.*

Loja das Conservas

Shop and sample more than 300 beautifully packed varieties of canned fish at this store-museum. Maps and other artifacts illuminate the craft of conserving fish in tins and you can guess the star ingredient of the adjoining café. ⊠ *Rua do Arsenal 130, Cais do Sodré*

BACK IN THE DAY

Lisbon's liveliest party street, Rua Nova do Carvalho, was known for a long time as a red-light area catering to the whims of the sailors who docked at the nearby waterfront. Gentrification began in 2011, when the houses of ill repute closed their doors, reopening as coffee shops, gin joints, and late-night clubs. It's now known as Rua Cor da Rosa (Pink Street)—one glimpse at the color of the brightly painted asphalt will tell you why.

☎ *91/118–1210* Ⓜ *Green line to Cais do Sodré.*

Zarzuela

$ | Portuguese. For a rare chance to sample a *pastel de nata* (custard tart) without wheat or gluten, step right up. Gluten-free goodies are the main reason to head to this welcoming coffee shop close to the famous Time Out Market. **Known for:** free-from products; cozy, unpretentious atmosphere; good coffee, ice cream, and pastries. *Average main: €6* ⊠ *Rua Bernadino Costa 23, Santos* ☎ *21/605–2532* ⊗ *Closed Tues.* Ⓜ *Green Line to Cais do Sodré; Tram 15E to Corpo Santo.*

☕ Coffee and Quick Bites

★ Buzz Lisboeta

$ | Café. Climb aboard a refurbished double-decker bus (the name's an apt pun on the vehicle and the buzz around this part of Lisbon) for salads, sandwiches, and good strong coffee (or good strong cocktails) in one of the city's liveliest creative spaces. **Known for:** weekend brunches; trendy clientele; vegetarian/vegan options. *Average main: €12* ✉ *Village Underground, Estação de Santo Amaro, Rua 1 de Maio 103, Alcântara* ☎ *91/111–5533* Ⓜ *Tram 15E or 18E to Calvário.*

Dear Breakfast
$ | Contemporary. However you like your eggs in the morning (or afternoon), Dear Breakfast will cook them to perfection, alongside a cheering range of home-baked breads, fresh juices, and jams. Eat them any which way, from omelets and eggs Benedict to huevos rancheros. **Known for:** cool, minimalist whitewashed interior and style mags to flick through; all-day breakfasts and brunches; organic juices, smoothies, and caffeine-free beetroot lattes. *Average main: €14* ✉ *Rua das Gaivotas 17, Santos* ☎ *21/228–1082* ⊕ *dearbreakfast.com* ⊘ *Closed Mon.* Ⓜ *Tram 25E to Conde Barão.*

Menina e Moça
$ | Café. This cute café-bar doubles as a bookstore, and it's not unusual to see local poets giving readings of their work. The bright primary colors and painted ceiling give it the look of a cozy kids' corner, but the coffees and mixed drinks are strictly for grown-ups. **Known for:** live music performances and book readings; good coffee and brunches; literary clientele. *Average main: €12* ✉ *Rua Nova do Carvalho 40–42, Cais do Sodré* ☎ *21/827–2331* Ⓜ *Green Line to Cais do Sodré.*

A Merendeira
$ | Portuguese. The late-night fueling stop of choice for many a hard-partying Lisboeta, A Merendeira's specialty is as simple as it is delicious: *pão com chouriço* (sausage baked into a bread roll). Grab one to go, or sit down and enjoy it with a bowl of caldo verde. **Known for:** being open all night; affordable prices; traditional Portuguese savory snacks. *Average main: €7* ✉ *Av. 24 de Julho 54G, Santos* ☎ *21/397–2726* ⊕ *www.amerendeira.com* Ⓜ *Train to Santos; Tram 15E or 18E to Santos.*

Mercado da Ribeira
$$ | Portuguese. Lisbon's main market since 1892, it has been divided into two different areas: one for the stalls that sell the city's freshest fruit, vegetables, and fish, the other for a very popular and noisy Time Out food hall, where Lisbon's top chefs and restaurants present their best creations. It's where tourists get an overview of local gastronomy and where locals find their favorite bites. **Known for:** people watching; noisy; good for grazing. *Average main: €20* ✉ *Av. 24 de Julho 49, Cais do Sodré* ☎ *21/395–1274* ⊕ *www.timeoutmarket.com* ▤ *No credit cards* Ⓜ *Green line to Cais do Sodré.*

🍴 Dining

Burger Factory
$ | Burger. The name may suggest production-line patties, but there's nothing mass produced about these burgers, which are made with top-

rate beef and topped with anything from crispy bacon and cheese to a fried egg (the name's a nod to the location inside trendy LX Factory). Vegan options are present and correct, the fries with garlic mayo are famous, and the late opening hours make this popular with late-night bar hoppers. **Known for:** attractively presented dishes with lots of Insta-appeal; contemporary decor and outdoor terrace at the heart of LX Factory; fast, friendly service. *Average main: €10 ⊠ LX Factory, Rua Rodrigues de Faria 103, Bldg. G, ground fl., Alcântara ☎ 21/408-7446 Ⓜ Tram 15E or 18E to Calvário.*

Cafe Boavida

$ | Café. The name translates as Good Life Cafe, and the cakes, croissants, wine, and cappuccinos at this minimalist-chic spot will certainly gladden the heart. There's a small exhibition space upstairs and weekly live music performances. **Known for:** friendly service and fair prices; organic, sustainably sourced ingredients; healthy breakfast and lunch options with vegan options. *Average main: €8 ⊠ Rua do Poço dos Negros 119, Cais do Sodré ☎ 93/119-1118 ⊟ No credit cards Ⓜ Tram 25E to Conde Barão.*

Cantina LX

$ | Portuguese. This industrial-chic former factory canteen now makes good use of original features (such as a wood-fired oven) to feed the pretty young things who hang in this part of town. It's right in the middle of LX Factory, and the hearty Portuguese dishes will fuel a day's

ART IN THE WILD

Lisbon is increasingly known as one of the best cities in Europe for street art, and props to the local authorities for encouraging local artists' creativity rather than stifling it. One of the biggest names on the city's street art scene is Bordalo II, known for his Trash Animals—giant 3-D murals made from discarded materials. Look out for his enormous wasp at LX Factory and his 2015 creation Peixes d'Alcântara—a big-eyed fish on a wall on Avenida de Ceuta, opposite Alcântara Terra rail station.

shopping or a night's socializing in the surrounding bars. **Known for:** casual-chic vibe; jazzed-up versions of traditional Portuguese dishes; oven-fired steaks and seafood. *Average main: €15 ⊠ LX Factory, Rua Rodrigues de Faria 103, Alcântara ☎ 21/362-8239 ⊕ www.cantinalx.com Ⓜ Tram 15E or 18E to Calvário.*

Comoba

$ | Café. This eco-conscious café, which opened in 2018, has a no-plastics policy and all its ingredients are sourced from local independent producers. There's abundant use of *matcha* (green tea powder), quinoa, and spirulina, and as there's no refined sugar in any of the cakes, cookies, and other sweet treats, they make a perfect guilt-free pick-me-up when combined with a cup of Comoba's excellent coffee. **Known for:** healthy breakfasts, brunches, and lunches with lots of vegan and GF options; bright,

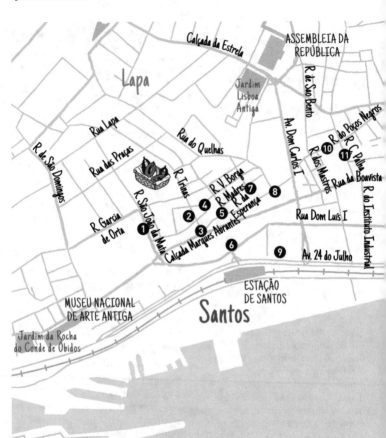

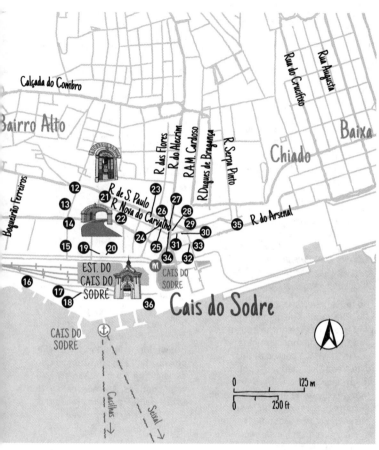

rustic-chic interior; excellent small-batch-roasted coffee. *Average main: €9 ⊠ Rua de Sao Paulo 101, Cais do Sodré ☎ 96/328–8453 Ⓜ Green Line to Cais do Sodré.*

Confraria LX

$$$ | **Sushi.** Occupying a bright and breezy downstairs room at the casual-chic hotel LX Boutique, Confraria LX is widely regarded as one of the best places in town to eat sushi. There is vegan and vegetarian options alongside the tuna and salmon rolls. **Known for:** casual-chic crowd at hip boutique hotel; good drinks list; location on the edge of nightlife district. *Average main: €23 ⊠ LX Boutique, Rua do Alecrim 12A, Cais do Sodré ☎ 21/342–6292 ⊕ www.lxboutiquehotel.com Ⓜ Green Line to Cais do Sodré.*

Doca Peixe

$$$ | **Seafood.** The display of the day's catch on ice at the entrance and the small aquarium clue you in to what's served at this well-regarded riverside spot. You might start with a tomato-and-mozzarella salad or prawns seared in cognac, then move on to sea bass with clams, or codfish baked in a cornbread crust served with turnip leaves. **Known for:** fresh-grilled fish; seafood stews; terrace with river views. *Average main: €23 ⊠ Doca de Santo Amaro, Armazém 14, Alcântara ☎ 21/397–3565 ⊕ www. docapeixe.com Ⓜ Tram 15E or 18E to Cais Rocha.*

Flora & Fauna

$ | **Eclectic.** Lisbon's late-night party scene inevitably leads to some very leisurely mornings, which helps this all-day brunch spot do a roaring trade in pancakes, smoothies, energy-boosting Brazilian açaí bowls, and other breakfast favorites. Lines are virtually inevitable at any time of day, but the flower-filled café is a pleasant place to wait. **Known for:** healthy menu with lots of fresh fruit and vegetables; good smoothies, coffee, and cocktails; bright interior and attractively presented dishes. *Average main: €12 ⊠ Rua da Esperança 33, Santos ☎ 96/164–5040 ⊗ Closed Mon.*

Heim Cafe

$ | **Café.** Lisbon's trendsetters head to this bright and breezy Ukrainian-owned café. Famed for its tasty brunches, there's usually a line but avocado toast on home-baked sourdough alone is worth the wait. **Known for:** trendy, largely foreign, crowd; choice of set brunches, served until 6 pm; gluten-free and vegan options. *Average main: €10 ⊠ Rua Santos-o-Velho 2–4, Santos ☎ 21/248–0763 Ⓜ Tram 25E to Santos-o-Velho.*

Ibo

$$$$ | **African.** Traditional fish and seafood dishes get a Mozambican makeover at this formal dining restaurant in a stylishly converted warehouse on the banks of the Tagus. The terrace is perfect for dinner with a sunset view, but the outdoor tables are hotly contested, so be sure to book ahead. **Known for:** spicy seafood curries; sophisticated ambience; extensive wine list. *Average main: €32* ✉ *Armazém A, Porta 2, Compartimento 2, Cais do Sodré* ☎ *96/133–2024* ⊕ *www. ibo-restaurante.pt* ⊘ *Closed Mon.* Ⓜ *Green Line to Cais do Sodré.*

Marisqueira O Palácio
$$ | **Seafood.** Staunchly traditional amid the flurry of modernization in the surrounding streets, this old-school *cervejaria* (beer hall) is the best of several local spots specializing in seafood and *cervejas* (beer). Priced by the kilo, the day's offer varies according to season and what the anglers have hauled in, but expect enormous crustaceans year-round. **Known for:** loyal local clientele; vast array of fresh fish and seafood; simple, traditional design. *Average main: €18* ✉ *Rua Prior do Crato 142, Alcântara* ☎ *21/396–1647* ⊘ *Closed Thurs.* Ⓜ *Tram 15E or 18E to Alcântara–Av. 24 de Julho.*

Monte Mar
$$$ | **Seafood.** A city-smart sister to the celebrated formal dining restaurant in Cascais, Monte Mar Lisboa offers the same superior seafood with a more relaxed riverfront ambience. Occupying one of the formerly disused warehouses along the revitalized docks, Monte Mar has a terrific view of the river, the 25 de Abril suspension bridge, and the Cristo Rei on the other side, while indoors it is all slick black and chrome. *Average main: €25* ✉ *Rua da Cintura do Porto de Lisboa Armazém 65, Cais do Sodré* ☎ *21/322–0160* ⊕ *www.mmlisboa. pt/en/restaurant-monte-mar-lisboa*

⊘ *Closed Mon.* Ⓜ *Green Line to Cais do Sodré.*

Osteria
$ | **Italian.** This tiny, welcoming Italian restaurant serves small plates designed to be shared among friends. There are excellent cheeses, sausages, and wines alongside mains and desserts typical of the Sardinia region. **Known for:** warm welcome and home-style cooking; affordable wine list and Italian liqueurs; cozy decor with lots of Italian flags and film posters. *Average main: €12* ✉ *Rua das Madres 52–54, Santos* ☎ *21/396–0584* ⊕ *www.osteria.pt.*

★ Pap'açorda
$$$ | **Portuguese.** A longtime favorite in the Bairro Alto, Pap'açorda has now moved to the laid-back-cool confines of the Time Out Mercado da Ribeira in Cais do Sodré, bringing its delicious dishes and its famously glitzy chandelier along for the ride. The menu still lists cutting-edge versions of Portuguese classics—grilled sole or John Dory; breaded veal cutlets; and a famous *açorda*, that bread-based stew rich in seafood (the luxury version contains lobster) and flavored with garlic and cilantro. **Known for:** casual-chic vibe; legendary chocolate mousse; strength on wine and cocktails. *Average main: €21* ✉ *Av. 24 de Julho 49, Mercado da Ribeira 1200–479, Cais do Sodré* ☎ *21/120–0479* ⊕ *papacorda.com* ⊘ *Closed Mon.* Ⓜ *Green Line to Cais do Sodré.*

Pesqueiro 25

$$ | Seafood. This restaurant brings the sea and traditional Portuguese recipes back to a neighborhood now full of international restaurants. A massive old black-and-white photo of Lisbon's fishwives takes you back to the Cais do Sodré of yesteryear, and the seafood is the freshest catch of the day from the Portuguese coast. **Known for:** lobster soup; shellfish platters; weekend seafood brunch. *Average main: €18* ⊠ *Rua Nova de Carvalho 15, Cais do Sodré* ☎ *96/882–8492* ⊘ *Closed Mon.* Ⓜ *Green Line to Cais do Sodré.*

★ Sala de Corte

$$$$ | Steakhouse. Sala de Corte is all about the meat, notably prime cuts of beef, grilled to perfection and accompanied by a yummy dipping sauce, like Stilton, chimmichurri, black truffle mayo, or béarnaise. Sip a cocktail at the stylishly lit long bar before taking a table. **Known for:** fine meat cooked in a specialist Josper oven; sophisticated, contemporary style; long lines. *Average main: €35* ⊠ *Praça de Dom Luis I 7, Cais do Sodré* ☎ *21/346–0030* ⊕ *www.saladecorte.pt* Ⓜ *Green Line to Cais do Sodré.*

Toscana Casa de Pasto

$ | Portuguese. Lisboetas consider this traditional *tasca* one of the best spots in the city for grilled fish. Take your pick from a seemingly unending list (choices vary according to the fishermen's daily haul), and staff will cook it to perfection on the charcoal grill. **Known for:** super fresh fish and seafood served with salad and boiled potatoes; affable staff and relaxed atmosphere; cheap and cheerful jugs of house wine. *Average main: €14* ⊠ *Rua do Sacramento A, Alcântara* ☎ *21/396-8633.*

A Travessa

$$$$ | Portuguese. The cloisters and courtyard of an 18th-century convent have been tastefully transformed into a grand setting for dinner at this hidden spot in the upper echelons of Santos. Traditional Portuguese dishes have absorbed culinary influences from the Belgian owners and there are daily surprises among the *entradas,* according to the best fresh produce of the day and the whims of the chef. **Known for:** romantic setting; excellent wine list and knowledgeable sommelier; rich meat and fish dishes. *Average main: €30* ⊠ *Travessa do Convento das Bernardas 12, Cais do Sodré* ☎ *21/390–2034* ⊕ *atravessa.com* Ⓜ *Tram 25E to Santos-o-Velho.*

Vegana

$ | Burger. A little off the main drag, Vegana's simple offer is a lifeline for hungry vegetarians. There are six types of burger to choose from (chickpeas and lentils keep the vegetables company in these meat-free patties) and sides like sweet potato fries, all of which helps soak up some of those drinks on a night out in Cais do Sodré. **Known for:** colorful spirulina/carob bread buns; inexpensive coffee; quick service and unpretentious vibe. *Average main: €7* ⊠ *Praça de Dom Luis I, 30, Cais do Sodré* ☎ *21/246-3511*

STREET ART

Lisbon's street art scene is striking, to say the least, with colorful murals and eye-catching sculptures cropping up everywhere, from the facades of flashy galleries and boutique hotels to the crumbling remains of once-grand buildings.

Sitting alongside the traditional azulejo tiles, the works further brighten an already colorful city. The explosion of urban art began with politically motivated motifs in the years following Portugal's Carnation Revolution in 1974, and in 2011 the city council began to actively encourage street artists to work their magic on rundown buildings across Lisbon. Talents such as Vhils (founder of urban art collective Underdogs) and Bordalo II rose to legendary status on the international street art scene, and international big hitters such as the Brazilian brothers Os Gemeos have also added their works to the colorful melting pot of styles.

The result is an open-air art gallery of mammoth proportions. Street art tours are increasingly popular but if you fancy going it alone, the state-sponsored Galeria de Arte Urbana (gau.cm-lisboa.pt/info.html) has pointers, including online maps.

⊘ Closed Sun. Ⓜ Green Line to Cais do Sodré.

Zuari
$ | African. Serving spicy samosas, curries, and other *picante* treats since the 1970s, Zuari was one of the first Goan restaurants to open in Lisbon (and many would argue it's still the best). It's a wonderful introduction to the flavors of the former Portuguese colony, and the very fair prices mean culinary adventures here won't break the bank. **Known for:** traditional Goan cuisine, strong on fish and meat dishes; excellent shrimp curries; very affordable wine list. *Average main: €11* ⊠ *Rua São João da Mata 41, Santos* ☎ *21/397–7149* ⊘ *Closed Mon.* Ⓜ *Tram 25E to Santos-o-Velho.*

Ⓨ Bars and Nightlife

★ O Bom O Mau e O Vilão
This film-themed bar (the name comes from the Portuguese title of *The Good, the Bad and the Ugly*) attracts an artsy young crowd thanks to its lengthy cocktail list and vintage-chic decor. DJs spin vinyl while patrons loaf in comfy armchairs or prop up the bar. ⊠ *Rua Do Alecrim 21, Cais do Sodré* ☎ *96/795–0287* Ⓜ *Green Line to Cais do Sodré.*

Crafty Corner
This beer-tasting room gives craft beer geeks something to get genuinely excited about. Spread over two floors of an artfully converted warehouse, it offers up to 12 locally produced ales per day, along with traditional salty accompaniments like the addictive *tremoços* (lupin beans). ⊠ *Travessa de Corpo Santo*

15, Cais do Sodré ☎ *96/993–4026*
⊕ *www.craftycornerbeer.com*
Ⓜ *Green Line to Cais do Sodré.*

Europa
A former brothel turned into a club, Europa was one of the early gentrifiers in transforming the former red-light district of Cais do Sodré into the place to be at night. The interior hasn't changed much, keeping the red-hot tones, but an added bar serves reasonably priced drinks. The official closing time is 4 am, but Europa is renowned for its after parties that can last until way past sunrise. There are different guest DJs on most nights, so the musical styles vary every time. ✉ *Rua Nova do Carvalho 16–20, Cais do Sodré* ☎ *91/848–9595* ⊕ *www.europabar.pt* Ⓜ *Green Line to Cais do Sodré.*

★ Lounge
This hip joint is where twenty- and thirtysomething vinyl junkies chat (or shout) to the pumping sound of dance music; there are regular live music events—think funky Brazilian or African sounds, not fado. It's a cozy space that gets packed on weekends. ✉ *Rua da Moeda 1, Cais do Sodré* ☎ *21/403–2712* ⊕ *www.loungelisboa.com.pt* Ⓜ *Green Line to Cais do Sodré.*

★ Matiz Pombalina
An upmarket cocktail bar whose decor is inspired by the Pombaline architecture of downtown Lisbon, Matiz Pombalina feels like the living room of an exceptionally stylish friend. The main focus is on gin but every cocktail on the extensive list

comes perfectly mixed. ✉ *Rua das Trinas 25, Santos* ☎ *21/404–3703* Ⓜ *Tram 15E or 18E to Santos.*

★ Microclub LX
As the name suggests, this is a nightclub of miniature proportions. Quality DJs play electronic dance music to a clued-in crowd, who jostle for space at the bar and on the tiny dance floor. ✉ *Rua Cascais 15, Alcântara* ☎ *91/288–0037* ⊕ *www.microclub.pt* Ⓜ *Tram 18E to Cemitério da Ajuda.*

★ Pensão Amor
There's no hipper place on Pink Street than this offbeat hangout housed in a former brothel with a decor that recalls its decadent past. Its warren of rooms houses a café, erotic bookshop, a bar serving cocktails for couples, and a dance floor. Burlesque shows add to the racy appeal, but it's more suggestive than sordid. ✉ *Rua do Alecrim 19, Cais do Sodré* ☎ *21/314–3399* ⊕ *www.pensaoamor.pt.*

★ Quimera Brewpub
If you choose just one craft beer spot in Lisbon, make it this one. Where else could you drink artisanal cervejas in a cavernous tunnel that once served as a passageway for the 18th-century royal cavalry? Substantial sandwiches and a series of live music events add to the

considerable appeal. ⊠ *Rua Prior do Crato 6, Alcântara* ☎ *91/707-0021* ⊕ *www.quimerabrewpub.com.*

★ Rio Maravilha

Occupying a space that was once a tea-break room for factory workers, Rio Maravilha now offers Lisbon's hardworking creative types a chance to eat, drink, and be merry. The Brazil-themed decor is colorful and the ambience relaxed, and the menu has plenty of creative small plates, but it's the views over the river and 25 de Abril suspension bridge that steal the show. It's open until late on weekends, and there are regular DJ sets and live music. ⊠ *LX Factory, Rua Rodrigues de Faria 103, 4th fl., Alcântara* ☎ *966/028-9229* ⊕ *www. riomaravilha.pt* Ⓜ *Tram 15E or 18E to Calvário.*

Sol e Pesca

This former fishing-tackle shop is now a trendy late-opening bar—with much of the original decoration— serving canned delicacies (mostly involving fish) and inexpensive draft beer. ⊠ *Rua Nova do Carvalho 44, Cais do Sodré* ☎ *21/346-7203* 🕙 *Closed Sun. and Mon.* Ⓜ *Green Line to Cais do Sodré.*

A Tabacaria

Killer cocktails are served with flair at this tiny former tobacconist (dating back to the 1880s) that feels a world away from the big, bold sidewalk bars nearby. Don't expect a seat—space is tight, and it's usually standing room only. ⊠ *Rua de Sao Paulo 75-77, Cais do Sodré* ☎ *21/342-0281* Ⓜ *Green Line to Cais do Sodré.*

 Performing Arts

Agua de Beber

This fun under-the-radar spot for live Brazilian music draws an extremely lively crowd of Brasileiros every weekend. The happy hours and excellent caipirinhas help get the party spirit flowing. ⊠ *Travessa de São Paulo 8, Cais do Sodré* ☎ *21/403-9956* Ⓜ *Green Line to Cais do Sodré.*

Bar a Barraca

A fabulous art deco cinema building now serves as a space for a range of performing arts events just a minute's walk from Santos train station. Expect everything from poetry recitals and jazz to tango lessons and music sessions from around the globe. ⊠ *Teatro CineArte, Largo do Santos 2, Santos* ☎ *21/396-5360* Ⓜ *Train to Santos; Tram 15E or 18E to Santos.*

B.Leza

Playing African beats for more than 20 years, B.Leza has moved several times, most recently into a riverfront warehouse. Always popular with the Lisbon party circuit, B.Leza has a strong Angolan influence, with *kizomba* dance workshops and regular live music and dance shows. ⊠ *Cais da Ribeira Nova, Armazém B, Cais do Sodré* ☎ *21/010-6837* Ⓜ *Green Line to Cais do Sodré.*

Dock's Club

Arrive after midnight and be prepared to dance until dawn at this dressy nightclub in a smart converted warehouse by the docks. Expect mainstream R&B and EDM, with some Angolan beats and Brazilian funk thrown in for good measure. Weekends are packed after 1 am, and Ladies Night drinks offers on Tuesday attract a decent crowd. ✉ *Rua da Cintura do Porto de Lisboa 226, Alcântara* ☎ *26/694–1927* Ⓜ *Tram 15E or 18E to Cais Rocha.*

★ MusicBox

Right in the middle of the party action, under the arches on Rua Cor da Rosa (as locals call this street), MusicBox is a packed party joint with a fast-revolving lineup of DJs, live music events, and themed nights. Get here after midnight—the fun goes on until dawn. ✉ *Rua Nova do Carvalho 24, Cais do Sodré* ☎ *21/347–3188* ⊕ *musicboxlisboa.com* Ⓜ *Green Line to Cais do Sodré.*

Titanic Sur Mer

Live music comes with a dash of Brazilian panache at this popular late-night dance spot. The famous Sunday-night Roda da Samba (musicians take turns to play) attracts fleet-footed *sambistas* from across the city. Hip-hop, rock, and Cuban jazz takes the stage as well, alongside themed events. Check listings in advance as this popular spot has one of the most eclectic musical menus in Lisbon. ✉ *Cais da Ribeira Nova, Armazém B, Cais do Sodré* ☎ *93/245–9860* Ⓜ *Green Line to Cais do Sodré.*

Sabotage

Rock out to live bands and DJs at Sabotage, where the sticky dance floor gets packed every weekend with an artsy, alternative crowd. As well as a lively international indie-rock playlist, this is one of the best places in Lisbon to catch up-and-coming Portuguese acts. ✉ *Rua de São Paulo, Cais do Sodré* ☎ *21/ 347–0235* ⊕ *www.sabotage.pt* Ⓜ *Green Line to Cais do Sodré.*

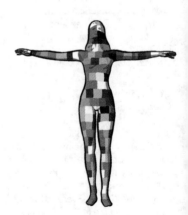

AMEIXOEIRA

CHARNECA

LUMIAR

SANTA MARIA DOS OLIVAIS

PARQUE DAS NAÇÕES

CARNIDE

AVENIDAS NOVAS

SÃO DOMINGOS DE BENFICA

MARVILA

BENFICA

CAMPOLIDE

BEATO

SÃO JOÃO

MARQUÊS DE POMPAL E AVENIDA DA LIBERDADE

ARROIOS

PENHA DE FRANÇA

SÃO MAMEDE

ANJOS

SANTA ENGRÁCIA

CAMPO DE OURIQUE

PRINCIPE REAL

INTENDENTE

GRAÇA

ESTRELA

MARTIM MONIZ

SÃO VICENTE

ALCÂNTARA

MOURARIA

ROSSIO

LAPA

BARRIO ALTO

BAIXA

ALFAMA

AJUDA

CHIADO

RESTELO

CAIS DO SODRE

SANTOS

BELÉM

Sightseeing ★★★☆☆ | Shopping ★★☆☆☆ | Dining ★★★★☆ | Nightlife ★☆☆☆☆

There are few tourists in this part of town, but those who do step off the tram and choose to wander around the neighborhoods of Estrela, Campo de Ourique, and Lapa will discover a side of Lisbon often only experienced by locals. The affluent district of Lapa was laid out shortly after the Great Earthquake of 1755, on what were then considered the outskirts of the city. It was where the wealthier classes built their mansions, most of which have since been turned into embassies or hotels (the most notable examples are down Rua do Sacramento à Lapa). Other buildings follow a neoclassical style, with many featuring beautiful decorative tiles on their facades. In fact, this was where the Portuguese tradition of covering buildings with tiles was born. Today, Lapa remains a peaceful residential neighborhood that eventually leads to Estrela, the site of a basilica whose large dome can be seen from almost anywhere in the city. Past the basilica runs the famous Tram 28, which ends in Campo de Ourique, a more modern district dating from the early 20th century.—*by Mario Fernandes*

Sights

Aqueduto das Águas Livres

Lisbon was formerly provided with clean drinking water by means of the Aqueduct of Free Waters (1729–48), built by Manuel da Maia and stretching for more than 18 km (11 miles) from the water source on the outskirts of the city. The most imposing section is the 35 arches that stride across the Alcântara river valley beyond the Amoreiras shopping complex; the largest of these is said to be the highest ogival (pointed) arch in the world. You can access this section from the Campolide neighborhood. Nearer the city center, another 14 arches run 200 feet along the Praça das Amoreiras, ending in the Mãe d'Agua, an internal reservoir capable of holding more than a million gallons of water. This extraordinary structure is open for visits, providing a chance to see the holding tank, lavish internal waterfall, and associated machinery. ⊠ *Calçada da Quintinha 6, Campo de Ourique* ☎ *21/810–0215* ⊕ *www.epal. pt/EPAL/en/menu/water-museum/* 💶 *€3* 🕙 *Closed Mon.* Ⓜ *Tram 24 to Campolide (last stop).*

Basílica da Estrela

A standout on Lisbon's skyline, this gleaming white basilica was built in the baroque and neoclassical styles, and its location at the top of one of Lisbon's seven hills makes for dramatic views from its rococo *zimbório* (dome). It was built at the end of the 18th century under the

Estrela, Lapa, and Campo de Ourique are about a 10- to 15-minute walk up Avenida Álvares Cabral from the Rato metro station, but the best way to reach this part of town is by tram. Trams 25 and 28 both go from the city center past the basilica in Estrela, ending their journey in Campo de Ourique.

command of Queen Maria I (whose tomb lies within the building) to fulfill a religious promise she made in praying (ultimately successfully) for a male heir. The interior is striking, too, with black-and-pink marble walls and floors and a famously elaborate nativity scene displayed year-round. Estrela is a short walk west of Largo do Rato, where the metro's Yellow Line terminates. You can also take the scenic route on Tram 28 from Praça Luís de Camões in the Chiado neighborhood; you'll pass through the São Bento district, dominated by Portugal's grand parliament building (a former monastery) on the way. ⊠ *Praça da Estrela, Lapa* 🎫 *Basilica free, dome €5* Ⓜ *Yellow Line to Rato; Tram 25 or 28 to Estrela.*

Casa Fernando Pessoa
Quotes by poet Fernando Pessoa cover the facade of the building where he lived for the last 15 years of his life (1920–35). Within his former apartment, visitors can see Pessoa's personal items, including his bed and the typewriter where he wrote many of his last works. There's also his personal library,

with more than 1,000 of his handwritten notebooks and a collection of Portuguese and international poetry. The site is also a cultural center that organizes literary debates and exhibitions. ⊠ *Rua Coelho da Rocha 16, Campo de Ourique* 🕾 *21/391-3270* ⊕ *www.casafernandopessoa.pt* 🕘 *Closed Sun.* Ⓜ *Tram 25 or 28 to Rua Saraiva Carvalho.*

English Cemetery
The English Cemetery is where Lisbon's once-sizeable English community was laid to rest over the years. Thanks to the Anglo-Portuguese alliance in the 14th century, the kingdoms of Portugal and England maintained close relationships, especially in trade, leading to the port wine industry in the city of Porto, which was mostly in British hands, and to a considerable number of British merchants settling in Lisbon. This cemetery, found behind a gate across from Jardim da Estrela, is filled with tombstones mixing English and Portuguese surnames, showing how British and Portuguese families intermarried over the centuries, but it's the tomb of novelist Henry Fielding (author of *Tom Jones*) that most visitors look for. Fielding

SIGHTS

Aqueduto das
Águas Livres...............1

Basílica da Estrela...18

Casa Fernando
Pessoa.....................12

English Cemetery 13

Jardim da Estrela 17

Mercado de Campo
de Ourique.................9

Museu Arpad Szenes –
Vieira da Silva 2

SHOPPING

Galeria Cristina
Guerra......................16

O Melhor Bolo
de Chocolate
do Mundo...................8

COFFEE & QUICK BITES

Aloma........................10

Amélia Lisboa 11

Lomar 5

DINING

Casa dos
Passarinhos 6

Clube de
Jornalistas 20

Come Prima 22

Ela Canela 7

Estórias na
Casa da Comida 3

Loco 19

Peixaria
da Esquina.................4

Tasca da Esquina.....14

BARS & NIGHTLIFE

A Paródia 15

Senhor Vinho...........21

moved to Lisbon hoping that better weather would improve his health but ended up dying in the city. A plaque also reveals that Thomas Barclay, appointed by George Washington as the first American consul in France, died in Lisbon in 1793 and is buried here. ⊠ *Rua de São Jorge, Estrela* ⊘ *Closed Sat.* Ⓜ *Yellow Line to Rato; Tram 25 or 28 to Estrela.*

Jardim da Estrela

Across the street from Basílica da Estrela is this romantic park dating back to 1852 and filled with exotic plants and trees. Although officially named after poet Guerra Junqueiro, everyone knows it as Jardim da Estrela. It's one of Lisbon's loveliest green spaces, where families take their kids to see ducks on the ponds and to run around on the playground, as they stay reading and others jog and do their daily workout. At the center is a 19th-century wrought-iron bandstand that once stood in the Passeio Público, now Avenida da Liberdade. There's a kiosk serving refreshments and a café with outdoor seating for light meals. ⊠ *Praça da Estrela, Campo de Ourique* Ⓜ *Tram 25 or 28 to Estrela.*

WORTH A TRIP

About a 15-minute walk from Campo de Ourique is Lisbon's remarkable aqueduct, which was one of the few structures left standing following the Great Earthquake of 1755. Still considered one of the greatest hydraulic and engineering works of all time, it had the world's tallest stone arches when it was built in 1732. You can now walk over the 14 largest arches (there are 109 in total), while enjoying views of the surrounding modern city. ⊠ *Calçada da Quintinha 6* ☎ *21/810–0215*

Mercado de Campo de Ourique

Started in 1934, this is one of Lisbon's oldest neighborhood markets and over the last few years has turned into one of the city's hottest food destinations. The stalls of fresh fruits and vegetables now surround tables where customers sit for meals prepared at the newer gourmet stalls. It's a lively place where you still find mostly locals, unlike at the bigger and more famous Mercado da Ribeira by the river. ⊠ *Rua Coelho da Rocha, Campo de Ourique* ☎ *21/132–3701* ⊕ *www.mercadodecampodeourique. pt* Ⓜ *Tram 25 or 28 to Igreja Sto. Condestável.*

Museu Arpad Szenes – Vieira da Silva

This small but beautiful museum in a former silk factory displays paintings, drawings, and prints by Maria Helena Vieira da Silva and her Hungarian husband, Arpad Szenes. The couple lived in Lisbon,

Paris, and Rio de Janeiro, and were influential artists after their participation in the 1937 World Exhibition in Paris. Most of Vieira da Silva's pieces are geometrical abstractions and can be seen over the two floors of the building that face the arches of the city's landmark aqueduct. Throughout the year the museum also hosts temporary exhibitions of 20th-century and contemporary art. ⊠ *Praça das Amoreiras 56, Amoreiras* ☎ *21/388–0044* ⊕ *www.fasvs.pt* ⊠ *€5* 🕒 *Closed Mon.* Ⓜ *Yellow Line to Rato.*

 Shopping

Galeria Cristina Guerra

This gallery regularly presents works by top Portuguese artists plus some big international names. Much of the artwork later appears in some of the world's leading art fairs. ⊠ *Rua Santo António à Estrela 33, Estrela* ☎ *21/395–9559* ⊕ *www. cristinaguerra.com* Ⓜ *Tram 25 or 28 to Rua Domingos Sequeira.*

O Melhor Bolo de Chocolate do Mundo

It's right there in the name: the best chocolate cake in the world can be found across from Campo de Ourique's popular market, or so says the baker who came up with his own chocolate recipe and has been selling it at this straightforwardly named shop since 2007. Everyone wants to judge for themselves, so the tiny shop is one of the neighborhood's most popular spots. Instead of flour, the bakers use layers of cocoa mousse, so it really is no ordinary chocolate cake. ⊠ *Rua Tenente Ferreira Durão 62A, Campo de Ourique* ☎ *21/396–5372* ⊕ *www. omelhorbolodechocolatedomundobycbl.com* Ⓜ *Tram 25 or 28 to Igreja Sto. Condestável.*

 Coffee and Quick Bites

Aloma

$ | **Portuguese.** In business since 1943, this was just another neighborhood pastry shop until it started receiving accolades for its excellent custard tarts, and ended up supplying those mouthwatering sweets to other shops in the city (and even to Paris's Galleries Lafayette!). This tart stands out for being creamier than most and for always being served cold. **Known for:** small 1940s interior; good-value sandwiches and snacks; famous custard tarts. *Average main: €2* ⊠ *Rua Francisco Metrass 67, Campo de Ourique* ☎ *21/396–3797* ⊕ *www. aloma.pt* Ⓜ *Tram 25 or 28 to Igreja Sto. Condestável.*

Amélia Lisboa

$ | **International.** Located on Campo de Ourique's main street, not far from the route of Trams 25 and 28, Amélia Lisboa is a good choice for a light meal. It attracts not only the people of the neighborhood but also Lisbon's young and trendy, who love the fun decor and the colorful healthy meals (which include power bowls and plenty of gluten-free and vegan options). **Known for:** brunch available throughout the day; inviting patio; plant-filled interior. *Average main: €8* ⊠ *Rua Ferreira Borges 101, Campo de Ourique*

☎ 21/385–0863 ⊕ www.ilovenicolau. com/pt/onde-estamos/amelia Ⓜ Tram 25 or 28 to Rua Domingos Sequeira.

Lomar

$ | Portuguese. Campo de Ourique residents head to this small pastry shop, in business since the 1970s, whenever they crave something sweet. It's found around the corner from the neighborhood's main square and park (Jardim da Parada), and not far from the popular Mercado de Campo de Ourique. **Known for:** good-value menus for light meals; brioche croissants; sugary pastries. *Average main: €3* ⊠ *Rua Tomás da Anunciação 72, Campo de Ourique* ☎ *21/385–8417* ⊘ *Closed Sun.* 🚫 *No credit cards* Ⓜ *Tram 25 or 28 to Igreja Sto. Condestável.*

🍴 Dining

Casa dos Passarinhos

$ | Portuguese. Serving tasty food at fair prices for more than 95 years, this traditional Portuguese restaurant is a lunchtime favorite for employees from the nearby Amoreiras office complex, and at night it draws mainly locals from the neighborhood. Come for the house specialties, which include a famous *naco na pedra* (steak cooked on a hot stone), *vitela barrosã* (tender veal from the north), grilled fish, and *açorda de gambas* (shrimp and bread stew). **Known for:** grilled fish; two dining rooms decorated in an old-fashioned rustic style; daily specials often at a good value. *Average main: €12* ⊠ *Rua Silva Carvalho 195, Campo*

de Ourique ☎ *21/388–2346* ⊕ *casa-dospassarinhos.com* ⊘ *Closed Sun. Closed 2 wks in Aug.*

Clube de Jornalistas

$$ | International. The "Press Club" is actually an excellent restaurant open to everyone, not just journalists. It does have a cozy reading room, but everyone usually heads straight to the pleasant garden in the back for outdoor dining. **Known for:** creative international menu; classic 18th-century interior; coisas doces for dessert (small servings of several desserts on one plate). *Average main: €18* ⊠ *Rua das Trinas 129, Lapa* ☎ *21/397-7138* ⊕ *www.restauranteclubedejornalistas.com* ♥ *Closed Sun.* Ⓜ *Tram 25 to Rua de São Domingos à Lapa.*

Come Prima
$ | Italian. Hidden in a residential area, Come Prima occupies a low-lit space split into two levels and is always packed with locals who love its distinguished Italian cuisine. If you're looking for a romantic place off the beaten path, this is a good choice. **Known for:** tasty Alba truffles; wood-oven pizzas; gigantic Parmigiano-Reggiano cheese used for pastas. *Average main: €14* ⊠ *Rua do Olival 258, Lapa* ☎ *21/390-2457* ⊕ *www.comeprima.pt* ♥ *Closed Sun. No lunch Sat.*

Ela Canela
$ | International. Located up the street from the last stop of Trams 25 and 28, this café serves healthy meals in a minimalist, light-filled space. It also has a few tables outside, where locals meet for brunch and where a few tourists who step off the trams and go off the beaten path through Campo de Ourique stop for a light meal. **Known for:** seasonal organic products; healthy cold and hot bowls; green and fruity juices and smoothies. *Average main: €15* ⊠ *Rua*

WORTH A TRIP

The ferry ride across the Tagus to Cacilhas is 10-minute hop from the ferry terminal in Cais do Sodré, and it's fun as well as fast. Ferries depart roughly every 15 minutes throughout the day and night, and passengers can sit on the open-air deck to catch dazzling views of the city, the river, and the 25 de Abril suspension bridge. Come hungry because just a few minutes' walk along the pier (past rather insalubrious-looking warehouses) are Ponto Final and Atire-te ao Rio, two unpretentious restaurants perched on the edge of the water. Their freshly grilled fish and jarrinhas (jug) of house wine are splendid companions to the dazzling sunset views.

Azedo Gneco 74B, Campo de Ourique ☎ *21/396-0475* ⊕ *www.elacanela.pt* ♥ *Closed Mon. and Tues.* Ⓜ *Tram 25 or 28 to Prazeres.*

★ Estórias na Casa da Comida
$$$ | Portuguese. An institution that's been serving up high-end cuisine for more than 35 years, Casa da Comida has been given a new lease on life thanks to the innovations of chef Duarte Lourenço and sommelier Ricardo Morais, as well a dramatic face-lift that has wowed interior design aficionados. Snack on a superior line of *petiscos* (light bites) in the bar area, go à la carte, or opt for the eight-course "Madness of the Chef" tasting menu that might feature treats like juniper-smoked rabbit or fish cake made from gooseneck barnacles and crab. **Known for:** classy interior

TILE HUNTING IN LISBON

Lisbon is basically an open-air museum of decorative tiles, and it all started in the neighborhood of Lapa.

The very first building to be covered in tiles can be found at Rua São João da Mata 19. Featuring just one color, it's now quite unremarkable compared to others around the city, but its historic significance can't be denied. The tiles were originally chosen to protect the building from humidity and to keep the interiors cooler in the summer. The trend caught on with other buildings in the neighborhood and eventually became a tradition not just in Lisbon but in all of Portugal and its colonies (particularly Brazil).

A common activity for tourists in Lisbon is to go tile hunting through the city streets, and a good place to start is Lapa and the nearby former fishing community of Madragoa. In these areas, you'll come across several picturesque examples of patterned tiles from the late 1700s and 1800s, especially on Rua das Trinas and Rua Vicente Borga. For the most monumental facades, you'll have to head to Chiado (Largo Rafael Bordalo Pinheiro), Alfama (Campo de Santa Clara), and Largo do Intendente, but it's around Lapa and Estrela that you'll find the largest concentration of photo-worthy buildings.

A few addresses to mark on your map: Rua do Sacramento à Lapa 24 (an 1800s mansion with windows covered in tiles and ceramics), Rua de São Domingos à Lapa 43–45 (covered with floral motifs), Rua das Janelas Verdes 70–78 (rare art nouveau tiles with reliefs), Rua do Jardim à Estrela 25 (with a facade from the 1800s completely covered with Asian faces), and Rua do Possolo 76 (colorful tiles from the 1700s).

design and a romantic terrace; contemporary Portuguese cuisine with an international flavor; excellent service. *Average main: €25* ✉ *Travessa das Amoreiras 1, Amoreiras* ☎ *21/386–0889* ⊕ *www. casadacomida.pt* ⊘ *Closed Sun. No lunch* Ⓜ *Yellow Line to Rato.*

Loco
$$$$ | **Portuguese.** Neighboring Basílica da Estrela, this Michelin-starred restaurant offers tasting menus by chef Alexandre Silva, who changes them every two weeks so that only the freshest seasonal ingredients are used. Occasionally, he invites other top chefs from Lisbon and beyond to create special one-night-only menus. **Known for:** fun dishes inspired by traditional Portuguese cuisine; high-quality yet little-known Portuguese wines; gorgeous design. *Average main: €80* ✉ *Rua dos Navegantes 53B, Estrela* ☎ *21/395–1861* ⊕ *www.loco. pt* ⊘ *Closed Sun. and Mon. No lunch* Ⓜ *Tram 25 or 28 to Estrela.*

Peixaria da Esquina

$$ | Seafood. After the success of his Tasca da Esquina in the same neighborhood, chef Vítor Sobral decided to open a spot where he could focus on fish and seafood coming straight from the Portuguese coast. It's all served in different ways (baked, grilled, cured, or marinated) in a casual atmosphere. **Known for:** oysters from the Algarve; delicious açordas; good Portuguese wines. *Average main: €17* ⊠ *Rua Correia Teles 56, Campo de Ourique* ☎ *21/387-4644* ⊕ *www. peixariadaesquina.com* ⊘ *Closed Mon. No lunch weekdays* Ⓜ *Tram 25 or 28 to Igreja Sto. Condestável.*

Tasca da Esquina

$$ | Portuguese. One of the country's most famous chefs, Vítor Sobral , has recreated a traditional Portuguese neighborhood eatery for modern palates. The glass-walled space is found on a corner up the road from Basílica da Estrela and is always packed, so be sure to book in advance. **Known for:** small plates blending tradition and modern creativity; surprise menu option selected by the chef; good selection of wines. *Average main: €18* ⊠ *Rua Domingos Sequeira 41C, Campo de Ourique* ☎ *21/099-3939* ⊕ *www.tasca-daesquina.com* Ⓜ *Tram 25 or 28 to Rua Saraiva Carvalho.*

🍸 Bars and Nightlife

A Paródia

Despite being one of Lisbon's oldest bars, A Paródia remains one of the city's best secrets. You must ring a bell to go inside, where you'll find a 1920s atmosphere and art nouveau decor. There are old mirrors, vintage furniture, and red velvet sofas where you can sit to enjoy fruity cocktails and snacks like toasted sandwiches. ⊠ *Rua do Patrocinio 26B, Campo de Ourique* ☎ *21/396-4724* ⊕ *www. aparodia.com* Ⓜ *Tram 25 or 28 to Rua Saraiva Carvalho.*

★ Senhor Vinho

This Lisbon institution attracts some of Portugal's most accomplished fado singers. It also serves better food than many *casas de fado* and is one of the few touristic spots that still attracts local fado fans. The name literally means "Mister Wine," and as expected, there are some good bottles to choose from. A voucher on the website gets you a 10% discount on dinner. ⊠ *Rua do Meio à Lapa 18, Lapa* ☎ *21/397-2681* ⊕ *www.srvinho.com* Ⓜ *Tram 25 to Rua de São Domingos à Lapa.*

GO FOR

Multicultural and vibrant atmosphere

Historic neighborhood

Youthful energy

AMEIXOEIRA

CHARNECA

LUMIAR

SANTA MARIA DOS OLIVAIS

PARQUE DAS NAÇÕES

CARNIDE

SÃO DOMINGOS DE BENFICA

AVENIDAS NOVAS

MARVILA

BENFICA

CAMPOLIDE

BEATO

MARQUÊS DE POMPAL E AVENIDA DA LIBERDADE

ARROIOS

SÃO JOÃO

PENHA DE FRANÇA

ANJOS

SÃO MAMEDE

INTENDENTE

SANTA ENGRÁCIA

CAMPO DE OURIQUE

PRINCIPE REAL

MARTIM MONIZ

GRAÇA

SÃO VICENTE

ALCÂNTARA

ESTRELA

MOURARIA

ROSSIO

RESTELO

AJUDA

LAPA

BARRIO ALTO

BAIXA CHIADO

ALFAMA

CAIS DO SODRE

SANTOS

BELÉM

Situated on the hillside below the São Jorge castle, these three neighborhoods are among the oldest in Lisbon and a walk around their narrow hilly lanes can feel like a step back in time. And although there are no palaces and little cultural patrimony here, getting lost in the winding lanes, where the scent of grilled fish mingles with Asian spices and the sound of fado drifts from balconies overhead, is a true Lisbon experience.—*by Trish Lorenz*

These areas, along with neighboring Alfama, were among the only to survive the devastating earthquake of 1755, and the higgledy-piggledy streets, with laundry lines flapping between buildings, continue to evoke medieval Lisbon. In the past these areas were outside the city walls so traditionally only the poorest people lived here, but today, although rapidly gentrifying, they remain working-class neighborhoods. Many Asian and African immigrants live in the area as well, contributing to the lively, multicultural feel. You'll also find artists and other creatives living here, which also gives these neighborhoods a slightly alternative vibe—vintage stores, designer ateliers, and speakeasy-style bars rub shoulders with traditional restaurants, Chinese supermarkets, and sari shops. If you're looking to hear some fado, Portuguese folk music, Mouraria is its birthplace and remains one of the best places in the city to hear it sung.

Sights

Igreja de São Cristóvão
(St. Christopher's Church)
Originally dating from the 13th century but reconstructed after a fire in the 16th century, this church was largely untouched by the 1755 earthquake. Its interior, with a painted ceiling and many gilded frame paintings, illustrates the baroque splendor of Portuguese churches before the earthquake robbed the city of much of its heritage and wealth. ⊠ *Largo São Cristóvão 4, Lisbon* ☏ *21/599–8801* ⊕ *www.arteporsaocristovao.org* ☾ *Closed Sun. and Mon.*

Largo do Intendente
This large square at the heart of Intendente is one of the most striking in the city. Neglected for many years, it's recently experienced a rebirth, and the buildings that surround it feature beautifully tiled facades and interesting architecture, including Lisbon's answer to New York's Flatiron Building, which is now a hotel at the top end of the square. Cafés with terraces offer plenty of opportunity for people-watching. ⊠ *Largo do*

Intendente, Intendente Ⓜ *Green Line to Intendente; Tram 28 to Largo do Intendente.*

Praça Martim Moniz

This large square at the heart of Lisbon's multicultural Martim Moniz neighborhood is the terminus of the 28 tram. There are fountains and shady benches perfect for relaxing and there's a small street food market with stalls serving Chinese, Indian, African, and Portuguese food and drinks. On weekends and special holidays, such as Chinese New Year, there are often dance and music performances and a craft market. ⊠ *Praça Martim Moniz, Lisbon* Ⓜ *Green Line to Martim Moniz; Tram 28 or Tram 12 to Martim Moniz.*

Rua da Guia

Fado, the mournful Portuguese folk music, is said to have been born in the Lisbon suburbs of Alfama and Mouraria. This street is redolent with its history, with large black-and-white photographs and information about famous *fadistas* pasted on its walls. One famous fadista, Maria Severa, lived on this street, and her former home is now a performance space, Maria da Mouraria (see listing). Mariza, one of contemporary fado's biggest stars, also hails from the area. ⊠ *Rua da Guia, Lisbon.*

★ Viúva Lamego

The prices at Lisbon's largest purveyor of vintage tiles and pottery are competitive. It is possible to arrange a visit to the factory outside the city, in Sintra. Even if you have no interest in tiles and ceramics,

GETTING HERE

Intendente and Martim Moniz have metro stops on the Green Line, but Mouraria is less well served by public transport. The 28 tram does run along the edge of Intendente and the 12 tram runs from Martim Moniz up Rua Cavaleiro, which saves you a few minutes' uphill walk into Mouraria, but its hilly location is unfortunately best reached on foot. From the Baixa you can also take the elevator (free) from Rua dos Fanqueiros to Rua da Madalena, at the base of Mouraria.

be sure to pass by this store—it's in one of Lisbon's most famous and beautifully tiled buildings. ⊠ *Largo do Intendente 25, Intendente* ☎ *21/231-4274* ⊕ *www.viuvalamego. com* ⊗ *Closed weekends* Ⓜ *Green Line to Intendente.*

Zambeze Patio

For some of the most dramatic views in Lisbon, this patio is hard to beat as it overlooks the heart of the city's historic center and the river Tagus as it stretches out to sea. This is a great place to take pictures and enjoy the view. If you'd like a drink, snack, or full meal, there are outdoor tables, also with great views, that belong to the neighboring Zambeze restaurant. ⊠ *Edifício EMEL, Mercado Chão do Loureiro, Calçada Marquês de Tancos, Lisbon* ☎ *21/887-7056 for restaurant reservations.*

SIGHTS
Igreja de
São Cristóvão 31
Largo do
Intendente 6
Praça
Martim Moniz 12
Rua da Guia 17
Viúva Lamego 4
Zambeze Patio 32

SHOPPING
A Vida Portuguesa 7
Atelier
Joana Simao.............24
Cortiço & Netos 20
Lupa 19
Prado Mercearia......33
Retro City Lisboa 1
Retrox 2
Tropical Bairro.........30

COFFEE & QUICK BITES
Bruta Flor.................15
Cafe O Corvo 23
Cafe O das Joanas 3
Infame......................9
O Ninho....................29
Union Lab 28

DINING
Cantina Baldracca ...27
Cantinho do Aziz 22
Cervejaria
do Ramiro.................10
The Food Temple 16
O Zé da Mouraria 13
Palanca Gigante.......21
Prado 34
Zé dos Cornos 25

BARS & NIGHTLIFE
Bar Flamingo 18
Bar 1908 8
Casa
Independente 5
Topo 11

PERFORMING ARTS
Maria da Mouraria ...14
Renovar a
Mouraria 26

Graça

CONVENTO
DA GRAÇA

Jardim
Augusto Gil

IGREJA DE
SÃO VICENTE
DE FORA

São Vicente

Alfama

0   250 m
0   500 ft

Shopping

Atelier Joana Simão

Local ceramics artist Joana Simão works and sells from this atelier, which is perfectly located on a pretty square in the heart of Mouraria. Her pieces are simple and contemporary, often in white and gray glazes, with interesting details such as rope handles. She also runs occasional workshops. ⊠ *Largo dos Trigueiros 16B, Lisbon.*

★ Cortiço & Netos

The Portuguese love affair with tiles is evident on buildings across the country but taking home a tile as a memento has implications, as many of those for sale have been stolen from historic buildings. For a more ethical option, Cortiço & Netos sells distinct and beautiful discontinued tiles from the 1950s onward. You can buy just one tile or by the square meter. ⊠ *Calçada de Santo André 66, Lisbon* ☎ *21/136–2376* ⊕ *www.corticoenetos.com* ⊙ *Closed Sun.* Ⓜ *Tram 12 to Calçada de Santo André.*

Lupa

This tiny shop with its pretty tiled floor features the work of a number of young local designers. Pieces for sale—backpacks and wallets, scarves in muted colors, hand-drawn postcards, and jewelry—have a minimalist and modern style. ⊠ *Calçada de Santo André 82, Lisbon* ☎ *967/851573* ⊙ *Closed Sun.* Ⓜ *Tram 12 to Calçada de Santo André.*

★ Prado Mercearia

With tiled floors and vintage fittings, this beautifully designed grocery store would fit right in in Brooklyn, as the shelves are stocked with seasonal, often organic, and all locally sourced products. Items include cheeses, tinned fish, bread, fruits and vegetables, and dry goods. There are also sandwiches, coffee, and homemade cake to take away or eat in. ⊠ *Rua Pedras Negras 35, Lisbon* ☎ *960/280492* ⊙ *Closed Sun.*

Retro City Lisboa

This store has a wide selection of vintage clothing, mostly dating from the 1980s onward. Its well-curated selection has been chosen to appeal particularly to younger fashion-forward buyers. ⊠ *Rua Maria Andrade 43, Intendente* ☎ *21/809–9932* ⊙ *Closed Sun.* Ⓜ *Green Line to Intendente; Tram 23 to Largo do Intendente.*

Retrox

This little vintage store specializes in furniture, books, and collectibles from the 1950s through 1970s. As with all vintage stores, what you find depends on luck and an eye, but you can often find good Portuguese design and international mid-century-modern pieces. ⊠ *Rua dos Anjos 4C, Intendente* ☎ *918/303991* ⊙ *Closed Sun.* Ⓜ *Green Line to Intendente; Tram 28 to Largo do Intendente.*

Tropical Bairro

This small vintage store is run by an Italian DJ and features a well-curated selection of vintage clothing, including the occasional high-fashion label, along with a broad variety of Latin and "tropical" records from the 1950s to '70s. ⊠ *Rua de São Cristóvão 3, Lisbon* ⊙ *Closed Sun.*

★ A Vida Portuguesa

This large emporium stocks beautifully designed and finely packaged traditional Portuguese goods at every price point that range from soaps and shaving cream to glassware, ceramics, textiles, notebooks, food, and olive oils. Airy and spacious, this contemporary shop is a must-visit for gifts and mementos that truly reflect Portuguese life. ⊠ *Largo do Intendente Pina Manique 23, Intendente* ☎ *21/197–4512* ⊕ *www. avidaportuguesa.com* Ⓜ *Green Line to Intendente; Tram 28 to Largo do Intendente.*

☕ Coffee and Quick Bites

Bruta Flor

$ | **Café.** This little café is notable for being open late—you can order snacks, coffee, beer, and wine until midnight. Along with cakes and croissants there are also savory snacks that include vegan and vegetarian options. **Known for:** vegan specials; vegetarian burger; gluten-free hot chocolate. *Average main: €10* ⊠ *Largo Severa 7A, Lisbon* ☎ *21/093–6099* ⊙ *Closed Tues.*

Cafe O Corvo

$ | **Café.** Situated on one of Mouraria's prettiest squares, O Corvo is a great place to recharge after a day of wandering the area's

hilly streets. There are outdoor tables under shady trees, friendly staff, and a menu that includes brunch, burgers, sandwiches, and snacks. **Known for:** brunch; salads; pretty shaded terrace. *Average main: €10* ⊠ *Largo dos Trigueiros 15A, Lisbon* ☎ *21/886–0545.*

Cafe O das Joanas

$ | **Café.** This local institution, popular with the artsy crowd, offers light breakfast and lunch options for reasonable prices. The terrace is great spot to relax and enjoy a beer or snack or both. **Known for:** snacks, salads, and sandwiches; alternative crowd; cheap draft beer. *Average main: €7* ⊠ *Largo do Intendente Pina Manique, Intendente* ☎ *21/887–9401* ⊙ *Closed Tues.* Ⓜ *Green Line to Intendente; Tram 28 to Largo do Intendente.*

Infame

$$ | **Contemporary.** This stylish and welcoming restaurant has been tastefully designed to make the most of its historical building with a striking tiled floor, high ceilings, an exposed metal staircase, and windows on three sides. A pleasant place for brunch, lunch, or dinner, the eclectic menu features seafood, meat, and vegetarian options, many with Asian influences. **Known for:** modern, Asian-influenced menu; stylish and contemporary decor; weekend brunch that includes vegetarian options. *Average main: €19 ⊠ Largo do Intendente Pina Manique 4, Intendente ☎ 21/880–4008 ⊕ infame.pt Ⓜ Green Line to Intendente; Tram 28 to Largo do Intendente.*

O Ninho

$ | Café. A good selection of pastries, a decent brunch menu, great coffee, and friendly service make this French-style café a good choice at the start of your day, whatever time that may be. Brunch is served until 3, and light lunch options are also available. **Known for:** good coffee; French-style pastries; healthy menu options such as fruit and granola. *Average main: €13 ⊠ Rua São Cristóvão 17–19, Lisbon ☎ 21/136–1664 ⊘ Closed Wed. and Thurs.*

Union Lab

$ | Argentine. Empanadas are the main menu item here. Freshly baked, the bite-size pastries (with meat, chicken, or vegetable fillings) are delicious, but juices, smoothies, and cocktails are also available. **Known for:** empanadas, including vegan options; friendly staff; well-priced cocktails. *Average main: €5 ⊠ Rua das Farinhas 16, Lisbon ☎ 918 /979014 ⊕ www.unionportugal.com ▭ No credit cards.*

🍴 Dining

Cantina Baldracca

$ | Pizza. Sometimes you just feel like eating a pizza, and this little restaurant does pizzas well, with thin crusts and traditional toppings in the Italian style—you won't find a Hawaiian on the menu here. Pasta, salads, and risottos are also available, as is a drinkable glass of red wine for €1.50. **Known for:** thin-crust traditional pizza; cozy interior; popularity as a student hangout. *Average main: €9 ⊠ Rue das Farinhas 1, Lisbon ☎ 918/751784 ⊘ Closed Sun. ▭ No credit cards.*

Cantinho do Aziz

$ | African. This Mozambican restaurant is a local institution and one of the best places in Lisbon to try African cuisine. The menu at this casual, low-key restaurant features fragrant and spicy meat dishes and usually one vegetarian dish. **Known for:** traditional Mozambican dishes like nhama (beef with manioc, okra, and coconut) and bakra (spicy lamb ribs); needing reservations; drawing large crowds. *Average main: €12 ⊠ Rua de São Lourenço 5, Lisbon ☎ 21/887–6472 ⊕ cantinhodoaziz. com.*

Cervejaria do Ramiro

$$ | Seafood. This traditional *cervejaria* (which literally translates to "beer house") is one of the most famous places in Lisbon to eat well-priced, fresh seafood. The

PORTUGAL'S BEAUTIFUL TILES

Although not a Portuguese invention, tiles have been used more imaginatively and consistently in Portugal than almost anywhere else in the world. Called azulejos, these beautiful tiles decorate everything from the walls of churches and palaces to the facades of ordinary houses, storefronts, public spaces, and train stations.

The History of Azulejos
The term "azulejo" comes not from the word azul ("blue" in Portuguese) but from the Arabic word for tiles, az-zulayj. The very earliest tiles on Portuguese buildings were imported from Andalusia. They're usually geometric in design and were most frequently used to form panels of repeated patterns. As Portugal's prosperity increased in the 16th century, the growing number of palaces, churches, and sumptuous mansions created a demand for more tile. Local production was small at first, and Holland and Italy were the main suppliers. The first Portuguese-made tiles had begun to appear in the last quarter of the 15th century, when a number of small factories were established, but three centuries were to pass before Portuguese tile making reached its peak. The first tiles produced in Portugal were geometric in pattern, as in the Moorish tradition, but by the 17th century, Portuguese tiles had evolved

their own style: maximalist and decorative, often in blue and white, with Christian motifs and other imagery, such as hunting and city scenes.

The medium is well suited to the deeply rooted Portuguese taste for intricate, ornate decoration. And, aesthetics aside, glazed tiling is ideally suited to the country's more practical needs. Durable, waterproof, and easily cleaned, the tile provides cool interiors during Portugal's hot summers and exterior protection from the dampness of Atlantic winters.

Where to Find Them
Intendente and Mouraria are two of the best places in Lisbon to see azulejos. Start in Largo do Intendente at Fabrica de Viuva Lamego's ornate and beautifully tiled 19th-century exterior and its more modest neighboring buildings. Then wander up the hill and turn right into Mouraria, camera at the ready, to see how many different designs you can spot on the area's buildings.

Portuguese tile making declined in quality in the 19th century, but a revival occurred in the 20th century, spearheaded by leading artists such as Almada Negreiros and Maria Keil. Today, some notable examples of modern tile use by contemporary artists can be seen in many of Lisbon's metro stations.

atmosphere is casual, frenetic, and buzzy—the restaurant's popularity and no-reservations policy means there's almost always a wait for tables, so it's best to arrive early. **Known for:** garlic shrimp; fresh lobster; no-reservations policy.

Average main: €20 ⊠ Av. Almirante Reis 1, Intendente ☎ 21/885-1024 ⊕ www.cervejariaramiro.pt ☉ Closed Mon. Ⓜ Green Line to Intendente; Tram 28 to Largo do Intendente.

The Food Temple

$ | **Vegetarian.** This easy-to-miss vegetarian tapas place is little more than a door in the wall halfway up a public stairway. Despite its location, it's worth the search for its vegetarian and vegan soups, salads, and tapas and its pretty tables on the outdoor stairway terrace on summer evenings. **Known for:** vegetarian tapas; outdoor tables; fresh smoothies and juices. *Average main: €9* ⊠ *Beco do Jasmim 18, Lisbon* ☎ *21/887–4397* ⊕ *www. thefoodtemple.com* ⊘ *Closed Mon. and Tues.* ▭ *No credit cards.*

Palanca Gigante

$ | **African.** This simple two-room Angolan restaurant is a good place to try typical dishes from the former Portuguese colony. Along with traditional Angolan stews such as *muamba*, there are dishes that reflect the historical and culinary interrelationship between Portugal and Angola, such as the grilled *chouriço* (smoked pork sausage). **Known for:** traditional Angolan muamba; funge, a kind of polenta made with cassava; budget-friendly prices. *Average main: €6* ⊠ *Beco do Cascalho, Lisbon* ☎ *924/426693* ⊘ *Closed Sun.* ▭ *No credit cards* Ⓜ *Green Line to Martim Moniz; Tram 28 to Martim Moniz.*

★ Prado

$$$ | **Contemporary.** Seasonal, locally grown ingredients are combined in unusual ways to create noteworthy dishes at this charming restaurant, where plants hang from the ceiling and Scandinavian furniture and a pale green color scheme

WORTH A TRIP

Fabrica do Gelado At Anjos, one stop beyond Intendente on the Green Line, this lovely little artisanal ice-cream parlor is located in a stylishly renovated mid-20th-century shop. It offers a variety of interesting and unusual flavors such as pineapple with ginger or lime with mint that are hand made daily on the premises. **Known for:** handmade ice creams; unusual flavor combinations; friendly and knowledgeable service. ⊠ Rua do Forno do Tijolo 26B ☎ 21/814–0051 ⊘ Closed Mon. ▭ No credit cards Ⓜ Green Line to Anjos.

keep things feeling serene. The wine list features only organic, biodynamic, and natural wines. **Known for:** fresh farm-to-table produce; natural and biodynamic Portuguese wines; trendy crowd. *Average main: €25* ⊠ *Travessa das Pedras Negras 2, Lisbon* ☎ *210/534649* ⊕ *pradorestaurante.com* ⊘ *Closed Mon. and Tues.* Ⓜ *Tram 28.*

O Zé da Mouraria

$ | **Portuguese.** One of the city's best *tascas* (a bar that serves food), O Zé da Mouraria features hearty, traditional fare every lunchtime. It's a no-frills kind of place but the servings are large, the wine list is decent, and the food is an excellent value. **Known for:** bacalhau (salted cod); grilled meats and stews; traditional Portuguese desserts such as arroz doce (rice pudding). *Average main: €12* ⊠ *Rua João do Outeiro 24, Lisbon* ☎ *21/886–5436* ⊘ *Closed Sun.* ▭ *No credit cards.*

Zé dos Cornos

$ | Portuguese. You'll probably need to wait on the stairs outside for a table and then perch on benches or at tightly packed tables, but it's worth the wait for the excellent Portuguese dishes served at this little local tasca. The menu changes daily with a selection of fish and meat options (no vegetarian options). **Known for:** small space that's always busy; their pork "piano" bones; good rice and bean sides. *Average main: €10* ⊠ *Beco dos Surradores 5, Lisbon* ☎ *21/886–9641* ⊗ *Closed Sun.* ⊟ *No credit cards* Ⓜ *Green Line to Martim Moniz.*

 Bars and Nightlife

Bar Flamingo

For a lively, late night with a local vibe, head to Bar Flamingo, an eclectic space that offers cocktails, music, dancing, and a party atmosphere. Totally unpretentious, the crowd is friendly and laid back. ⊠ *Largo do Terreirinho 16, Lisbon* ☎ *925/197865.*

Bar 1908

This hotel bar exudes a youthful, upmarket vibe and features striking artwork by local street artist Bordalo II; the combination makes it a great spot to enjoy a cocktail, a glass of wine, or a beer. The outdoor terrace is another great spot for a drink and a bite to eat—the small menu includes snacks and burgers. ⊠ *1908 Lisboa Hotel, Largo do Intendente Pina Manique 6, Intendente* ☎ *21/880–4004* ⊕ *www.1908lisboahotel.com* Ⓜ *Green*

Line to Intendente; Tram 28 to Largo do Intendente.

★ Casa Independente

This venue, styled as a series of rooms—a nod to its former life as an apartment building—attracts a young and stylish crowd for drinks, live music, and DJ sets. The upstairs rooms are more intimate, with a vintage-store aesthetic, and there's a roof terrace and downstairs bar and dance space. ⊠ *Largo do Intendente Pina Manique 45, Intendente* ☎ *21/887–2842* ⊕ *casa-independente.com* Ⓜ *Green Line to Intendente; Tram 28 to Largo do Intendente.*

Topo

This unpretentious rooftop bar has great views of the castle and the ancient neighborhoods that sit on the hill beneath it. It can be a little hard to find, but persevere and you'll be rewarded with fine views and a wide selection of drinks along with a young, laid-back crowd. ⊠ *Commercial Center Martim Moniz, 6th fl., Lisbon* ☎ *21/588–1322* ⊕ *www.topo-lisboa.pt* Ⓜ *Green Line to Martim Moniz; Tram 28 to Martim Moniz.*

 Performing Arts

★ Maria da Mouraria

This small restaurant is one of the most authentic venues in Lisbon for listening to mournful and soulful fado music. On the site of the former house of famous fadista Maria Severa, the venue hosts regular concerts, sometimes luring big-name singers to perform. You can dine in the restaurant, which serves traditional Portuguese dishes, while you listen, or try your luck arriving just for the concert, but tables may be sold out. ✉ *Largo Severa 2B, Lisbon* ☎ *21/886–0165* ⊕ *mariadamouraria.pt.*

Renovar a Mouraria

This not-for-profit association has a pretty terrace and small bar that hosts events celebrating the diversity of Mouraria's community. From Brazilian samba nights to Cuban, African, and Portuguese national holidays, the parties attract a lively, diverse crowd that often spills out on the steps around the terrace. ✉ *Beco do Rosendo 8, Lisbon* ☎ *21/888–5203* ⊕ *www.renovaramou-raria.pt.*

GO FOR

Big monuments

Cool cultural
centers

Trains to
beaches

AMEIXOEIRA

CHARNECA

LUMIAR

SANTA MARIA
DOS OLIVAIS

PARQUE
DAS
NAÇÕES

CARNIDE

SÃO DOMINGOS
DE BENFICA

AVENIDAS
NOVAS

MARVILA

BENFICA

CAMPOLIDE

BEATO

MARQUÊS DE POMPAL E
AVENIDA DA LIBERDADE

ARROIOS

SÃO JOÃO
PENHA DE
FRANÇA

SÃO
MAMEDE

ANJOS

INTENDENTE

SANTA
ENGRÁCIA

CAMPO DE
OURIQUE

ALCÂNTARA

PRÍNCIPE
REAL

MARTIM
MONIZ

MOURARIA

GRAÇA

SÃO
VICENTE

ESTRELA

ROSSIO

BAIXA

CHIADO

ALFAMA

LAPA

BARRIO
ALTO

RESTELO

AJUDA

CAIS DO
SODRÉ

SANTOS

BELÉM

Sightseeing ★★★★★ | Shopping ★★★☆☆ | Dining ★★★★☆ | Nightlife ★★☆☆☆

Beautiful Belém is home to some of Lisbon's most awe-inspiring architecture, and it's also home to some of the most important museums and cultural centers in the city. The open riverside promenade and green open spaces feel a world away from the tightly packed streets of central Lisbon, and it's a favorite spot for joggers, starry-eyed couples, and strolling local families. The enormous, late-Gothic Jerónimos Monastery is perhaps Lisbon's most photogenic building, while Belém Tower and the Monument to the Discoveries are two major waterfront landmarks. The ultramodern Museum of Art, Architecture and Technology (MAAT) brings things bang up-to-date, and there are several smart hotels and upmarket drinking and dining opportunities alongside the traditional seafood restaurants. Oh, and Belém is also home to the most famous pasteis de nata (custard tarts) in the whole of Portugal; don't miss the opportunity to sample one (or several), fresh from the oven, sprinkled with cinnamon, and enjoyed with a strong coffee.—by Lucy Bryson

. . . .

◉ Sights

Champlimaud Centre for the Unknown

In a prime riverside location, this giant medical research and clinical facility, completed in 2010 from a design by Pritzker Prize winner Charles Correa, has become a pilgrimage site for architecture buffs. Its Darwin's Café restaurant is open to the public and has stunning river views, not least from its charming esplanade café. ✉ *Av. Brasília, Belém* ☎ *21/048–0200* ⊕ *fchampalimaud.org* Ⓜ *Tram 15E at Pedrouços.*

★ Mosteiro dos Jerónimos

If you see only one building in Belém, make it this magnificent monastery. This UNESCO World Heritage Site is a supreme example of the Manueline style of building (named after King Dom Manuel I), which represented a marked departure from earlier Gothic architecture. Much of it is characterized by elaborate sculptural details, often with a maritime motif. João de Castilho was responsible for the southern portal, which forms the main entrance to the church: the figure on the central pillar is Henry the Navigator. Inside, the spacious interior contrasts with the riot of decoration on the six nave columns and complex latticework ceiling. This is the resting place of both explorer Vasco da Gama and national poet Luís de Camões. Don't miss the Gothic- and Renaissance-style double cloister, also designed

to stunning effect by Castilho.
✉ *Praça do Império, Belém* ☎ *21/362–0034* ⊕ *www.mosteirojeronimos.pt* 🎫 *Church free, cloister €10 (free 1st Sun. of month), €12 Discovery ticket includes Torre de Belém* ⊙ *Closed Mon.* Ⓜ *Tram 15E to Mosteiro Jerónimos.*

★ **Museum of Art, Architecture and Technology (MAAT)**
The 2016 opening of this ultra-modern art museum provided yet another reason for culture vultures to head to Belém. Perched on the edge of the Tagus, the building's dramatic wave formation (designed by British architect Amanda Levete) battles for attention with the back-drop of the equally eye-catching 25 de Abril Bridge. The permanent and visiting exhibitions aren't too shabby, either. ✉ *Av. Brasília, Central Tejo, Belém* ☎ *21/002–8130* ⊕ *www.maat.pt/pt* 🎫 *From €5* ⊙ *Closed Tues.* Ⓜ *Tram 15E to Altinho.*

Museu Berardo
Housed in the minimalist Belém Cultural Center, the Museu Berardo is a showcase for one of Europe's most important private collections of modern art. Works from this treasure trove—which ranges from Picasso and Warhol to Portugal's own Paula Rego—are regularly rotated through the galleries, and there are also excellent visiting exhibitions. The complex has a restaurant and several cafés.
✉ *Praça do Império, Belém* ☎ *21/361–2400* ⊕ *en.museuberardo.pt* 🎫 *€5 (free on Sat.)* Ⓜ *Tram 15E to Centro Cultural Belém.*

GETTING HERE

Walking to Belém along the 5-mile, flat coastal path from Cais do Sodré via Alcântara is one way to arrive. Belém is also easy to reach by public transport. The 15 tram from the Baixa to Belém takes around 35 minutes but it's a fun, scenic ride. The main attractions can be explored on foot and there are fewer hills to navigate.

Museu de Marinha
One of Lisbon's oldest museums (it was founded in 1853), the large, navy-run Maritime Museum showcases the importance of the seafaring tradition in Portugal. With its thousands of maps and maritime codes, navigational equipment, full-size and model ships, uniforms, and weapons, the museum appeals to visitors young and old. ✉ *Praça do Império, Belém* ☎ *21/097–7388* ⊕ *museu.marinha.pt* 🎫 *€5* Ⓜ *Tram 15E to Mosteiro Jerónimos.*

Museu Nacional dos Coches (National Coach Museum)
In a former royal riding school with a gorgeous painted ceiling, the National Coach Museum has a dazzling collection of gloriously gilded horse-drawn carriages. The oldest on display was made for Philip II of Spain in the late 1500s; the most stunning are three conveyances created in Rome for King John V in 1716. The museum, Portugal's most visited, is right next door to the official residence of the president of the republic, whose **Museu da Presidência** tells

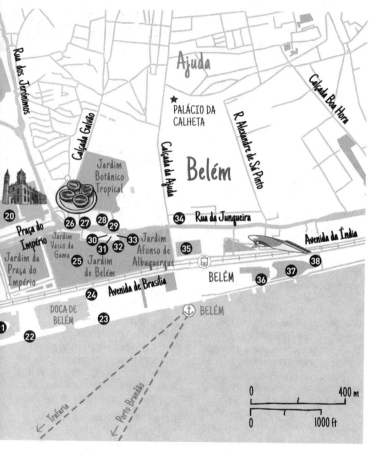

the story of the presidency, profiles the officeholders, and displays gifts they have received on state visits. The Coach Museum has moved across the road into a purpose-built structure designed by Brazilian Pritzker Prize winner Paulo Mendes da Rocha. ⊠ *Av. da Índia 136, Belém* ☎ *21/049–2400* ⊕ *www.museudoscoches.pt* 🎟 *€8* 🕓 *Closed Mon.* Ⓜ *Tram 15E to Altinho.*

Padrão dos Descobrimentos

The white, monolithic Monument of the Discoveries was erected in 1960 to commemorate the 500th anniversary of the death of Prince Henry the Navigator. It was built on what was the departure point for many voyages of discovery, including those of Vasco da Gama for India and—during Spain's occupation of Portugal—of the Spanish Armada for England in 1588. Henry is at the prow of the monument, facing the water; lined up behind him are the Portuguese explorers of Brazil and Asia, as well as other national heroes. On the ground adjacent to the monument, an inlaid map shows the extent of the explorations undertaken by the 15th- and 16th-century Portuguese sailors. Walk inside and take the elevator to the top for river views. ⊠ *Av. Brasília, Belém* ☎ *21/303–1950* ⊕ *www. padraodosdescobrimentos.pt* 🎟 *€5* 🕓 *Closed Mon. Sept.–Mar.* Ⓜ *Tram 15E to Mosteiro dos Jerónimos.*

Planetário Calouste Gulbenkian

Although it's looking a little run-down, the Calouste Gulbenkian Planetarium presents interesting astronomical films with various

themes several times a week. Headphones can be used to translate the presentations into English. A full program of events and screenings can be found on the website. ⊠ *Praça do Império, Belém* ☎ *21/362–0002* ⊕ *ccm.marinha.pt/pt/ planetario* 🎟 *€5* 🕓 *Closed Mon.*

Sala Thai Pavilion

Your eyes do not deceive you—there really is an ornate, gilded Thai pavilion beneath the jacaranda trees in Belém's Vasco da Gama Gardens. Built to celebrate 500 years of diplomatic relations between Thailand and Portugal, the structure was opened by Thai princess Maha Chakri Sirindhorn. Instagram opportunities abound. ⊠ *Jardim Vasco da Gama, Belém* ✛ *Next to* children's playground M Tram 15E to Mosteiro dos Jerónimos.

★ Torre de Belém

Another UNESCO World Heritage Site, the openwork balconies and domed turrets of the fanciful Belém Tower make it perhaps the country's purest Manueline structure. It was built between 1514 and 1520 on what was an island in the middle of the river Tagus, to defend the port entrance, and dedicated to St. Vincent, the patron saint of Lisbon. Today the chalk-white tower stands near the north bank—evidence of the river's changing course. Cross the wood gangway and walk inside to admire the cannons and descend to the former dungeons, before climbing the steep, narrow, winding staircase to the top of the tower for a bird's-eye view across the Tagus and over the city. ⊠ Av. Brasília, Belém ☎ 21/362–0034 ⊕ www. torrebelem.pt ⊠ €6 (free 1st Sun. of month) ☉ Closed Mon. M Tram 15E to Largo da Princesa.

 Shopping

Coisas do Arco do Vinho

Next to the Centro Cultural de Belém, Coisas do Arco do Vinho sells prize-winning wines. The owners, wine connoisseurs, can give you expert advice. ⊠ Rua Bartolomeu Dias, Lojas 7–8, Belém ☎ 21/364–2031 M Tram 15E to Centro Cultural Belém.

Galeria Arte Periférica

This gallery and arts store at the Centro Cultural de Belém is a good source of contemporary art, particu-

larly by emerging young talent. ⊠ Centro Cultural de Belém, Praça do Imperio , Loja 3, Belém ☎ 21/361–7100 ⊕ www.arteperiferica.pt M Tram 15E to Centro Cultural Belém.

MAAT Shop

Inside the cool confines of the Museum of Art, Architecture and Technology (MAAT), this small store sells contemporary artworks and art materials, as well as designer stationery, ceramics, and choco-lates from Portuguese chocolatier Arcádia. ⊠ MAAT, Av. Brasília, Central Tejo, Belém ☎ 21/002–8130 ⊠ maat@ edp.pt ☉ Closed Tues. M Tram 15E to Altinho.

★ Margarida Pimentel Jewellery

Accessories meet art at Margarida Pimentel. The Portuguese designer crafts gold and silver into incred-ible shapes for showstopping rings, bracelets, and necklaces. ⊠ Centro Cultural do Belém, Praça do Imperio, Belém ☎ 21/366–0034 M Tram 15E to Centro Cultural Belém.

☕ Coffee and Quick Bites

Café do Forte

$ | Portuguese. Take a seat on the terrace to catch the sun dip over the river Tagus as you sip a coffee, fresh fruit juice, or a cold beer. There are good pizzas, salads, and pastries, but it's the riverfront setting that's the draw here. **Known for:** spacious terrace close to Belém Tower; wine by the glass; tasty ice creams. Average main: €7 ⊠ Forte do Bom Successo, Av. Brasília, Belém ✛ Between Belém Tower and Fort

☎ 96/502–3819 ⊕ cafedoforte.com
Ⓜ Tram 15E to Largo da Princesa.

O Careca
$ | **Café.** Many a Lisboeta would argue that O Careca, which has been cooking up pastries since the 1950s, serves the best croissants in town. Try them for yourself at this simple-but-smart café—best enjoyed outside on the terrace with a coffee or pot of tea. **Known for:** delicious sweet and savory pastries; friendly service; casual vibe. *Average main:* €7 ⊠ Rua Duarte Pacheco Pereira, 11D, Restelo, Belém ☎ 21/301–0987 ⊗ Closed Tues. ▭ No credit cards Ⓜ Tram 15E to Pedrouços.

Pão Pão Queijo Queijo
$ | **Deli.** Pão Pão Queijo Queijo (Bread Bread Cheese Cheese) serves a huge variety of sandwiches, wraps, salads, and burgers, catering to everyone from staunch vegans to dedicated carnivores. **Known for:** excellent salads and falafels; fair prices; popularity with locals. *Average main:* €10 ⊠ Rua de Belém 126, Belém ☎ 21/362–6369 Ⓜ Tram 15E to Mosteiro dos Jerónimos.

★ Pasteis de Belém
$ | **Café.** This bakery-café specializes in pasteis de nata, delicious, warm custard pastries sprinkled with cinnamon and powdered sugar. Although the sweet treats are ubiquitous in Portugal, the version here is the most celebrated. **Known for:** the most famous custard tarts in Portugal; distinctive azulejo tiling; good espressos. *Average main:* €8 ⊠ Rua de Belém 84–92, Belém ☎ 21/363–7423 ⊕ www.pasteisde-belem.pt Ⓜ Tram 15E to Mosteiro Jerónimos.

Pasteis de Cerveja de Belém
$ | **Portuguese.** Belém's pasteis de nata may be the most famous custard tarts on the planet, but the specialty here are *pasteis de cerveja* (beer tarts), and they're surprisingly delicious. Wash one down with a coffee, or even a beer. They serve substantial lunches, too. **Known for:** the only homemade beer tarts in town; friendly service; simple, unpretentious decor. *Average main:*€12 ⊠ Rua de Belém 15, Belém ☎ 21/363–4338 Ⓜ Tram 15E to Mosteiro dos Jerónimos.

WORTH A TRIP

Jardim Botânico da Ajuda Portugal's oldest botanical garden—laid out in 1768 by the Italian botanist Domenico Vandelli (1735–1816)—is a relaxing place to spend an hour or so. You can stroll up here from the river at Belém, or take Tram 18 from the Cais do Sodré station (it terminates near here). Ornate fountains and meandering peacocks create a sense of splendor, and many species of flora, labeled in Latin, can be viewed in several greenhouses covering 4 acres.The larger Jardim Botânico Tropical at the bottom of the hill, whose entrance is just opposite the Mosterio dos Jerónimos, was created later and contains hundreds of species from the Azores, Madeira, and Portugal's former colonies. ⊠ Calçada da Ajuda, Ajuda ☎ 21/362–2503 ⊕ www.isa.ulisboa.pt/en/visitors/ajuda-botanical-garden ☑ €2.

Pastelaria Nau de Belém

$ | Café. It's certainly not the most famous pastry café in town, but Pastelaria Nau has quietly cultivated a reputation for deliciously sweet desserts and speedy, friendly service. The beer cakes are a treat and the custard tarts are arguably as good as the more famous ones from Pasteis de Belém. **Known for:** no lines; casual and friendly atmosphere; good coffee and cold beers. *Average main: €6 ⊠ Rua de Belém 29, Belém ☎ 21/362-1778 ⊟ No credit cards Ⓜ Tram 15E to Mosteiro dos Jerónimos.*

Queijadas de Belém

$ | Portuguese. The namesake tarts, *queijadas*, are supersweet cheese cakes, but this is also a good place to satisfy more substantial hunger, because it serves a mean lunch plate, too. Don't miss the grilled sardines when they're in season. **Known for:** good coffee and delicious pastries; affordable main meals; friendly service. *Average main: €11 ⊠ Rua de Belém 1, Belém ☎ 21/363-0034 Ⓜ Tram 15E to Mosteiro dos Jerónimos.*

🍴 Dining

Alecrim & Manjerona

$ | Portuguese. A combination café-deli-wine bar, Alecrim & Manjerona (Rosemary & Marjoram) is a quiet little spot with a purely Portuguese menu. From specialty sausages to sandwiches made from local goat cheeses, everything is sourced, and prepared, with love. **Known for:** mini grocery store selling Portuguese products; good vegetarian options; good, well-priced local wines. *Average main: €7 ⊠ Rua do Embaixador 123, Belém ☎ 21/362-0642 ⊘ Closed Sun. Ⓜ Tram 15E to Altinho.*

★ Espaço Espelho D'Agua

$$ | Fusion. A favorite with the fashion press, this multipurpose space on the banks of the river serves up fusion food, cocktails, and small plates to a stylish clientele. There's a vertical garden, a concert and exhibition space, and a café, as well as the main restaurant. **Known for:** terrace with river views; live music and cultural events; elegantly presented plates. *Average main:€17 ⊠ Edifício Espelho D'Agua, Av. Brasília, Belém ✥ Next to Padrao dos Descobrimentos ☎ 21/301-0510*

WORTH A TRIP

Estufa Real

Every Sunday starting at noon, a wonderful brunch buffet with lots of salads (€37 per person, half price for children under 11) is served inside the 18th-century "Royal Greenhouse" of the Ajuda Botanical Gardens. Surrounded by exotic trees and plants, you will be cordially welcomed with a glass of orange juice or sparkling wine on the house. ⊠ Jardim Botânico da Ajuda, Calçada do Galvão, Calçada do Galvão, Ajuda ☎ 21/361-9400 ⊕ www.estufareal.com ⊘ Closed Sat. No dinner.

⊕ www.espacoespelhodagua.com
Ⓜ Tram 15E to Centro Cultural Belém.

Feitoria

$$$$ | **Fusion.** Expect culinary wizardry at this Michelin-starred restaurant headed by one of Portugal's most acclaimed chefs, João Rodrigues. The casual-chic style applies to everything, from the interior of the restaurant to the staff's attire, and the dishes are presented with incredible flair. **Known for:** high-end gastronomy; river views; inventive vegetarian/ vegan options. *Average main: €26* ⊠ Hotel Altis Belém, Doca do Bom Successo, Belém ☎ 21/040-0208 Ⓜ Tram 15E to Centro Cultural Belém.

★ Nau de Restelo

$ | **Indian.** Fans of spicy food should head to this relaxed restaurant specializing in dishes from the former Portuguese colony of Goa. Goan cuisine mixes traditional Portuguese ingredients with Indian seasonings and cooking techniques, and diners can buy bags of spices to take home. **Known for:** delicious samosas; fiery curries; off-the-tourist-track location. *Average main: €15* ⊠ Rua de Pedrouços 1A, Belém ☎ 21/302-0675 ⊕ www.naudores-telo.com ⊗ Closed Sun. No dinner Mon.–Thurs. Ⓜ Tram 15E to Largo da Princesa.

Nikkei

$$$ | **Japanese Fusion.** A dressy crowd gathers at this ultramodern, dimly lit restaurant specializing in Japanese-Peruvian fusion food. Nikkei opened in 2018 and quickly attracted a fashionable crowd keen to sample the many varieties of ceviche, as well as *tiraditos* (a sashimi-shaped raw fish dish that blends Peruvian and Japanese culinary traditions). **Known for:** excellent sushi, sashimi, and ceviche; location close to Belém Tower; smaller crowds than at nearby restaurants. *Average main: €22* ⊠ Doca de Bom Successo, Belém ☎ 21/301-7118 ⊕ www.velalatina.pt/ Ⓜ Tram 15E to Largo da Princesa.

Nune's Real Marisqueira

$$ | **Seafood.** Crustaceans of every shape and size are the specialty at this relaxed beer hall–restaurant, but the steaks and the fish are also delicious. The atmosphere is relaxed, the chefs take their work seriously, and the restaurant attracts locals in droves. **Known for:** super fresh fish and seafood; ice-cold beers; lively atmosphere. *Average main: €20* ⊠ Rua Bartolomeu Dias 112, Belém ☎ 21/301-9899 ⊕ www.nunesmarisqueira.pt ⊗ Closed Mon. Ⓜ Tram 15E to Largo da Princesa.

Restaurante Belém 2-8

$$ | **Portuguese.** Even though it's located right at the heart of Belém's sightseeing action, this traditional Portuguese restaurant has avoided becoming a tourist trap. The space is light and airy and the relaxed café downstairs and formal dining room upstairs serve everything from pastries and *petiscos* (small plates) to full meals. **Known for:** well-prepared fish and seafood; welcoming atmosphere; popular location close to major sites. *Average main: €19* ⊠ Rua de Belém

WHO WAS HENRY THE NAVIGATOR?

Eternally looking out to sea from the prow of Belém's ship-shaped Monument to the Discoveries, Prince Henry the Navigator (1394–1460) was one of the originators of Portugal's Age of Discovery.

Henry was in fact neither a navigator nor a sailor but funded and organized great voyages. Born in Porto to John I of Portugal and Phillipa of Lancaster, Prince Henry reached adulthood at the end of a period of battle for Portuguese royalty, when the decimated nobility were beginning to look abroad for new sources of riches. Henry researched and funded journeys to lands previously unexplored by Europeans, establishing

a colony in Madeira and encouraging Portuguese sailors to explore uncharted territories beyond the west coast of Africa.

He also established at school for navigation in Sagres, southern Portugal, and it was from this region that many of his sailors' epic journeys began. History looks back less fondly on his involvement in founding the European slave trade: Henry funded Antao Goncalves's expedition to the African coast in 1441, in which he captured several African men and brought them back to Portugal, prompting a string of negotiations that led to Portugal's deep involvement in slavery and the slave trade.

2, Belém ☎ 21/363–9055 ⊕ www. restaurantebelem2a8.com ⊗ No dinner Mon. Ⓜ Tram 15E to Mosteiro dos Jerónimos.

Restaurante do Clube Naval de Lisboa

$ | Portuguese. On the banks of the Tagus and with a suitably nautical theme to the decor, this restaurant is owned by Lisbon's Naval Club and offers excellent fish, simply served. Floor-to-ceiling windows allow diners to enjoy the view when it's too cool for the terrace. **Known for:** fair prices; traditional Portuguese dishes; sunny terrace. *Average main:* €15 ⊠ Edifício do Clube Naval de Lisboa, Av. Brasília, Belém ☎ 21/363–6014 ⊗ Closed Tues. Ⓜ Tram 15E to Mosteiro dos Jerónimos.

 Bars and Nightlife

Bar 38°41

Perfectly mixed drinks and equally perfect views over the river entice chic Lisboetas to the terrace cocktail bar at the luxurious Altis Belém Hotel and Spa. It's open to nonguests, so get here well ahead of time if you want to bag a table at sunset. ⊠ Altis Belém Hotel and Spa, Doca de Bom Successo, Belém ☎ 21/040–0210 ⊕ www.altishotels. com Ⓜ Tram 15E to Centro Cultural Belém.

★ Enoteca de Belém

Wine buffs should seek out this hidden spot, tucked away on a little alleyway that houses gallery and exhibition spaces. Staff at the cozy wine bar can offer tasting sessions and advice on which wines to pair with the very good Portuguese dishes on the food menu. ⊠ *Travessa Marta Pinto 10, Belém* ☎ *21/363–1511* Ⓜ *Tram 15E to Mosteiro dos Jerónimos.*

Á Margem

The perfect place for a sundowner, Á Margem is a minimalist white cube of a bar-restaurant perched on the banks of the Tagus. The salads and small plates are good, too. ⊠ *Doca de Bom Successo, Av. Brasília, Belém* ☎ *91/862–0032* ⊕ *www.amargem.com* Ⓜ *Tram 15E to Centro Cultural Belém.*

Quiosque Belém

Sipping a drink at one of Lisbon's many outdoor kiosks is key to enjoying the city's fine views, and fine weather and Belém's own *quiosque*is perfect for sipping a sundown *ginjinha* (sour cherry liqueur) or a chilled white wine and enjoying the leafy location. ⊠ *Rua Vieira Portuense 1, Belém* ☎ *91/665–2660* Ⓜ *Linha de Cascais train to Belém.*

SUD Lisboa

A bar, restaurant, and swimming pool all enjoy gorgeous views at this super fancy, contemporary space. By day visitors can eat, drink, and swim; at night saxophonists play under the twinkling lights of the poolside bar. ⊠ *Pavilhão Poente, Av. Brasília, Belém* ✛ *Next to MAAT* ☎ *21/159–2700* ⊕ *www.sudlisboa.com* Ⓜ *Tram 15E to Altinho.*

Topo Belém

With two renowned rooftop bar–restaurants in Martim Moniz and Chiado, the team behind Topo snagged a third spot with killer views when it took over the roof terrace space at Belém Cultural Center. ⊠ *Centro Cultural de Belém, Praça do Império, Belém* ☎ *21/301–0524* Ⓜ *Tram 15E to Centro Cultural Belém.*

The View Rooftop

Live music, DJ sets, cocktails, and views over the river to Lisbon attract a hip young crowd to this lively hangout. The View Rooftop organizes summer boat parties—check its Facebook page for full listings. ⊠ *Rua de Alcolena 9–12, Restelo, Belém* ☎ *96/276–8434.*

★ Wine with a View

Grab a glass of good wine to go at this amply stocked mobile wine bar. Wine with a View's smart vintage cart has a near-permanent pitch in the gardens of Belém Tower. It peddles Portuguese wines of every style and hue, to be sipped from disposable wine glasses while sightseeing. ⊠ *Av. Brasília, Belém* ✛ *Easily visible in corner of gardens in front of tower* ☎ *93/931–5778* ⊕ *www.winewithaview.pt* Ⓜ *Tram 15E to Largo da Princesa.*

 Performing Arts

Terraço de Belém

One of several esplanade bar-restaurants in Belém, this one has a reputation for lively live music and dance events, from daytime jazz jamborees to all-night EDM dance-offs. ⊠ *Edifício Polo Náutico S/N , Av. Brasília, Belém* ☎ *21/404–0036* Ⓜ *Linha de Cascais train to Belém.*

GO FOR

Surprising
attractions

The Gulbenkian

Local
restaurants

AMEIXOEIRA

CHARNECA

LUMIAR

SANTA MARIA
DOS OLIVAIS

PARQUE
DAS
NAÇÕES

CARNIDE

SÃO DOMINGOS
DE BENFICA

AVENIDAS
NOVAS

MARVILA

BENFICA

CAMPOLIDE

BEATO

MARQUÊS DE POMPAL E
AVENIDA DA LIBERDADE

ARROIOS

SÃO JOÃO

PENHA DE
FRANÇA

SÃO
MAMEDE

ANJOS

INTENDENTE

SANTA
ENGRÁCIA

CAMPO DE
OURIQUE

PRINCIPE
REAL

MARTIM
MONIZ

GRAÇA

SÃO
VICENTE

ESTRELA

ROSSIO

MOURARIA

ALCÂNTARA

LAPA

BARRIO
ALTO

BAIXA

CHIADO

ALFAMA

RESTELO

AJUDA

CAIS DO
SODRE

SANTOS

BELÉM

Sightseeing ★★★☆☆ | Shopping ★☆☆☆☆ | Dining ★★★☆☆ | Nightlife ★☆☆☆☆

Farmland with a few mansions scattered around became a sprawling modern residential and business district in the early 20th century.

Long, broad avenues radiated from Marquês de Pombal Square and spread to the northern and eastern parts of city, at first lined with elegant buildings but later taken over by dull office and apartment blocks. People referred to them as the avenidas novas (new avenues), and that's what this district is officially called today. In the 1950s it was chosen as the site of the city's greatest museum (the Calouste Gulbenkian Museum), which is the main reason many tourists head to this part of town. While it may lack the soul of old Lisbon and doesn't have other major attractions besides the Gulbenkian, it's home to several large hotels, so it's also where many end up staying. Wider sidewalks and more pedestrian space created in 2016 have made the area much more inviting and led to the opening of new restaurants with outdoor seating and some kiosks serving light meals, like in the city's older neighborhoods.—*by Mario Fernandes*

....

⊙ Sights

Casa-Museu Anastácio Gonçalves
The former home of renowned 20th-century doctor and art collector Anastácio Gonçalves was turned into a museum in 1980 and houses around 3,000 of his most prized pieces. Those include paintings by major Portuguese artists like Columbano Bordalo Pinheiro and José Malhoa, ancient Chinese porcelain, and 19th-century furniture from around Europe. The building is an art nouveau mansion from 1904, which was just one of several in the neighborhood at the time. The others are now gone, leaving Gonçalves's home dwarfed by the tall office buildings and hotels that surround it. ⊠ *Av. 5 de Outubro 6–8, Lisbon* ☎ *21/354–0923* ⊙ *Closed Mon.* Ⓜ *Yellow Line to Picoas.*

Fonte Luminosa
This monumental fountain was built from 1938 to 1948, when World War II raged across Europe but Portugal remained a neutral, war-free country. It's called "luminous fountain" because of a light show that takes place daily after the sun sets, until 9 pm. The water falls from an upper platform to a large basin, but also only at set times— during the light show in the evening, and at lunchtime, between noon and 3. In the water are four sculptures of mermaids and another showing Triton on horseback. On either side of the monument are stairs that take you to a terrace at the top,

with views over the Avenidas Novas. ⊠ *Alameda D. Afonso Henriques, Lisbon* Ⓜ *Green or Red Line to Alameda*.

Galeria 111

This high-profile gallery is one of the few dating back to before the 1974 revolution, presenting some of the best contemporary Portuguese artists from the 1960s to today. You may find works by big names like Paula Reo and Vieira da Silva together with pieces by emerging artists. ⊠ *Campo Grande 113, Lisbon* ☎ *21/797-7418* ⊕ *www.111. pt* Ⓜ *Green or Yellow Line to Campo Grande*.

Igreja de São Sebastião

The only centuries-old attraction in this mostly modern neighborhood, this church was built in 1652 and is one of the few survivors of the Great Earthquake of 1755. It was surrounded by farmland but is now almost hidden by tall apartment and office buildings. Behind a plain exterior is typical Portuguese baroque decoration, with walls lined with 18th-century paintings and tile panels illustrating the life of St. Sebastian. The 17th-century giltwork of the main altar has been carefully restored and shines as you enter. ⊠ *Rua Tomás Ribeiro 64, Lisbon* Ⓜ *Blue or Red Line to São Sebastião*.

Jardim Zoológico

Families should set aside a full day to explore this deservedly popular and immaculately maintained zoo, which is home to more than 3,000 animals from more than 330

GETTING HERE

The Metro is the best way to reach Avenidas Novas. All four lines go through the district, but it's the Yellow Line that stops at the main avenues and squares. Unlike the other parts of the city, it does not have tram services, but Buses 736, 738, and 744 connect it to downtown and beyond.

species. The grounds are huge, but visitors can leap aboard a cable car to whiz from one attraction to another. Those who don't have a head for heights can board a miniature train (not included in entrance price) that trundles around the gardens. Highlights include a "Tigers' Valley," a gorilla house, a petting zoo, and twice-daily animal shows (you have your pick of those that feature parrots, pelicans, dolphins, sea lions, reptiles, or lemurs). There are several cafés on the grounds, as well as picnic areas for those who prefer a packed lunch. ⊠ *Praça Marechal Humberto Delgado, Sete Rios* ☎ *21/723-2900* ⊕ *www. zoo.pt* ⊠ *€22* Ⓜ *Blue Line to Jardim Zoológico*.

Museu Bordalo Pinheiro

Rafael Bordalo Pinheiro was the older brother of one of Portugal's greatest artists, Columbano, and was himself a prominent artist but much more multifaceted. Born in Lisbon in 1846, he excelled not just as a painter but above all as an outrageous caricaturist and ceramist. He satirized Portugal's political and social climate and put

great wit in everything he did. He invented the iconic peasant figure Zé Povinho, who had the habit of bluntly saying exactly what he thought and who came to be represented in newspaper cartoons and ceramics. At this museum, housed in the former home of a friend of the artist, there are drawings, paintings, and fantastically designed ceramics, often featuring animals and plants. There's also a library with some of Bordalo Pinheiro's original publications and a video explaining the art and times of the artist. ⊠ *Campo Grande 382, Lisbon* ☎ *21/581–8540* ⊕ *www.museubordalopinheiro.pt* ☽ *Closed Mon.* Ⓜ *Green or Yellow Line to Campo Grande.*

⭐ Museu Calouste Gulbenkian

Set in lovely gardens filled with leafy walkways, blooming flowers, and waddling ducks, the museum of the celebrated Calouste Gulbenkian Foundation houses treasures collected by Armenian oil magnate Calouste Gulbenkian. The collection is split in two: one part is devoted to Egyptian, Greek, Roman, Islamic, and Asian art, and the other to European acquisitions. The quality of the pieces is magnificent, and you should aim to spend at least two hours here. English-language notes are available throughout. Varied and interesting temporary exhibitions are also often staged in the Foundation's main building, and the summer months see live classical music performances on the grounds. A walk through the gardens leads to the foundation's Modern Collection: 9,000 pieces from the 20th and 21st centuries, including sculptures, paintings, and photography. Portuguese artists make up the bulk of the collection, along with some big-name international artists including British artist David Hockney and renowned sculptor Antony Gormley. ⊠ *Av. de Berna 45, Lisbon* ☎ *21/782–3000* ⊕ *gulbenkian.pt/en* ☒ *Museum (Founder's Collection plus Modern Collection), €10; temporary exhibitions vary (free Sun. from 2)* ☽ *Closed Tues.* Ⓜ *Blue Line to São Sebastião or Praça de Espanha.*

Palácio Pimenta–Museu de Lisboa

A palace built in the 1700s for a nun, who just so happened to be one of the king's mistresses, is now the main branch of the Lisbon Museum. The king spent summers at the palace, so a formal garden was laid out behind the building. There are peacocks roaming around, as well as a few ceramic animals created by the great 19th-century sculptor and satirist Rafael Bordalo Pinheiro. The museum houses a collection of archaeological finds, historic tile panels, paintings, and sculptures, all related to the history of Lisbon. A highlight is a model of the city, showing it as it was before it was laid to ruins in the 1755 earthquake. ⊠ *Campo Grande 245, Lisbon* ☎ *21/751–3200* ⊕ *www.museudelisboa.pt* ☽ *Closed Mon.* Ⓜ *Green or Yellow Line to Campo Grande.*

Praça de Touros do Campo Pequeno

Built in 1892, Lisbon's circular, redbrick, Moorish-style bullring is an eye-opening site. Encompassing esplanades and an underground mall, the ring holds about 9,000 people, who crowd in to watch Portuguese-style bullfights (in which the bull is never killed in the ring) in season (April–October). The arena is also used as a venue for concerts and other events. Tickets for all are sold from a booth in the new shopping mall under the building, which is open daily from 10 am to 11 pm. (On show nights only, the little ticket windows on either side of the bullring's main gate are also open.) There's also a small museum that describes the building and gives background into bullfighting in Lisbon. ⌂ *Campo Pequeno, Campo Pequeno* ☎ *21/799-8450 arena and show/bullfighting tickets, 21/799-8456 museum* ⊕ *www.campopequeno.com* 🎫 *Visit from €3, bullfights from €16* Ⓜ *Yellow Line to Campo Pequeno.*

Coffee and Quick Bites

Choupana Caffé

$ | **International.** It's always difficult to get a table at this café, as it's a favorite of young crowds who apparently crave its pancakes and pastries all day. By the entrance is a display of Portuguese and international gourmet products to take home. **Known for:** weekend brunch; organic yogurt; craft beer. *Average main: €10* ⌂ *Av. da República 25A,*

Avenida da República once rivaled Avenida da Liberdade as Lisbon's grandest avenue. It was also lined with monumental buildings but, sadly, most of those were demolished in the 1950s and '60s, and replaced with office and apartment blocks. It was also home to a few beautiful cafés, but of those only Versailles (Av. da República 15A, Avenidas Novas, Yellow or Red Line to Saldanha) survives.

Lisbon ☎ *21/357-0140* ⊕ *www.choupanacaffe.pt* Ⓜ *Yellow or Red Line to Saldanha.*

L'éclair

$ | **French Fusion.** No one could predict the success of this Portuguese-French pastry shop when it opened not far from the Calouste Gulbenkian Museum. In a city with so many traditional pastries, a menu dedicated exclusively to French éclairs and macarons certainly didn't seem to have great appeal. **Known for:** special salted éclairs served only at lunchtime; organic juices; international teas. *Average main: €5* ⌂ *Av. Duque de Ávila 44, Lisbon* ☎ *21/136-3877* ⊕ *www.l-eclair.pt* Ⓜ *Yellow or Red Line to Saldanha.*

Versailles

$ | Portuguese. Open since 1922, this is one of Lisbon's surviving grand cafés and arguably its most beautiful. Unlike the others, in Baixa and Chiado, it's still mostly a place for locals, who often meet here and stay chatting for hours over coffee. **Known for:** palatial, mirrored interior; variety of Portuguese pastries; lunch menus of traditional Portuguese food. *Average main: €6 ⊠ Av. da República 15A, Lisbon* ☎ *21/354–6340* Ⓜ *Yellow or Red Line to Saldanha.*

🍴 Dining

Ground Burger

$$ | American. Located next to the Calouste Gulbenkian Museum, this is largely considered Lisbon's best burger joint. It serves American-style burgers, and there's a new one on the menu every month, plus a vegetarian option. **Known for:** 100% Black Angus burgers; American-style milk shakes; craft beers. *Average main: €16 ⊠ Av. António Augusto de Aguiar 148A, Lisbon* ☎ *21/371–7171* ⊕ *www.groundburger. com* Ⓜ *Blue or Red Line to São Sebastião.*

Laurentina

$$ | Portuguese. In business since 1976, this is one of the top restaurants for traditional Portuguese food in the Avenidas Novas district. The plant-filled interior has been modernized, but the menu has been left largely untouched and includes a few Mozambican specialties (the restaurant's founder learned to cook in the former Portuguese colony). **Known for:** variety of cod dishes; good-value daily specials at lunchtime; long list of Portuguese wines. *Average main: €16 ⊠ Av. Conde Valbom 71A, Lisbon* ☎ *21/796–0260* ⊕ *www.restaurantelaurentina.com* Ⓜ *Blue or Red Line to São Sebastião.*

Lucca

$ | Italian. This restaurant's two dining rooms fill up quickly with local families who come for the traditional Italian pizzas. Located way off the beaten tourist path, it's worth a detour—it truly serves some of the best wood-fired pies in town. **Known for:** thin-crust pizzas; spicy pastas; Italian desserts. *Average main: €11 ⊠ Travessa Henrique Cardoso 19B, Lisbon* ☎ *21/797–2687* ⊕ *www.lucca.pt* Ⓜ *Green Line to Roma.*

Mercantina

$ | Italian. Shortly after opening, this restaurant was distinguished with the Associazione Verace Pizza Napoletana certificate, meaning the city of Naples certifies that the pizzas served here are real Neapolitan pizzas. The ingredients are imported directly from Naples and used not just in the pizzas but in all the Italian specialties. **Known for:** good-value lunch menus; cocktails; Italian desserts. *Average main: €12 ⊠ Praça de Alvalade 6B, Lisbon* ☎ *21/796–0313* ⊕ *www.mercantina.pt* Ⓜ *Green Line to Alvalade.*

O Prego da Peixaria

$ | Portuguese. When, unexpectedly, the *prego* (steak sandwich) became one of the most popular items at the trendy seafood restaurant Sea Me in Chiado, the owners decided to open a spot devoted exclusively to pregos and other traditional sandwiches. Some old standards are modernized with different flavors and combinations, including fish and vegetarian options. **Known for:** bolo de caco (traditional bread from Madeira); attractive industrial-style space; smoothies and all-natural juices. *Average main: €11* ⊠ *Av. Praia da Vitória 77B, Lisbon* ☎ *21/354–0360* ⊕ *www.opregodapeixaria.com* Ⓜ *Yellow or Red Line to Saldanha.*

O Talho

$$ | International. Chef Kiko has several restaurants in Lisbon, each with its own specialty, but this was his first. O Talho means "The Butcher Shop," and this elegant, meat-centric restaurant actually does double-duty as a working butcher shop. **Known for:** signature drinks; dry-aged meat; inventive, international dishes. *Average main: €20* ⊠ *Rua Carlos Testa 1B, Lisbon* ☎ *21/315–4105* Ⓜ *Blue or Red Line to São Sebastião.*

Paladar Zen

$ | Vegetarian. Located between the Calouste Gulbenkian Museum and the Campo Pequeno arena, this restaurant serves a vegetarian (largely vegan) fixed-priced buffet. Dishes change daily and there are always cold and hot options, labeled in Portuguese and English. **Known for:** good-value lunches; veggie sushi; vegan desserts. *Average main: €10* ⊠ *Av. Barbosa du Bocage 107, Lisbon* ☎ *21/795–0009* ⊙ *Closed Sun.* Ⓜ *Yellow or Red Line to Saldanha.*

Panorama

$$$$ | Portuguese. Located at the top of the Sheraton Lisboa Hotel, this restaurant offers bird's-eye views of Lisbon. A number of the city's top chefs had their start here before moving on to their own restaurants, and it has always been the place to try contemporary Portuguese cuisine that's mindful of the gastronomic traditions of Portugal's different regions. **Known for:** grilled fish and meat; good selection of international wines; cocktails. *Average main: €50* ⊠ *Sheraton Lisboa Hotel, Rua Latino Coelho 1, Lisbon* ☎ *21/312–0000* ⊕ *www.panorama-restaurante.com* ⊙ *No lunch Mon.–Sat.* Ⓜ *Yellow Line to Picoas.*

Psi

$ | Vegetarian. Blessed by the Dalai Lama on one of his visits to Lisbon, this is one of the city's oldest vegetarian restaurants. It's now mostly vegan but has maintained its Asian-inspired menus. **Known for:** seating in a covered Zen garden; sugar-free desserts; good selection of teas. *Average main: €11* ⊠ *Alameda Santo António dos Capuchos, Lisbon* ☎ *21/359–0573* ⊕ *www.restaurante-psi.com* ⊙ *Closed Sun.* Ⓜ *Blue Line to Avenida.*

⅄ Bars and Nightlife

Jupiter Lisboa Rooftop Bar

One of Lisbon's least-known rooftop bars, this one is located at the top of the Jupiter Lisboa Hotel, on one of the busiest avenidas of the Avenidas Novas. Open for drinks and light meals throughout the day, it attracts workers from the neighboring offices, who relax by the pool (which only guests of the hotel can dive into). ✉ *Jupiter Lisboa Hotel, Av. da República 46, Lisbon* ☎ *21/073–0104* Ⓜ *Yellow or Red Line to Saldanha.*

Old Vic

A decades-old secret, Old Vic is one of Lisbon's oldest and most beautiful bars, but it's hidden between apartment buildings and you have to ring a bell to get in. Red velvet booths and the low-lit, Victorian-inspired interior are conducive to sipping cocktails late into the night. ✉ *Travessa Henrique Cardoso 41, Lisbon* ☎ *91/407–6170* Ⓜ *Yellow Line to Entre Campos.*

12 | # South of the River

GO FOR

Great seafood

Incredible beaches

Under-the-radar experiences

LISBON
RIO TEJO
ALMADA
CACILHAS
TRAFARIA
CAPARICA
PRAGAL
COVA DA PIEDADE
COVA DO VAPOR
SOBREDA
FEIJÓ
LARANJEIRO
SEIXAL
COSTA DA CAPARICA
CHARNECA DE CAPARICA
CORROIOS
AMORA
ARRENTELA
ALDEIA DE PAIO PIRES
FERNÃO FERRO
QUINTA DO CONDE
LAGOA DE ALBUFEIRA
SESIMBRA (CASTELO)
SÃO LOURENÇO
MECO
AZEITÃO
ARRÁBIDA
SESIMBRA (SANTIAGO)

Sightseeing ★★★★★ | Shopping ★★☆☆☆ | Dining ★★★★★ | Nightlife ★★★☆☆

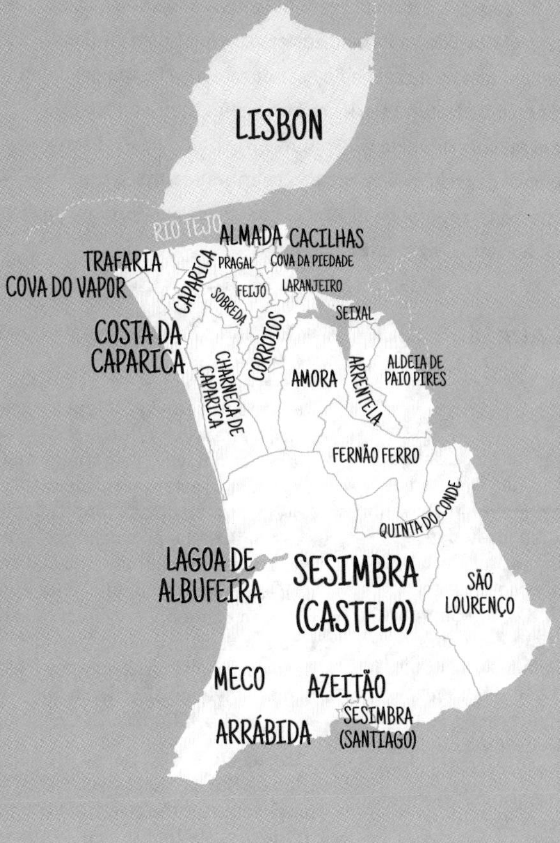

L isbon's secret is well and truly out, but it's still possible to dodge the crowds if you make the short hop across the river Tagus. A short ferry ride from downtown Lisbon, colorful Cacilhas is increasingly enticing Lisboeta night owls, while the views and handsome old buildings of Almada Velha offer a wealth of photo-snapping opportunities. Local foodies like to make the similarly short ferry hop from Belém to Trafaria, a fishing town known for its superior seafood. From here it's a short Uber ride to the fishing village of Cova do Vapor and surfer hangout Costa da Caparica. A little farther afield and best reached by car or motorcycle, the secluded beaches of the Arrábida Natural Park are famous for their crystal-clear turquoise waters and proximity to wild nature. The pretty beach town of Sesimbra is an easy day trip by bus and has calm waters that are perfect for swimming, as well as a reputation as one of best places in Portugal for fish and seafood restaurants.—*by Lucy Bryson*

Cacilhas & Almada Velha

 Sights

★ Cristo Rei

Lisbon's answer to Rio de Janeiro's Christ the Redeemer sits atop a giant concrete plinth high above the Tagus. It was inaugurated in 1959 as a mark of thanks for Portugal's safety during the violence of World War II. Today, the Santuário Nacional do Cristo Rei is an important religious site, but most casual visitors come here primarily for the spectacular views from the 262-foot-high viewing platform, which is reached by elevator. The peaceful, scenic grounds are free to visit. ⊠ *Praceta do Cristo Rei 27A, Almada* ☎ *21/275–1000* 💰 *€6.*

★ Elevador Panorâmico da Boca do Vento

This eye-catching elevator is a fun, free, and extremely photogenic way to travel between Almada Velha and the riverfront, with its gardens and noteworthy restaurants. Enjoy the views from the glass-fronted cabin as you make the ascent or descent. The lift was inaugurated in 2000 and its design is something of a fusion between contemporary minimalism, traditional azulejo tiling, and art deco curves. It runs every day from 8 am to midnight. ⊠ *Rua do Ginjal 72, Almada* ☎ *22/031–5755* 💰 *€1.*

Olho de Boi

Olho de Boi, or Bull's Eye, is the local name for the riverfront area at the foot of Almada's Panoramic Elevator. The views over the 25 de Abril suspension bridge and across the shimmering river to Lisbon are incredible. Stroll through the pleasant green space at Jardim do Rio and past a rather ramshackle collection of warehouses to reach the area's Naval Museum in one direction and the famous Ponto Final riverfront restaurant in the other. Watch your step after dark. ⊠ *Olho de Boi, Rua do Gingal, Almada.*

 Shopping

★ Casa da Avó Berta
Grandma Berta's House is as welcoming and cozy as the name suggests, and it's packed full of retro-chic Portuguese products that make lovely souvenirs or gifts. From beautifully packaged soaps and ceramic sardines to handcrafted jewelry and gourmet treats, this fragrant store appeals to browsers and serious shoppers alike. You can even sink into a comfy chair for coffee and cake. ⊠ *Rua Cândido dos Reis 51A, Almada* ☎ *21/ 596–3696.*

Mama Flores
Locally produced arts and crafts jostle for shelf space with fresh flowers and potted plants at this colorful little shop and gallery on Cacilhas's main strip. The friendly Spanish owner is an enthusiastic source of local information. ⊠ *Rua Cmte. António Feio 9, Cacilhas* ☎ *21/096–5691* ☾ *Closed Mon.*

Petisco da Lata Loja Gourmet
The Portuguese have turned canned fish into an art form, and this shop-café has a huge range of tinned tuna and sardines, all beautifully packaged. The tinned fish appear

GETTING HERE

Take the 10-minute passenger ferry from Cais do Sodré to Cacilhas (departures roughly every 20 minutes, 5 am–1 am), and there is a connecting bus (203) from Cacilhas to Sesimbra and Caparica. Ferries between Belém and Trafaria are a little less regular and take around 20 minutes (6 am–9 pm). Trains, buses, and cars cross the 25 de Abril suspension bridge or the sweeping Ponte Vasco da Gama. Drivers should expect to pay a couple of euros in tolls on either bridge. Regular buses leave from the Transportes Sul do Tejo (TST) terminal in Praça da Espanha for Sesimbra, calling at Alcântara Terra before crossing the river. There are also regular TST services between Alcântara Terra and Costa da Caparica.

in various guises at the in-store café, so shoppers can try before they buy. There's a good range of wines and Portuguese spirits, too, which can be bought by the bottle to go or sipped in the café. ⊠ *Rua da Judiaria 22A, Almada* ☎ *91/755–9953* ⊕ *petisco-da-lata.business.site* ☾ *Closed Mon.*

Retro Queen
Lisbon's vintage junkies often make the hop across the river to browse the racks at this small but well-stocked store. Although the name may suggest otherwise, there's a good range of vintage menswear in addition to some killer dresses, handbags, and jewelry. ⊠ *Rua Cândido dos Reis 60A, Cacilhas* ☎ *96/421–8591.*

☕ Coffee and Quick Bites

Cervejaria a Madrugada
$ | Portuguese. The crowds that pack the esplanade at this simple snack bar are testament to its status as a solid *bom e barato* (good and cheap) choice. Grab a *bifana* (roast pork sandwich) or a cheese salad and wash it down with strong coffee or a glass of local wine. **Known for:** plates of seasonal, summertime snails; simple, well-made Portuguese snacks; tapas-style plates of cheeses and cured meats. *Average main: €5 ⊠ Rua Cândido dos Reis 120, Almada ▭ No credit cards.*

★ Chá de Histórias
$$ | Café. This is a retro-chic spot for tea and cakes or cocktails and *petiscos* (small plates). The kitsch collectibles and bottle-filled cabinets make the space feel like being at someone's grandparents' house, and the board games and comic books add to the charm. **Known for:** delicious homemade cakes; toasted sandwiches with huge variety of fillings; weekend DJ sessions. *Average main: €6 ⊠ Rua Cândido dos Reis 129, Cacilhas ☎ 21/274-4084 ⊙ No lunch.*

Dá Cá Cilhas
$ | Café. This bright red kiosk directly in front of the ferry terminal is hard to miss, and there are few better spots for a quick coffee, beer, or *ginjinha* (sour cherry liqueur) while waiting for a boat. There are bikes for hire, and although the food offer is limited, toasted sandwiches, nuts, and potato chips will keep hunger pangs at bay while you soak up the sun. **Known for:** cheap coffee and beer; location in the middle of Cacilhas's main square; friendly staff. *Average main: €4 ⊠ Largo Alfredo Diniz Cacilhas, Cacilhas ☎ 96/570-3579.*

GETTING HERE

Thanks to soaring prices in the city, Lisboetas are increasingly making the quick and easy ferry trip across the river for a night out in Cacilhas and Almada Velha. Ferries run roughly every 20 minutes, 5 am–1 am, between Cacilhas and the transport hub at Cais do Sodré, and it's just a few minutes' walk to the main bar and restaurant strip. Almada's old town is also within walking distance. It's a slightly rough walk along the sea edge to famed waterside restaurants like Ponto Final, or take the free tram from Almada Old Town to the riverfront.

🍴 Dining

Cabrinha
$$ | Portuguese. The largest of Cacilhas's many *marisqueiras* (traditional seafood restaurants), Cabrinha has been doing a roaring business among locals and out-of-towners for over 40 years. Crustaceans of all shapes and sizes are priced by weight, while steaks, grilled fish, and the famous seafood stew will satisfy a hearty appetite without blowing the budget. **Known for:** brisk, friendly service; lobster and giant prawns; seafood rice. *Average main: €19 ⊠ Beco Bom*

Sucesso 4, Cacilhas ☎ *21/ 272–2240* ⊕ *www.cabrinha.com.pt.*

Estaminé 1955

$ | **Fast Food.** The burgers at this modern café are all proudly Portuguese, whether they're made from lamb, beef, chicken, or chickpeas and vegetables. The patties, cheese toppings, and bread buns are locally sourced and Lusitano in flavor, and there's a wide range of cocktails (both boozy and saintly) to choose from. **Known for:** several types of vegetarian burger; excellent sangria and cocktails; inventive menu. *Average main: €9* ✉ *Rua Cândido dos Reis 130A, Cacilhas* ☎ *21/297–0370* ⊕ *estamine1955.pt.*

O Farol

$$ | **Portuguese.** The oldest *cervejaria* (relaxed dining and drinking spot) in the region, O Farol has been serving cold beer, rich seafood stews, and delicious shellfish since 1890. The brightly lit space feels more functional than fashionable, but the crowds eating here are a testament to the outstanding seafood, and the sunset views over the river to Lisbon are magical. **Known for:** grilled fish and shrimp; efficient, friendly service; excellent location just steps from ferry terminal. *Average main: €20* ✉ *Largo Alfredo Dinis 1, Cacilhas* ☎ *21 /276–5248* ⊕ *restaurantefarol.com.*

★ Mafia das Pizzas

$ | **Italian.** Napoli's organized crime gangs are mercifully absent from this trendy joint, but the superfine, slightly blackened, wood-fired pizza crust calls to mind the Italian city's famously excellent pies. For a local flavor, top with Portuguese *alheira* sausage and wash it down with a jug of the famous sangria. **Known for:** youthful clientele; modern decor; imported Italian pizza flour for super authentic crust. *Average main: €12* ✉ *Rua Cândido dos Reis 81, Cacilhas* ☎ *21/274–0774* ⊘ *Closed Mon. No lunch Tues.–Fri.*

Maui Poké & Sushi House

$ | **Modern Hawaiian.** Hawaiian-style *poké* (diced raw fish) bowls are the stars of the show at this funky little restaurant, which also has a nice line of colorful cocktails. The sushi, ceviche, and sashimi are spot on, there are plenty of vegetarian and vegan options, and the *rodizio* (all you can eat) option is a good value. **Known for:** cheery staff; modern decor blending Japanese, Hawaiian, and Portuguese styles; pleasant terrace. *Average main: €14* ✉ *Rua Cândido dos Reis 55B, Cacilhas* ☎ *97/757–1012* ⊘ *Closed Tues.*

Tasca do Paulinho

$ | **Portuguese.** Petiscos and people-watching are the order of the day at this informal hangout on Cacilhas's pedestrian main drag. Paulinho is a modern take on the traditional Portuguese *tasca* (tavern), with a funky tiled interior. **Known for:** good, affordable wine by the glass; pleasant terrace; steaks, hamburgers, and small plates. *Average main: €9* ✉ *Rua Cândido dos Reis 96, Cacilhas* ☎ *21/ 259–1449* ⊘ *Closed Tues.*

Veg-e-Tal

$ | Vegetarian. Vegans and vegetarians no longer need to go hungry in fish-focused Almada, as the ongoing gentrification of the old town has brought with it a new type of diner. Veg-e-Tal serves vegetarian set lunches, always with vegan and gluten-free options, alongside tasty cakes and very well-priced wines by the glass. **Known for:** children's menu; good coffee and cakes; pleasant terrace and good location in Almada's old town. *Average main: €7* ✉ *Avenida Dom Afonso Henriques 8A, Almada* ☎ *21/274-5784* ⊕ *www. vegetal.pt* ⊘ *Closed Sun.*

☚ Bars and Nightlife

Birraria Beer & Gin

Tapping into trendy Lisboetas' fondness for gin and craft beers, Birraria is one of several bars tempting city folk across the river for a night out. The centuries-old building has been jazzed up with colorful artworks, but in warmer weather it's all about enjoying the mingling opportunities provided by the outdoor tables and chairs on this lively car-free strip. ✉ *Rua Cândido dos Reis 140, Cacilhas* ☎ *21/274-5938.*

Boca do Vento Bar & Tapas

There's a decent range of gin-based cocktails and light meals at Boca do Vento (Mouth of the Wind), but the views are the real stars of the show. Perched high above the river Tagus, at the entrance to the elevator that zips people between Almada Velha and the riverfront, it's a spectacular place for sunset drinks on the terrace. ✉ *Largo da Boca do Vento, Almada* ☎ *91/440-6981.*

Boteco 47

A bright and breezy spot with a nice line of cocktails and petiscos , Boteco 47 is another of the Cacilhas bars that buzzes with Lisboetas after dark. Order a bottle of wine and some small plates to share, pull up a seat outside, and watch the party unfold after dark. ✉ *Rua Cândido dos Reis 47, Cacilhas.*

A Piratta

Embrace your inner pirate and order a rum cocktail at one of the liveliest bars on Cacilhas's main drag. With a nautically themed interior and staff in full pirate regalia, A Piratta isn't aiming to be chic, but fun is definitely to be had after dark on the weekends. ✉ *Rua Cândido dos Reis 16, Cacilhas.*

☚ Performing Arts

★ Casa da Cerca

A contemporary art museum and live music venue set in a beautiful 18th-century building and surrounded by immaculately maintained grounds, Casa da Cerca more than merits the quick trip across the river. Permanent and visiting exhibitions and installations will appeal to art lovers, and a café-bar with incredible views across the Tagus and the 25 de Abril Bridge adds considerably to the appeal. From March to September, the Há Música na Casa da Cerca program hosts weekly, free live music ranging from jazz and blues to fado. ✉ *Rua Cerca*

SURREAL SIGHTSEEING

Overlooking the ocean in the middle of the Serra da Arrábida, graffiti-covered giant cannons stand poised for battle, artillery stores sit gathering rust, and spiders scuttle through enormous underground bunkers that were once the sleeping quarters of Portuguese soldiers. It's a truly surreal sight in the middle of this tranquil nature reserve. Built just after World War II, the abandoned barracks of the 7ª Bataria do Outão, tucked away just off the 25 de Abril highway through the hills, are open to explorers. With the backdrop of mountains and the ocean, this is a spectacular photo opportunity. A 10-minute walk from Portinho da Arrábida Beach, a hidden trail leads to a 200-step descent and the Lapa da Santa Margarida, a chapel and shrine in a natural cave that is filled with flowers, statues, and other offerings from religious visitors. Less hidden, but no less spectacular, is the enormous pilgrims' sanctuary at Cabo Espichel, a barren cliff on the very edge of Europe. The views of the church and the abandoned pilgrims' quarters, stark against the ocean backdrop, are well worth a visit. While it's possible to go it alone, difficult access means exploring Arrábida Natural Park is easiest with a guide. Daniel Coelho, who runs jeep, Vespa, and sidecar tours of the area with Bike My Side (⊕ www.bikemyside.com), says, "Lisbon's sights are packed with visitors, but south of the river there are some really intriguing attractions and no crowds at all."

2, Almada ☎ 21/272-4950 ⊕ www.m-almada.pt.

★ Cine Incrível

The colorful art deco building is reason enough to visit this cinema-turned-arts-venue, which was the first place in town to show films when it opened its doors in 1926 under the grand-sounding moniker Cinema da Sociedade Filarmónica Incrivel Almadense (Cinema of the Incredible Almadense Philharmonic Society). Today, cool kids sip drinks at the bar, nod appreciatively at poetry readings, and move to the sound of live music. It's closed Sunday–Wednesday. ⊠ Rua Capitão Leitão 1, Almada ☎ 93/207-2937 ⊕ cineincrivel.pt.

SFIA Almadense

The Sociedade Filarmónica Incrível Almadense has been entertaining Almada locals since 1848 and continues to put on a diverse array of music and arts events. Brass bands, vocal choirs, and classical performances draw large crowds, as do the photographic exhibitions and theater performances (in Portuguese, but there are some entertaining performances for young children). ⊠ Rua Capitão Leitão 3, Almada ☎ 21/275-0929 ⊕ incrivelalmadense.pt.

Costa da Caparica, Trafaria & Cova do Vapor

👁 Sights

Costa da Caparica Beach

When Lisboetas want to go to the beach, more often than not their preferred spot is the Costa da Caparica, which is packed in summer. Formerly a fishing village, the town itself is rather lacking in charm these days, but the beachfront is lively with surf schools, cafés, and bars catering to a relaxed, sandy-footed clientele. You may be able to avoid the crowds by heading south toward the less accessible dunes and coves at the end of the peninsula. Each beach is different: the areas nearest Caparica are family oriented, whereas the more southerly ones tend to attract a younger crowd (there are some nudist beaches, too). The Mélia Aldeia dos Capuchos Hotel offers some seclusion without being too far from the action. Beach erosion is a problem in winter (March through October is the best time to visit). **Amenities:** food and drink; lifeguards; parking (fee); showers; toilets; water sports. **Best for:** partiers; sunset; swimming; walking. ⊠ *Costa da Caparica*.

⭐ **Praia da Cova do Vapor**

Still under the radar even among locals, Cova do Vapor is a fishing hamlet perched at the point where the river Tagus meets the Atlantic Ocean. The soft-sand beach is Caparica's closest point to Lisbon, and there are glorious views over

GETTING HERE

Bus 161 to Caparica leaves every 15-20 minutes from the TST stand near Alcântara Terra railway station between 9 am and 6 pm. The Costa da Caparica stretches for 18 miles and is roughly divided into beaches popular with families, partiers, surfers, etc., but visitors are essentially welcome to lay their towel wherever they choose. A fun hop-on, hop-off beach train travels much of the coast during the summer high season, but a car is needed to reach farther-flung beaches. Trafaria, a riverfront fishing town famed for its seafood restaurants, can be reached by 20-minute ferry ride from Belém between 6 am and 9 pm, and it's a short cab ride or half-hour walk from there to the colorful fishing village of Cova do Vapor, where the beautiful white sands mark the beginning of Costa da Caparica.

the city's domes and towers, but its rustic beach shacks and hand-constructed wooden playground make Cova do Vapor Beach feel like another world. While crowds of surfers pack out most of the Costa , there are still vast swaths of space on the sands and gentle dunes here. **Amenities:** food and drink; parking (no fee). **Best for:** solitude; swimming; walking. ⊠ *Praia da Cova do Vapor*.

☕ Coffee and Quick Bites

Choco Frrito Orriginal
$ | **Portuguese.** *Choco frito* (breaded and fried cuttlefish) is a south-of-the-Tagus staple and a dish that tends to divide opinion among foreign visitors. Unusual spelling aside, there are few better places to try the dish than this funky little kiosk on the beach, where it comes freshly made and served in small, medium, and large portions. **Known for:** family-friendly seating on the beach; delicious French fries and hot sauce; lively atmosphere with sunset DJ sets. *Average main: €9* ⊠ *Praia da Saúde, Costa da Caparica* ✛ *Next to Bar do Golfinho* ☎ *21/387–5839* ⊙ *Closed Nov.–Mar.* ⊟ *No credit cards.*

Koa
$ | **Eclectic.** A healthy newcomer, Koa has become a favorite with surfers, yogis, and party people alike thanks to its energy-boosting all-day brunch menus. The perfectly plated granola bowls, colorful fruit salads, and frothy cappuccinos look as good as they taste, making the menu here a big hit with the Instagram set. **Known for:** vegetarian, vegan, and gluten-free options; young, trendy clientele; delicious fresh juices and strong coffee. *Average main: €10* ⊠ *Rua João Inácio 22B, Costa da Caparica* ☎ *21/193–4795* ⊙ *Closed Mon. and Tues.*

🍴 Dining

Borda D' Água
$$ | **Eclectic.** Whether you drive to Praia Morena or catch the small train at Caparica, stop at this restaurant—a glassed-in wooden cabana built in the sand dunes. The laid-back beach vibe is enticing, with colorful pillows, hammocks, and weathered wooden tables, and a caipirinha will add to the holiday vibe as you study the menu of suitably unpretentious fare such as salads, sweet crepes, and hamburgers, as well as daily fish specials, served with boiled potatoes and vegetables. **Known for:** caipirinhas; relaxed vibe; vegetarian and vegan dishes. *Average main: €18* ⊠ *Praia da Morena, Costa da Caparica* ☎ *212/975213* ⊕ *www.bordadagua.com.pt* ⊙ *Closed Dec.–mid-Jan.*

Princesa
$$ | **Seafood.** Charge your camera: this is one of the most picturesque spots for a meal anywhere in the region. A vast outdoor space is filled with sunloungers and comfy chairs, so you can relax with a sangria and enjoy views across Fonte de Telha Beach as you browse the menu of simple-yet-tasty salads, seafood, and grilled fish. **Known for:** good caipirinhas; spectacular sunset views; family-friendly ambience. *Average main: €17* ⊠ *Estrada das Praias, Costa da Caparica* ☎ *21/154–1242* ⊙ *No dinner Oct.–May.*

Retiro do Pescador
This simple, homey beach shack serves freshly caught fish and seafood to a relaxed clientele. It's

one of few beachfront spots to open year-round (bundle up from October to May, as things get chilly after sunset). ⊠ *Av. 1º de Maio 242, Costa da Caparica* ☎ *21/296–2725.*

★ Sentido do Mar

$$ | **Asian Fusion.** This highly regarded sushi spot has sea views, speedy service, and a bright, modern interior with lots of colorful mosaics. Grab a table on the esplanade to dine with the sea breeze in your hair and magical sunsets over the crashing waves just steps away. **Known for:** super fresh fish; excellent sushi and ceviche; tasty cocktails. *Average main: €18* ⊠ *Rua Muralha da Praia 7, Praia do Norte, Costa da Caparica* ☎ *21/290–0473.*

O Xéxéxé

$ | **Portuguese.** A haven for vegetarians and vegans amid a sea of fish restaurants, O Xéxéxé is a cozy bistro serving delicious meat-free meals as well as home-baked pies and pastries. With creative use of fresh, seasonal ingredients, there are several choices of set meals each day. **Known for:** gluten-free options; enthusiastic and helpful staff; colorful and creative salads. *Average main: €10* ⊠ *Rua Grupo Desportivo dos Pescadores 1, Costa da Caparica* ☎ *21/243–5031* ⊙ *Closed Mon. and Tues. No dinner Sun.*

Bars and Nightlife

Bambu Bar

Make like the locals and duck inside this simple, unpretentious beach bar to escape the chilly sea breezes

in cooler weather, or sip a glass of local wine with a gorgeous beach view during the summer. The food is a little underwhelming, but the beach backdrop, friendly service, and lively local vibe more than make up for it. ⊠ *Rua de São Martinho 348, Fonte da Telha, Costa da Caparica* ☎ *91/680–0055.*

Leblon

Named for Rio de Janeiro's most upmarket beach neighborhood, Leblon attracts the same type of well-groomed beachgoer as its Brazilian namesake. Young, fashionable folk in expensive swimwear come here for tasty post-swim petiscos and strong caipirinhas, with things getting very busy on the weekends. Open until late during the summer, it's day drinking only from October to May. ⊠ *Praia Das Palmeiras, Costa da Caparica* ☎ *96/423–0203.*

Waikiki

Steps from the water at the popular Praia da Sereia, Waikiki is the place to come for late-night summer beach parties, or for daytime drinking and sunbathing during the warm spring months. There are sandwiches, salads, and fruit smoothies on the food menu, which could come in handy after one of the bar's summer surf classes. Like many Costa da Caparica beach bars, it's closed October through March. ⊠ *Praia da Sereia, Costa da Caparica* ☎ *21/296–2129* ⊕ *www.waikiki.com.pt.*

Sesimbra and Arrábida

 Sights

Praia da California

Sesimbra's beachfront stretches the entire length of the historic downtown area, divided in the middle by a whitewashed fort jutting out to sea. The eastern side, known as Praia da California, is rocky at the far end, with some currents and small waves. During the summer it's packed with sunloungers, pedal boats, and splashing families but it's blissfully quiet from mid-October through June. **Amenities:** food and drink; lifeguards (summer); showers (summer); toilets (summer). **Best for:** snorkeling; swimming; walking. ⊠ *Rua Heliodoro Salgado 2C, Sesimbra.*

GETTING HERE

Buses run roughly once an hour from the TST bus terminal at Praça da Espanha and Sesimbra, also calling at Alcântara. The 207 bus takes around 45 minutes; avoid the 260 bus because it takes a long, slow route around the outskirts of Almada. Buses are slightly more frequent in the summer (be sure to double-check the timetable), but there are no buses in either direction after 9 pm. Another option is to take the ferry from Cais do Sodré to Cacilhas, where the 203 bus runs out to Sesimbra (the last bus is at 10:30 pm from Cacilhas and 8:30 pm from Sesimbra). Exploring Arrábida requires a car or an organized day trip, as there are very few public transport options.

★ Praia de Galapinhos

Frequently cited as one of the most beautiful beaches in Portugal, Galapinhos has such white sand and crystalline water that it appears almost Caribbean. Surrounded by the wild nature of Arrábida's hills (wild boar have been spotted taking a dip here during the heat of summer), it's best visited outside the July–September summer season, when things get busy and access to vehicles is restricted. There's parking nearby for the rest of the year, but you'll need to follow a rough path to reach the beach itself. **Amenities:** food and drink (summer). **Best for:** snorkeling; solitude; swimming; walking. ⊠ *Praia dos Galapinhos, Sesimbra.*

★ Praia do Ouro

Calm and clear water, a workout station, and a diving platform make the western stretch of Sesimbra Beach a favorite with families and athletic young folk. Boats docking here in the summer whisk beach-hoppers off to hard-to-reach strands, but with the pine-covered hills stretching right down to the sand and a café-bar doing a brisk trade in wine, ice cream, and seafood, there's plenty of reason to stay put. The beach has wheelchairs and an access point during the July–September high season and has won national awards for accessibility. **Amenities:** food and drink; lifeguards (summer); parking (fee); showers; toilets (summer). **Best for:** snorkeling; swimming. ⊠ *Avenida dos Náufragos 20, Sesimbra.*

Praia do Portinho da Arrábida

One of the most celebrated of the famous Arrábida beaches, Portinho (as it's known locally), is an absurdly photogenic crescent of golden sand and turquoise waters, flanked on all sides by pine-covered hills. There's no public transport, and a high-season car ban makes access tough throughout July and August, but it's a joy to visit at any other time of year. There are several decent seafood restaurants right behind the beach. **Amenities:** food and drink. **Best for:** snorkeling; swimming; walking. ⊠ *Praia do Portinho da Arrábida, Sesimbra.*

Praia do Ribeiro do Cavalo

Dubbed "the most Thai beach in Portugal," the wild, hard-to-reach Ribeiro do Cavalo has dazzling white sands and crystal-clear water in several shades of turquoise. Curiously formed rocks jutting out of the water are encircled by all manner of colorful fish, so bring your snorkel gear. Until recently a genuine hidden treasure, the beach is now well known among beach lovers. During the summer, regular boat services speed sunseekers to and from the beach and Praia do Ouro in Sesimbra (a 5–10-minute ride), but for the rest of the year it can only be reached by private boat, kayak, or by a half-hour walk/scramble along a very rough track. Look out for the purple markings on the rocks that indicate which way to go. **Amenities:** none. **Best for:** snorkeling; swimming. ⊠ *Praia do Ribeiro do Cavalo, Sesimbra* ✛ *Follow the main road from Sesimbra, west past Praia do Ouro. Drive or walk and keep a close eye out for the sign for the beach. From here it's a steep clamber downhill. Wear sneakers (not flip-flops) and watch your step.*

☕ Coffee and Quick Bites

Fini

$ | Café. There's no shortage of places to eat ice cream in Sesimbra, but Fini serves superior Italian scoops and has a sunny patio over-looking the sea. Flavors vary from day to day (the banana and peanut butter, when available, is particu-larly delicious), there's a huge range of toppings, and there's good coffee, too. **Known for:** fresh, contemporary decor; huge range of fresh fruit and nut toppings; jars of ice cream to go. *Average main: €5 ⊠ Avenida dos Náufragos 15, Sesimbra ☎ 91/380–5885 ⊕ fini.pt ⊘ Closed Tues.*

★ Galé
$ | Seafood. A short flight of steps up from the beachfront road leads to this friendly café-bar, which has a wonderful vantage point over the sea. The seafood, toasted sand-wiches, and house white wine are all good, but the main attraction is the sheltered terrace, which allows drinkers and diners to gaze out to the ocean even on rainy days. **Known for:** very friendly family owners; good shellfish; popularity with locals. *Average main: €13 ⊠ Rua Capitão Leitão 7, Sesimbra ☎ 21/223–3170 ⊘ Closed Tues. ⊟ No credit cards.*

🍴 Dining

★ Tasca do Isaias
$ | Seafood. The huge queues that form outside this tiny, family-run tavern are a testament to the fact that the fish served here is the best in town. The daily catch is written on a blackboard and cooked to perfec-tion on a charcoal grill out on the flagstones. **Known for:** family-run business; lively local atmosphere; long queues and shared tables if it's busy. *Average main: €12 ⊠ Rua Coronel Barreto 2, Sesimbra ☎ 91/457–4373 ⊘ Closed Sun. ⊟ No credit cards.*

WORTH A TRIP

The historic town of Azeitão is famous for its culinary and boozy treats as well as its dramatic hillside setting. Increasingly popular with wine lovers keen to do some sipping and sightseeing, it's an easy day trip from Lisbon. Several buses make the 40-minute journey daily from the TST bus terminal at Praça de Espanha to Vila Nogueira do Azeitão, the historic center. From there, a handful of wineries are within easy walking distance. The José Maria de Fonseca Wine Museum offers a chance to poke around the cellars and gardens of a 200-year-old family winery (one of the most established in Portugal), and a 15-minute walk leads to the astonishing Bacalhôa Vinhos de Portugal, famed for both its incred-ible art collection and gardens as well as the wines themselves.

Azeitão, Meco & Lagoa de Albufeira

👁 Sights

José Maria da Fonseca Company
For a close look at the wine business, seek out the original headquarters of the José Maria da Fonseca Company; its manor house and cellars stand on the main road through town. The intriguing tours talk about the long history of the winery and allow you to see all stages of production, including a peek into its dark and mysterious prized Moscatel cellars, where 200-plus-year-old bottles are still aging gracefully. The tour takes

GETTING HERE

Regular TST buses (number 754) run between Lisbon's Praça da Espanha and Setúbal and stop at Azeitão, though the service ends around 7:30 pm. The ride takes around 35 minutes. There's a very limited bus service between Sesimbra, Meco, and Lagao de Albufeira, but if time is of the essence, it's easier to hire a car or take a trip with a guide. Driving in the region is lovely, with lots of scenic small villages, rolling hills, and dramatic ocean views.

around 20–40 minutes, depending on the size of the group, and at the end you are brought to the wine-shop, where select products can be tasted and bought. ✉ *Rua José Augusto Coelho 11–13, Vila Nogueira de Azeitão* ☏ *212/198940* ⊕ *www.jmf. pt* ✆ *Free.*

Praia da Lagoa de Albufeira

Mammoth white sand dunes separate the calm lake at Lagoa do Albufeira from the crashing Atlantic waves on the other side. Kitesurfers whiz by, families splash in the waters, and locals wade through the shallows, harvesting shellfish. It's a fascinating scene that gets very busy in summer, but the sunbathing and people-watching opportunities at this beautiful spot are unparalleled. **Amenities:** food and drink; parking (fee) **Best for:** walking; water sports. ✉ *Praia de Lagoa de Albufeira, Sesimbra.*

Praia do Meco

Crashing waves, jagged cliffs, and tall dunes make for a dramatic view at Praia do Meco, which found fame in the 1970s as one of the first nudist beaches in Portugal. Today, this 3-mile sweep of beach is a popular spot with surfers and day-tripping families, but those keen to get an all-over tan can head due south to Rio da Prata, a clothing-optional section of the beach. **Amenities:** food and drink; parking (fee). **Best for:** solitude; surfing; walking. ✉ *Praia do Meco, Aldeia do Meco.*

Quinta da Bacalhoa

The jewel in the crown of this late-16th-century L-shape mansion is its box-hedged garden and striking azulejo-lined paths. Although the grand home here is a private residence, visitors can take tours of the gardens—bookings are necessary and can be made online. Among the highlights are three pyramidal towers—including the so-called Casa do Fresco, which houses the country's oldest azulejo panel. Dating to 1565, it depicts the story of Susannah and the Elders. Scattered elsewhere are Moorish-influenced panels, fragrant groves of fruit trees, and enough restful spots to while away an afternoon. ✉ *4 km (2½ miles) east of Vila Nogueira de Azeitão on N1, Vila Nogueira de Azeitão* ☏ *212/198060* ⊕ *www.bacalhoa.com* ✆ *Weekdays €4, Sat. €8* ☾ *Closed Sun.*

Shopping

Azulejos de Azeitão

Stop here if you're eager to get your hands on some of those decorative and distinctive Portuguese tiles. The company uses traditional European methods to sketch, fabricate, hand-paint, and glaze each of the tiles sold in the shop. Reproduction Portuguese styles and murals range from the 16th to the 19th century (Spanish, Islamic, Hispano-Moorish, French, Italian, English, and Dutch styles from similar periods are also available). Choose from premade selections or design your own to be made and framed. They ship to the United States. ⊠ *Rua dos Trabalhadores da Empresa Setubalense 15, Vila Nogueira de Azeitão* ✛ *To get to the store from Azeitão, follow N10 to the split with N379 and bear right, staying on N10; the turnoff is the second left* ☎ *212/180013* ⊕ *www.azulejos-deazeitao.com* ⊘ *Closed Mon.*

Mercado do Azeitão

Vila Nogueira de Azeitão's agricultural traditions are trumpeted on the first Sunday of every month, when a country market is held in the center of town. Apart from the locally produced wine, you can buy *queijo fresco* (light, soft cheese made from cow, sheep, or goat milk) and the renowned local *queijo de Azeitão*, a handmade D.O.P. (Designated Product of Origin) certified cheese made from sheep milk and cured for a period of 20–40 days. This short curing process gives the cheese a very soft and creamy *amanteigado* (butter-like) texture, and it should be served like butter. It's sold in small rounds of various sizes; slice the top rind off and spoon the spread on a big hunk of excellent fresh bread from one of the market's bakery stalls. ▧ TIP➔ You can buy everything you need here to make the perfect picnic lunch. ⊠ *Vila Nogueira de Azeitão.*

 ## Coffee and Quick Bites

★ **Fábrica de Tortas Azeitonense** $ | **Portuguese.** Aside from great cheese and wine, visitors should be sure to sample the local sweet treat, *tortas de Azeitão* (little rolled tortes filled with an egg-and-cinnamon custard). Fábrica de Tortas Azeitonense started making this regional delicacy along with other varieties of egg-custard pastries in 1995 and is now the best-known producer in the area. **Known for:** sweet snacks to go; wine and cheese; egg pastries and tortas de Azeitão. *Average main: €8* ⊠ *N10, Km 17, Sesimbra* ☎ *212/190418* ⊕ *www.tortasdeazeitao.com* ▭ *No credit cards.*

🍴 Dining

Bar do Peixe
$$ | **Seafood.** Meco's most famous
restaurant draws seafood fans
from across the region. The freshly
caught sea bass, swordfish, and
huge variety of crustaceans are part
of the appeal, but the setting in front
of wild, windswept Meco Beach adds
to the charm. **Known for:** great sea
views; oysters in summer season;
late opening. *Average main: €18*
✉ *Praia do Moinho de Baixo, Aldeia do
Meco* ☎ *21/268–4732* 🕓 *Closed Tues.*

Estoril, Cascais, and Guincho

GO FOR

Great beaches

Boutique shops

Casino high life

GUINCHO

CASCAIS   ESTORIL

LISBON

ATLANTIC
OCEAN

Sightseeing ★ ★ ★ ☆ ☆ | Shopping ★ ★ ☆ ☆ ☆ | Dining ★ ★ ★ ☆ ☆ | Nightlife ★ ★ ★ ☆ ☆

Situated 30 km (18 miles) west of Lisbon, the district of Cascais stretches from the surf beaches of Guincho to the upmarket neighborhood of Estoril and beyond. With some 25 km (15½ miles) of coastline, its many and varied beaches are a principal attraction. Guincho, wild and windy, with plenty of waves, attracts surfers, kitesurfers, and those who prefer a less citified feel to their beach experience. Cascais has a host of sandy bays that are perfect for families, whereas Estoril's casino and Tamariz beach club attract an upmarket crowd. The town of Cascais itself has a discrete grandeur, faded glamour, and just a hint of playboy charm: the James Bond film Casino Royale was modeled on the Estoril Casino, inspired by the period during World War II when spies of every nationality and beleaguered refugee gentry occupied the town's villas and palaces, rubbing shoulders with the Portuguese aristocracy, for whom it has been a summer holiday destination for more than 150 years. Today, you'll still find sailing, tennis competitions, and motor racing on the annual calendar, but wealthy families make up most of the residents who enjoy the beaches, sunny climate, and laid-back lifestyle. Just 30 minutes by train from central Lisbon, Cascais is a great place to base yourself if you're traveling with children and well worth a day trip otherwise.—*by Lucy Bryson*

....

Estoril

 Sights

Espaço Memória dos Exílios

Inaugurated in 1999 and located above the post office in a striking 1942 modernist building, this museum focuses on Estoril's community of aristocratic exiles, who fled here from northern Europe during World War II, but its collection of memorabilia relates broadly to Portugal's mid-20th-century history. The exhibit consists mostly of black-and-white photos with captions in Portuguese, and there's also an exhibit devoted to the Nazi persecution of the Jews. ✉ *Av. Marginal 7152B, Estoril* ☎ *21/481–5930* ⊕ *www.cm-cascais.pt/equipamento/espaco-memoria-dos-exilios* 🎫 *Free* ⏱ *Closed weekends.*

★ Estoril Casino

The glitzy Estoril Casino retains a glamorous allure. In addition to having gambling salons, the casino is one of the largest in Europe and has a nightclub, bars, and restaurants. Tour groups often make an evening of it here, with dinner and a floor show, but it's a pricey night out. Most visitors are content to feed one of the 700 slot machines in the main complex and then check out the other entertainment options: art exhibits, movies, nightly cabaret performances, concerts, and ballets (in summer). To enter the gaming rooms you must pay a small fee (slots are free) and show your passport to prove that you're at least 21. Reservations are essential for the restaurant and floor show. Drink and show packages are available. ⊠ *Av. Dr. Stlanley Ho, Parque do Estoril, Estoril* ☎ *21/466–7700* ⊕ *www. casino-estoril.pt* 🛍 *gaming rooms €4, slot machines free.*

🛍 Shopping

Feira do Artesanato
Each summer (late June–early September), Estoril hosts a huge open-air arts-and-crafts fair near the casino. Vendors sell local art, crafts, fashion, and food and drink every evening until midnight. With live music, dancing, and kid-friendly shows, it's a major event on Estoril's cultural calendar. ⊠ *Av. Amaral Estoril, Estoril* ☎ *21/467–8210.*

Galeria do Casino Estoril
The Galeria do Casino Estoril holds three big art exhibitions during the year. In spring, talented young artists from Portuguese art schools are featured; native art is the theme in summer; in October, Portuguese and international artists grab the spotlight. During the year there are also eight individual exhibitions.

All the works—paintings, bronzes, ceramics, drawings, and sculptures, including marble pieces by Portugal's most famous sculptor, João Cutileiro—are for sale. ⊠ *Casino Estoril, Largo José Teodoro dos Santos, Estoril* ☎ *21/466–7700 (ask for art gallery)* ⊕ *www.casino-estoril.pt.*

🍴 Dining

A Choupana
$$$ | **Seafood.** Just east of town, this restaurant, with English-speaking staff, has views of Cascais Bay from its picture windows and is a reliably good place to eat. The cuisine is primarily Italian, but there are good Portuguese dishes, too. **Known for:** pasta; Portuguese dishes; live piano recitals accompanying dinner on Friday and Saturday night. *Average main: €25* ⊠ *Estrada Marginal 5579, Estoril* ☎ *21/466–4123* ⊕ *www.choupanagordinni.com.*

Cimas
$$ | **Eclectic.** You're in for a good meal in these baronial surroundings of burnished wood, heavy drapes, and oak beams that have played host to royalty, high-ranking politicians, and other celebrities. The menu is a traditional and international hybrid, with everything from French and British to Indian and Indonesian selections on offer. **Known for:** game; fresh fish; traditional atmosphere. *Average main: €20* ⊠ *Av. Marginal, Estoril* ☎ *21/468–1254* ⊕ *www.cimas.com.pt* 🕑 *Closed Sun.*

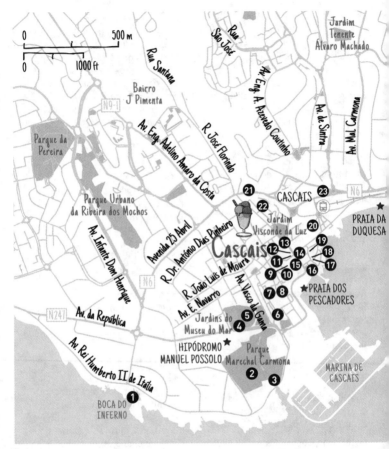

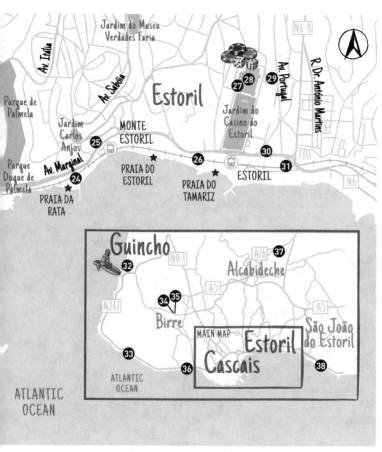

Bars and Nightlife

Piano & Co

Owned by well-known Portuguese singer and actor Vítor Espadinha, this spacious late-night venue (10 pm–4 am most nights) attracts a mixed-age crowd for regular live music. The walls are hung with images of old-school greats like Sinatra, but many of the performances are from young local talent—check the Facebook page for up-to-date listings. A separate bar area is popular with those wanting to chat without the musical backdrop. ⊠ *Rua de Olivença 6, Estoril* ☏ *939/103654.*

Tamariz Beach Club

Hugely popular during the summer (it's closed in the off-season), this enormous beachfront nightspot has eight bars and three dance floors. Resident and visiting DJs play the latest dance tunes to a young, fashionable crowd. This is strictly for night owls as things don't get busy until well after midnight. ⊠ *Praia da Tamariz, Av. Marginal 7669, Estoril.*

Cascais

◉ Sights

★ **Boca do Inferno** *(Mouth of Hell)*
The most visited attraction in the area around Cascais is the forbiddingly named Mouth of Hell, one of several natural grottoes in the rugged coastline. Located just 2 km (1 mile) west of town, it is best appreciated at high tide or in stormy

GETTING HERE

Cascais and Estoril are a 30-minute train ride from Lisbon's Cais do Sodré station. The station for Estoril is a 5-minute walk from the casino. Cascais's town center and its beaches are just a few minutes' walk from the station, but much of the accommodation requires a short taxi ride. There's a bus from Cascais station to Guincho, or you can rent a bike or taxi (around €10) for the 10-km (6-mile) journey.

weather, when the waves are thrust high onto the surrounding cliffs. You can walk along the fenced paths to the viewing platforms above the grotto and peer into the abyss. A path leads down to secluded spots on the rocks below, where fishermen cast their lines. Afterward, shop for lace, leather items, and other handicrafts at roadside stalls, or linger in one of the nearby cafés. ⊠ *Cascais.*

Museu do Mar *(Sea Museum)*
For an understanding of development in Cascais, visit this modern, single-story museum. Here, the town's former role as a fishing village is traced through model boats and fishing gear, period clothing, analysis of local fish, paintings, and old photographs. ⊠ *Rua Júlio Pereira de Melho, Cascais* ☏ *21/481–5906* ⊕ *www.cm-cascais.pt/museumar* 🎟 *Free* ⊘ *Closed Mon.*

FAMOUS LOCAL: PAULA REGO

Portuguese artist Paula Rego is widely regarded as one of the world's great figurative artists. Her work—paintings, pastel drawings, and prints—is valued in the millions and she is one of only a few living artists to have a museum dedicated to her work: the House of Stories in Cascais (see listing), which encompasses 50 years of her art and offers a fascinating glimpse into her unique mind-set.

Rego was born in Lisbon in 1935 but spent her early childhood living with her grandmother and aunt in Cascais. It was during this time that she absorbed the local dramatic folk stories, fragments of which are still strongly evident in her work today. Wider Portugal, too, remains an influence, examples of which can be seen in the deep blue skies, shapely big-bottomed women, and Catholic iconography that often feature in her pieces. Other themes in her work allude to the authoritarian years of the 1940s and '50s and the Colonial Wars that triggered the 1974 revolution.

Museu dos Condes Castro Guimarães *(Counts of Castro Guimarães Museum)*

One of Cascais's 19th-century town houses serves as the museum's home with displays of 18th- and 19th-century paintings, ceramics, and furniture, as well as artifacts from nearby archaeological excavations. ⊠ *Av. Rei Humberto II de Itália, Cascais* ☎ *21/481–5304* ⊕ *www.cm-cascais.pt/mccg* ⊠ *€3* ⊗ *Closed Mon.*

Parque do Marechal Carmona

The most relaxing spot in Cascais is this municipal park, which has a shallow lake, a café, a small zoo, plus tables and chairs under the trees for picnickers. ⊠ *Praceta Domingos D'Avilez, Av. da Republica, Cascais* ⊕ *www.cm-cascais.pt/equipamento/parque-marechal-carmona.*

 Shopping

Casa da Guia

Housed in a grand old building, Casa da Guia is a pretty outdoor shopping center that sits on a cliff right on the ocean at the far end of Cascais after Boca do Inferno. The shops are all high-end, brand-name boutiques, and there are several restaurants, bars, bakeries, and delis with large outdoor terraces scattered throughout the property. ⊠ *Av. Nossa Senhora do Cabo 101, Cascais* ☎ *21/484–3215.*

Cascais Villa

Cascais Villa is on the Marginal (coastal road) into Cascais from Lisbon. The shopping center has a cinema, restaurants, and shops carrying internationally known brands. ⊠ *Av. Dom Pedro I, Cascais* ☎ *21/482–8250.*

Ceramicarte

Fátima and Luís Soares present their carefully executed, modern ceramic designs alongside more traditional jugs and plates at Ceramicarte. There's also a small selection of tapestries and artworks. The store is near the main Catholic church in the old town. ⊠ *Largo da Assunção 3–4, Cascais* ☎ *21/484–0170* ⊕ *www.ceramicarte.pt.*

Fnac

In the Cascais shopping mall on the road between Cascais and Sintra, the book-computer-record shop Fnac sells English-language books as well as tickets to cultural events. ⊠ *Estrada Nacional 9, Alcabideche, Cascais* ☎ *707/313435* ⊕ *www.fnac.pt.*

Torres

For typical Portuguese handmade jewelry such as filigree, go to Torres, which has its own designers and trademark brand. ⊠ *Alameda Combatentes da Grande Guerra 147, Cascais* ☎ *21/013–1717* ⊕ *www. torres.pt.*

Vista Alegre Atlantis

Portugal has a long tradition of ceramics, and Vista Alegre, founded in 1824, is one of the country's premium brands. It makes everything from functional pieces such as plates and cups to more decorative and art-led collections. ⊠ *Estrada Nacional 9, Lojas 0055/56, Cascais* ☎ *21/469–2397* ⊕ *vistaalegre.com.*

WORTH A TRIP

Mercado de Carcavelos In the nearby town of Carcavelos, 7 km (4½ miles) southeast of Estoril, the busy Mercado de Carcavelos sells food, clothes, and crafts; you can reach it by local train. Also in Carcavelos, on the other side of the station toward the beach, Praça do Junqueiro is a pretty square with a surf shop, vintage store, cafés, and restaurants and is a nice spot for lunch or coffee and cake. ⊠ Rua do Mercado, Parede.

☕ Coffee and Quick Bites

Pastelaria a Bijou de Cascais

$ | Portuguese. The Portuguese have a sweet tooth—not a morning, or afternoon, goes by without a stop for a coffee and pastry—and this traditional little shop, with its wide selection of tarts, cakes, biscuits, and croissants is a great introduction to typical Portuguese sweets. It's also a good spot for a light breakfast. **Known for:** Portuguese pastries; coffee; reputation as a local favorite. *Average main: €4* ⊠ *Rua Regimento Infantaria Dezanove 55, Cascais* ☎ *21/483–0283* ⊕ *www. bijoudecascais.pt.*

⭐ Santini Cascais

In the heart of old-town Cascais, Santini Cascais is Portugal's most famous ice-cream parlor and has what many people consider to be the country's best Italian-style gelato. Try classics like chocolate, strawberry, pistachio, and hazelnut or seasonal favorites like blood-orange sherbet, made from imported Sicilian blood oranges. Branches have now opened across Lisbon and in Porto, but Santini Cascais is where it all began. ⊠ *Av. Valbom 28F, Cascais* ☎ *21/483-3709* ⊕ *www.santini.pt.*

🍴 Dining

Beira Mar
$$$$ | Seafood. One of several well-established restaurants behind the fish market, Beira Mar has won a string of awards for the quality of its fish and seafood. An impressive glass display shows off the best of the day's catch, although (as always) you can end up paying top dollar for dinner if you're not careful, because it's sold by weight, so make sure you know the price first, or stick to dishes with fixed prices. **Known for:** fresh seafood, including lobster; grilled fish; vegetarian options like vegetable risotto. *Average main: €27* ⊠ *Rua das Flores 6, Cascais* ☎ *21/482-7380* ⊕ *www.restaurante-beiramar.pt* ⊘ *Closed Tues.*

Caffe Itália
$$ | Pizza. There are plenty of other pizza joints in Cascais, but Caffe Itália is probably the best of the bunch. In its indoor dining rooms or on its sunny terrace you can choose from a range of authentic thin-crust pizzas and fresh homemade pasta dishes. **Known for:** thin-crust pizza; outdoor terrace with views; homemade tiramisu. *Average main: €20* ⊠ *Rua Marques Leal Pancada*

WORTH A TRIP

Quinta do Pisão is a 1,112-acre natural park and farm situated on the outskirts of Cascais that makes for a pleasant day out if you tire of the beach. Along with walking trails across meadows and through forests, it has a farm where visitors can pick their own vegetables and fruit to buy and take home. There's also a small herd of endangered woolly Portuguese Asinina de Miranda donkeys, which children can ride.

16A, Cascais ☎ *21/483-0151* ⊘ *Closed Wed. No lunch Thurs.*

Dom Manolo
$ | Fast Food. The surroundings aren't sophisticated in this Spanish-owned grill-restaurant, but for down-to-earth fare it's a good choice. The waiters charge back and forth delivering excellent *frango* (spit-roasted chicken) and grilled fish to a largely local clientele. **Known for:** spit-roasted chicken; reputation as a local favorite; outdoor tables. *Average main: €15* ⊠ *Av. Marginal 11, Cascais* ☎ *21/483-1126* ⊟ *No credit cards.*

★ Monte Mar
$$$$ | Seafood. Superior seafood and steaks come with equally impressive sea views at this highly regarded, formal restaurant in Cascais, where reservations are recommended. Situated right at the edge of the ocean, the terrace is the perfect spot for taking in those amazing ocean views or for outdoor dining on warm days. **Known for:**

grilled fish and fresh shellfish; amazing ocean views; attracting everyone from rock stars to visiting politicians (including Bill Clinton, Rudy Giuliani, and Bryan Adams). *Average main: €35 ⊠ Av. Nossa Senhora do Cabo, Cascais ☎ 21/486–9270 ⊕ www.montemarrestaurante. com ⊙ Closed Mon.*

★ O Pescador

$ | Seafood. Fresh seafood fills the menu at this folksy restaurant, where a cluttered ceiling and maritime-related artifacts distract the eye. Sole and *bacalhau* (salted cod) are specialties, but there are usually one or two vegetarian options, such as a salad with tofu and asparagus. **Known for:** seafood like bacalhau assado (baked salted cod); famously well-stocked wine cellar; reputation as a local favorite since 1964. *Average main: €15 ⊠ Rua das Flores 10, Cascais ☎ 21/483–2054 ⊕ www. restaurantepescador.com ⊙ No lunch Wed.*

★ Restaurante Pereira

$ | Portuguese. Popular though it may be, this restaurant remains low-key, with checked cotton tablecloths, very simple decor, and a cheap, but very good, menu that includes dishes from every region in Portugal. The owner's cooking attracts many customers, so get there early—12:30 for lunch and 7:30 for dinner—especially during summer when competition for the outdoor tables is fierce, and the interior is packed with locals all year round. **Known for:** traditional Portuguese dishes; reputation as a local favorite; outdoor tables.

Average main: €13 ⊠ Travessa Bela Vista 42, Cascais ☎ 21/483–1215 ⊕ restaurantepereira.pai.pt ▭ No credit cards ⊙ Closed Thurs.

🍸 Bars and Nightlife

Chequers

The bar at Chequers restaurant is a popular spot to drink and dance the night away among a mixed crowd of locals and out-of-towners. ⊠ Largo Luís de Camões 7, Cascais ☎ 21/483–0926.

Forte Dom Rodrigo

You can hear fado, the mournful Portuguese folk music, as you dine at Forte Dom Rodrigo. It's one of the most famous *casas de fado* in the region, owned by popular *fadisto* Rodrigo Ferreira. It opens at 7 pm; closing time depends on the performances. ⊠ Rua Madressilvas 8, Cascais ☎ 21/487–1373.

John Bull

On hot summer nights, customers of the English-style pub-restaurant John Bull spill out into the square. ⊠ Largo Luís de Camões 4, Cascais ☎ 21/483–3319.

🎭 Performing Arts

Teatro Gil Vicente

Watching a performance at this beautiful 19th-century theater, with its ornate ceiling and gilded balcony, is like stepping back in time. Programming is irregular but includes theater productions, as well as international dance and music performances. ✉ *Rua Gomes Freire 5, Cascais* ☎ *21/483-0522.*

Guincho

 Sights

★ Praia do Guincho *(Guincho Beach)*
Cars often line either side of the road behind Guincho Beach on weekends, and surfers can always be seen braving its waves, irrespective of the season or prevailing weather conditions. The surf can be trying and the undertow dangerous: even accomplished swimmers have had to summon Guincho's lifeguards—it's not an activity for the fainthearted. If you prefer something more sedate, this beach—with the Serra da Sintra serving as a backdrop—is an ideal spot to watch the sunset. The Fortaleza do Guincho and Estalagem Muchaxo are the obvious choices for those seeking accommodation close by.
Amenities: food and drink; parking (no fee); showers; toilets. **Best for:** sunset; surfing; windsurfing. ✉ *N247, Cascais.*

 Shopping

Auguri
Get into the Cascais spirit at this little boutique, which sells resort, sailing, and beachwear for men and women. There's a wide selection, from swimwear, floaty dresses, and beach cover-ups to casual men's polo shirts and T-shirts from international brands like Billabong and Scotch & Soda alongside local

brands such as Lisbon's Stessa. ✉ *Rua Frederico Arouca 7, Cascais* ☎ *917/227171.*

 Coffee and Quick Bites

Azimut
$ | Contemporary. There are plenty of beach bars and restaurants on the esplanade between Cascais and Estoril, but this one at Monte Estoril, a 10-minute walk from either town, is the pick of the bunch. Right by a small sandy beach called Das Moitas, the vibe is peaceful and there's a broad menu ranging from snacks, hamburgers, toasted sandwiches, and salads to seafood and fish. **Known for:** beachside dining; hamburgers, salads, and sandwiches; children's menu. *Average main: €12* ✉ *Praia das Moitas, Estoril* ☎ *21/482-0433* ⊕ *www.restaurantebarazimut.pt.*

Cafe Galeria House of Wonders
$ | Vegetarian. This vegetarian and vegan café has a pleasant rooftop terrace and a wide-ranging menu that includes snacks and sharing plates as well as a hot and cold meze-style buffet. Smoothies,

juices, teas, coffee, sangria, and beers are available to wash it all down. **Known for:** vegan and vegetarian snacks and meals; rooftop terrace; homemade cakes. *Average main: €13 ⊠ Rua da Misericórdia 53, Cascais ☎ 911/702428.*

🍸 Bars and Nightlife

Cascais Jazz Club
This soulful little bar presents live jazz, blues, and bossa nova jams and performances Thursday–Sunday evenings and attracts a slew of keen regulars along with visitors. Its diminutive size belies the quality of the musicians that it features. ⊠ *Largo Cidade de Vitória 36, Cascais* ☎ *962/773470* ⊕ *cascaisjazzclub.pt.*

 Performing Arts

⭐ Casa das Histórias Paula Rego
Designed by Eduardo Souto de Moura, one of Portugal's preeminent architects, the striking terra-cotta-color buildings of this museum are as intriguing as the notable work shown inside. The building houses some of the works of Portugal's best-known contemporary artist, Paula Rego, and there's a small amphitheater on-site that sometimes hosts speakers and literary and art events. ⊠ *Av. da República 300, Cascais* ☎ *21/482–6970* ⊕ *www. casadashistoriaspaularego.com/pt* 🎫 *€5.*

INDEX

Photo Credits

Chapter 2: Baixa (including Rossio): (43) tetiana_u/Shutterstock. Chapter 4: Avenida
da Liberdade, Príncipe Real, and Restauradores: (94) ThinAir/Shutterstock. Chapter 5:
Alfama: (104) Philip Rwankole, Lost Tribe Magazine. Chapter 6: Graça, São Vicente, Beato,
and Marvila: (120) S-F/Shutterstock. Chapter 8: Estrela, Campo de Ourique, and Lapa: (152)
joyfull/Shutterstock.

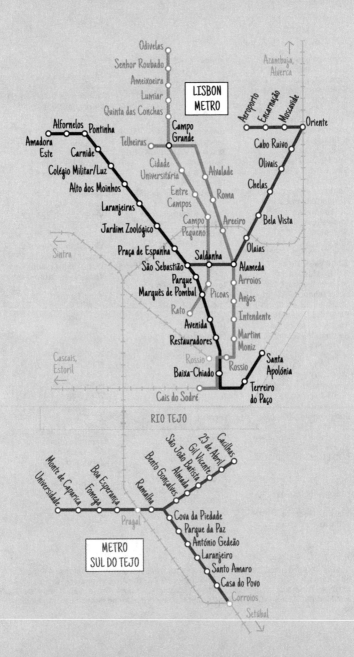

RESOURCES

Lisbon's transit system includes trams, buses, ferries, and funiculars, and elevators linking high and low parts of the city. It's operated by the public transportation company, Carris.

For all these forms of transport, paying as you board means paying much more (€1.80 a ride for the bus, €2.85 for the tram, €3.60 for the funicular, or €5 for the elevator), in cash. It's better to purchase a 7 Colinas or Viva Viagem travel card, both of which can also be used on the metro and ferries. Buy them at transport terminals and at the foot of the Elevador de Santa Justa.

Lisbon's modern metro system (station entrances are marked with a red "M") is cheap and speedy, though it misses many sights and gets crowded during rush hour and for big soccer matches. You can charge your Viva Viagem card with cash. For €1.40, you get one hour's access to buses, trams, and the metro: choose the "Zapping" option to load larger amounts onto your card if you intend to make multiple journeys.

The Lisboa Card is a special pass that allows free travel on all public transportation (including trains to Sintra, Cascais, and Estoril) as well as free or discounted entry into 27 museums, monuments, and galleries. The cards are valid for 24 hours (€18.50), 48 hours (€31.50), or 72 hours (€39). It's sold at the airport (in well-signed kiosks), across from the Mosteiro dos Jerónimos, in the Lisbon Welcome Centre, at the tourist office in the Palácio Foz, and at major hotels and other places around the city. Cardholders get to skip the line at many attractions, too.

Taxis in Lisbon are relatively cheap, and the airport is so close to the city center that many visitors make a beeline for a cab queue outside the terminal. To avoid any hassle over fares you can buy a prepaid voucher (which includes gratuity and luggage charges) from the tourist office booth in the arrivals hall. Expect to pay €10–€20 to most destinations in the city center and around €40 if you're headed for Estoril or Sintra. Uber is also very popular in Lisbon, and it's worth downloading the app even if you're not a regular user. Prices are at least a third cheaper than taxis on most journeys, and you won't have to fiddle around with cash. In addition, taxi drivers in Lisbon have the annoying habit of taking foreigners on circuitous routes around the city in order to bump up their fare. For this reason alone, Uber and pre-paid vouchers are recommended.

VISITOR INFORMATION

Visitors' first port of call in downtown Lisbon should be the Ask Me Lisboa welcome center at Terreiro do Paço, where English speakers offer advice on everything from public transport to booking wine tours and surf classes. There are pamphlets offering all types of officially approved trips and tours, along with free Wi-Fi. You can also pick up a Lisboa Card here, which offers unlimited travel on public transport as well as discounted or free access to many major tourist attractions. There's also a branch at the airport that's open daily 7 am to midnight, and booths at key spots including Santa Apolónia (daily 8–1 and 2–4), Rossio (Praça D. Pedro IV, 10–1 and 2–6), and across from Mosteiro de Jerónimos in Belém (10–6).

NOTES

NOTES

NOTES

NOTES

NOTES

NOTES

NOTES

NOTES

NOTES

Fodor's INSIDE LISBON

Editorial: Douglas Stallings, *Editorial Director;* Margaret Kelly, Jacinta O'Halloran, Amanda Sadlowski, *Senior Editors;* Kayla Becker, Alexis Kelly, Teddy Minford, Rachael Roth, *Editors;* Jeremy Tarr, *Fodors.com Editorial Director;* Rachael Levitt, *Fodors.com Managing Editor*

Design: Tina Malaney, *Design and Production Director;* Jessica Gonzalez, *Graphic Designer;* Mariana Tabares, *Design & Production Intern*

Production: Jennifer DePrima, *Editorial Production Manager;* Carrie Parker, *Senior Production Editor;* Elyse Rozelle, *Production Editor;* Jackson Pranica, *Editorial Production Assistant*

Maps: Rebecca Baer, *Senior Map Editor;* Andrew Murphy, *Cartographer*

Photography: Jill Krueger, *Director of Photo;* Namrata Aggarwal, Ashok Kumar, Carl Yu, *Photo Editors;* Rebecca Rimmer, *Photo Intern*

Business & Operations: Chuck Hoover, *Chief Marketing Officer;* Robert Ames, *General Manager;* Stephen Horowitz, *Director of Business Development and Revenue Operations;* Tara McCrillis, *Director of Publishing Operations*

Public Relations and Marketing: Joe Ewaskiw, *Senior Director Communications & Public Relations;* Esther Su, *Senior Marketing Manager;* Ryan Garcia, Thomas Talarico, Miranda Villalobos, *Marketing Specialists*

Technology: Jon Atkinson, *Director of Technology;* Rudresh Teotia, *Lead Developer;* Jacob Ashpis, *Content Operations Manager*

Illustrator: Pedro Brito

Writers: Lucy Bryson, Ann Abel, Mario Fernandes and Trish Lorenz

Lead Editor: Margaret Kelly

Editors: Alexis Kelly, Amanda Sadlowski, Douglas Stallings

Production Editor: Jennifer DePrima

Designers: Tina Malaney, Chie Ushio

Production Design: Jessica Gonzalez

1st Edition

ISBN 978-1-64097-146-2

ISSN 2640-6233

Library of Congress Control Number 2018914617

SPECIAL SALES

This book is available at special discounts for bulk purchases for sales promotions or premiums. For more information, e-mail SpecialMarkets@fodors.com.

PRINTED IN THE UNITED STATES OF AMERICA

10 9 8 7 6 5 4 3 2 1

ABOUT OUR WRITERS

Award-winning travel journalist **Ann Abel** writes for *Forbes, Conde Nast Traveller, Departures, Robb Report, Afar, Well + Good* and other publications. After a career in New York, she began her live-in love affair with Lisbon on Valentine's Day 2017.

Animation director, illustrator, and graphic designer **Pedro Brito** is a local artist who was born and raised on the other side of the Tagus River, just across the water from Lisbon. He's published seven graphic novels, including, *Pano Cru, Beraca* and *You are the Woman of My Life, She the Woman of My Dreams* with João Fazenda. The latter won the Best Portuguese Comic Book Award and the Audience Award at the BD Amadora Festival in 2001. Pedro also directed six short animated films, including *Pickpocket Blues* (2006) and *Fado of a Grown Men* (2011). His latest film project, *Assim, mas sem ser assim*, is set to debut in 2019. Pedro's collaborations on books, magazines, and illustrated children's books are too many to name here, but he's very proud of *A Casa Sincronizada*, written by Inês Pupo and Gonçalo Pratas, which won the SPA / RTP 2012 Award for Best Children's Book.

Lucy Bryson is a British freelance travel writer who moved to Lisbon in 2015 after nearly a decade living in Rio de Janeiro, Brazil. She provides Lisbon articles and hotel reviews for *Fodors.com* has written Lisbon content for Fodor's *Portugal* guidebooks, and writes about the city and its culture for *Vice, Atlas Obscura*, and *Urban Travel Blog*, among others. Lucy's work had also been published by *BBC Travel, Rough Guides, Footprint*, and *USA Today*. She now lives by the beach in nearby Sesimbra. When she's not swimming or trail running in Arrabida Natural Park, Lucy can often be found in Lisbon itself, where she particularly enjoys raising a glass to the city and its sunny climate at one of the many marvellous miradouros.

Mario Fernandes grew up in the United States but has been living in Lisbon since 2003, working as a blogger and travel writer. He has shared his passion for the Portuguese capital in several international publications, websites and guidebooks, and though he also covers other destinations as a writer and photographer, his main focus is still Lisbon. He regularly offers his expert advice and insider's knowledge on his website *Lisbon-Lux.com*, and now on this edition of Fodor's *Inside Lisbon*, highlighting the city's most authentic and noteworthy experiences in several of the best and up-and-coming neighborhoods.

A journalist with more than 15 years experience, **Trish Lorenz** has been based in Lisbon since January 2014. She is *Monocle* magazine's Portugal correspondent and writes about the culture, business, politics, and people of the Iberian Peninsula for titles including *The New York Times, The Financial Times, The Guardian, The Telegraph* and the *Sunday Times*. She lives in the historic heart of the city, is beginning to master the Portuguese language, and in her free time enjoys exploring Lisbon's cobbled lanes and discovering new places in which to expand her knowledge of Portuguese cuisine and sunny terraces on which to enjoy a local wine.